THE RHETORIC OF MENACHEM BEGIN

The Myth of Redemption Through Return

Robert C. Rowland

D1607691

UNIVERSITY
PRESS OF
AMERICA

LANHAM • NEW YORK • LONDON

Copyright © 1985 by

University Press of America,® Inc.

4720 Boston Way
Lanham. MD 20706

3 Henrietta Street
London WC2E 8LU England

Library of Congress Cataloging in Publication Data

Rowland, Robert C., 1954-
 The rhetoric of Menachem Begin.

 Bibliography: p.
 Includes index.
 1. Begin, Menachem, 1913-   —Oratory.
2. Prime ministers—Israel—Biography. 3. Revisionist
Zionism. 4. Israel—Politics and government.
5. Political oratory—Israel. I. Title.
DS126.6.B33R69   1985   956.94'054'0924   85-9128
ISBN 0-8191-4735-4 (alk. paper)
ISBN 0-8191-4736-2 (pbk. : alk. paper)

All University Press of America books are produced on acid-free
paper which exceeds the minimum standards set by the National
Historical Publications and Records Commission.

ACKNOWLEDGEMENTS

Without the help of a large number of people I could not have completed this project. First and foremost, I would like to thank Karlyn Campbell for the countless hours she spent on this project. Her comments on style, substance, and organization were always useful, if occasionally painful. It is from her example, more than anything else, that I have learned about the art of rhetorical criticism. I would also like to thank Wil Linkugel for his help in focusing my research. Daniel Breslauer provided guidance on Jewish culture and myth. Paul Campbell provided any number of helpful comments about both the style and substance of my research. I would like to thank Donn Parson not only for his insightful suggestions on this project, but also for his guidance and friendship.

Acknowledgement is made to the following publishers and authors for permission to quote:

Harry Hurwitz, _Menachem Begin_ (Johannesburg, South Africa: The Jewish Herald, December 1977).

Menachem Begin, _The Revolt_ (c Steimatzky Ltd., Israel, 1952, 1972, 1977).

Eliezer Berkovits, _Faith After the Holocaust_ (New York: KTAV, 1973).

Menachem Begin, statement following the Golan annexation, in "Israel Hits Back After U.S. Sanctions," _Jerusalem Post International Edition_, 20-26 December 1981, pp. 1-2, reprinted by permission of the _Jerusalem Post_.

A number of other individuals helped make this project possible. The librarians at the University of Kansas, the New York Public Library, and the Zionist Archives helped me obtain hard to find material on revisionist Zionism. Harry Hurwitz, the Minister of Information at the Israeli Embassy in Washington, sent me a number of important documents as well as his own book on Prime Minister Begin. I would also like to thank Prime Minister Menachem Begin, who personally answered a letter I had addressed to his staff and graciously granted permission to quote from his writings.

Finally, I would like to thank a number of people who provided the social climate that allowed me to complete this project. Mark Gidley, Rodger Payne, Zac Grant, and the other debaters made my years at the University of Kansas very rewarding. Fellow graduate students, Chuck Kauffman, Ed Hinck, Deanna Womack, Craig Dudczak, Helen Warren, David Williams, and Andy Rist provided intellectual stimulation in graduate school. Frank Cross, Jim Prentice, and Steve Griffin kept me aware of the real world away from my research. At Baylor, Bill English, Lee Polk, and the Baylor debaters provided the support and friendship I needed to complete the project. I also would like to thank one of my students and friends, Bonnie Dow, who assisted me as a proofreader and advised me on style.

TABLE OF CONTENTS

Page

INTRODUCTION

The event which led me to focus on Menachem Begin's rhetoric was the 1978 meeting between Prime Minister Begin, President Sadat, and President Carter at Camp David. My original aim was to study Begin's rhetoric as prime minister in the hope of elucidating the development of the peace negotiations between Israel and Egypt. However, my research on Begin and the peace process convinced me that this approach was too simplistic. Begin's rhetoric could not be understood outside of the context of Zionism and the history of the state of Israel. More important, Begin himself could not be understood apart from his years as commander of the underground organization, the Irgun Zvai Leumi.

In biographies of Begin, I found countless references to the influence of his years as commander of the Irgun on his life. Moreover, I found that Begin himself continues to refer to his role as a commander of the Irgun as the most important event in his life. As a result, I turned to Begin's memoir of the underground war against the British, The Revolt.

The Revolt is a fascinating and disappointing work. It is poorly organized, highly emotional, and lacks the personal details one expects in the memoir of an underground leader. It reveals Begin's obsession with the holocaust and his love for the soldiers of the Irgun. The work not only refers to the horror of the holocaust, but also makes bitter attacks on the passivity of the European Jewish community during Hitler's assault on the Jewish people. By contrast, Begin describes the soldiers of the Irgun as heroes unparalleled in human history. They are described as larger than life, men who drew their strength from the land of Israel. This facet of the memoir suggested that The Revolt could be explained as a mythic response to the moral problems created by the holocaust.

While the mythic dimension of The Revolt is important, I was not satisfied with this conclusion. I still wanted to evaluate the quality of Begin's contemporary rhetoric. The fact that The Revolt has a mythic dimension does not mean that Begin's modern rhetoric is also informed by myth or even that the rhetoric of the Irgun reflects the same mythic dimension found in The Revolt. In order to determine whether this mythic dimension informs all of Begin's rhetoric, I analyzed representative works of Irgun rhetoric and of Begin's rhetoric as prime minister of Israel. My analysis revealed that the same mythic pattern informs the rhetoric of the Irgun and The Revolt and that the ideology and policies of the Begin government are influenced by the mythic perspective through which Begin views the world.

The organization of this study reflects the process through which I discovered the mythic dimension in Begin's rhetoric. I begin by developing the theoretical background necessary for an understanding of Begin's world view. I then argue that The Revolt and the rhetoric of the Irgun are informed by a myth. Next, I analyze Begin's rhetoric as prime minister and explain how his mythic perspective has influenced his policies. Finally, I evaluate the quality of his myth.

CHAPTER I

MENACHEM BEGIN AND MYTH

Menachem Begin's importance in Zionist and Israeli history is undeniable. Begin was one of the leading figures in the youth movement of the revisionist wing of Zionism in the 1930s[1] and, since the death of Vladimir Jabotinsky, he has been the leading revisionist Zionist figure in the world. Begin is also important as an example of the suffering which the German and Soviet tyrannies inflicted on the Jewish people of Europe. While the Nazis were killing nearly everyone in his family, the Soviets imprisoned Begin in the Gulag. After his release from a Soviet work camp, Begin served as commander of the underground organization Irgun Zvai Leumi in its battle against the British in Palestine. A number of scholars now believe that Begin's Irgun played a major role in forcing the British to leave Palestine.[2] Following the establishment of the Jewish state, Begin served as an important opposition leader in the Knesset. After almost thirty years in the opposition, he was elected prime minister of Israel in 1977. As prime minister, he made a number of crucial policy decisions affecting the future of Israel: he ordered two invasions of Lebanon, a number of bombing attacks on Palestine Liberation Organization (PLO) camps, a bombing raid on an Iraqi nuclear reactor, and he officially annexed the Golan Heights and East Jerusalem. He also won the Nobel Peace Prize and negotiated a peace treaty with Egypt. Of all the leaders of Israel, only David Ben-Gurion can be said to have had more influence on the development of the Israeli state.

Through his forty years as a leading Zionist, rhetoric has been the primary tool Begin has used to generate and maintain his political power. During his years in the Zionist movement and in the Israeli Knesset, Begin rarely possessed the power to influence directly the policies of either. Revisionist Zionism was a splinter group denied power in Palestine by the "official" Jewish organizatons, the Jewish Agency, and Haganah.[3] Similarly, the Irgun was a tiny underground organization, bitterly opposed by the Zionist mainstream in Israel. From 1948 to 1967, Begin's party, Herut, was never even considered as a possible partner

1

in the coalition governments which ruled Israel. Even
after he joined the Government of National Unity in
1967, he served as Minister Without Portfolio and was
not responsible for any specific policy area. Following his resignation in 1970, he joined the opposition
until his election as Prime Minister in 1977. Throughout his career, Begin has been forced to rely on his
ability to persuade. Thus, Begin's political influence has come almost totally from his rhetorical
skills.

The importance of rhetoric in Begin's career is
obvious even in the Irgun's revolt against the British. In fact, the revolt, which Begin believes was
the most important event in his life,[4] was waged primarily with rhetoric. While the Irgun fought the
British with bombs and bullets, they used such weapons
for principally rhetorical, not military purposes.[5]

While the most typical rhetorical acts are public
speeches and essays, some rhetorical acts are based on
non-linguistic symbolism.[6] Picasso's "Guernica" is an
example of a non-verbal work which makes a powerful
rhetorical point. To millions throughout the world,
the painting symbolizes the evils of fascism. The
rhetorical intent of the painting is also obvious in
Picasso's refusal to allow it to be exhibited in Spain
as long as a fascist government remained in power.

Similarly, many of the para-military operations
of the Irgun were primarily rhetorical and only sec-
ondarily military operations. The Irgun had no chance
to defeat the British military in Palestine. There
were never more than a few score full-time soldiers
fighting for the Irgun against over 80,000 British
soldiers and policemen.[7] And over the five years of
the revolt, the Irgun killed only 200 British soldiers
and police.[8] However, despite these low casualty
figures, the Irgun is believed to have hastened the
British withdrawal from Palestine. The Irgun's success can be attributed to its strategy. The Irgun
never attempted to defeat the British on the battlefield; rather, its aim was to destroy the prestige of
Britain. In The Revolt Begin explains:

> History and our observation persuaded
> us that if we could succeed in de-
> stroying the government's prestige in
> Eretz Israel [the land of Israel] the
> removal of its rule would follow auto-

2

matically. Thenceforward, we gave no peace to this weak spot. Throughout all the years of our uprisings, we hit the British Government's prestige, deliberately, tirelessly, unceasingly.[9]

The operations of the Irgun were not aimed at a military victory, but at a rhetorical victory in which the ability of the "terrorists" to strike at will against the British Empire would symbolize the failure of that Empire and force the British to leave Palestine.

Not only were many of the operations of the Irgun inherently rhetorical, but Begin followed up those operations with extensive persuasive campaigns. He wrote speeches to be broadcast over the Irgun's clandestine radio station, copy for wall posters, and articles for the Irgun's newspapers. This rhetoric was essential to the operation of the Irgun:

> It was our duty to elucidate the principles of the struggle and its aims. The world must know what we are fighting for. The people should know why they must be prepared, through our operations, to endure recurring troubles. The youth must know why they are risking their lives. (p. 44)

As prime minister, he has continued to rely on rhetoric. Begin's recognition of the persuasive power of language is obvious in his refusal to refer to the West Bank as "occupied territory." Instead, Begin calls the West Bank by its biblical names, Judea and Samaria.[10] Haber's description of Begin's concern with language while serving as commander of the Irgun is applicable to the whole of Begin's career: "For Begin, the use of the word, whether written on walls or broadcast by the underground radio station, was an all-powerful weapon."[11]

The importance of rhetoric in Begin's career has been noted by all of his biographers. Begin first rose to prominence within the revisionist wing of Zionism because of his powerful oratory. Haber reports on the effects of his speaking: "His speeches were electrifying. He was learning to use the spoken word as a sharp and effective political weapon--one on which he would rely heavily in the years to come."[12] Begin's other biographers note that he has honed his rhetorical skills since his days in Betar [the youth organization of the revisionist movement] and is now one of the most acclaimed Israeli public speakers. Hirschler and Eckman write: "Though he hardly ever raises his voice nowadays, he keeps audiences spellbound, even when they do not agree with what he says."[13] Gervasi describes him as "one of Israel's three or four best speakers."[14] Hurwitz makes the same point: "He is the finest orator in the Knesset and one of the greatest orators we have today."[15]

Begin's importance as a political leader is undeniable. For over thirty-five years he has been one of the most important political figures in Israel. As prime minister he was involved in crucial peace negotiations which may determine Israel's future. Prior to the birth of Israel, he commanded an important underground organization and served as a leader of the revisionist movement. Nor is there any question about the importance of rhetoric to Begin's political career. Begin recognizes that the ultimate power of any politician in a democratic society is the word.

The Problem

While Begin's importance as a political leader and as a rhetor is clear, he remains an enigmatic figure in other ways. At times, the political positions he advocates seem to be based on inconsistent assumptions. He is willing to give up the strategic depth of the Sinai, but is unwilling to part with any of the West Bank, although much of it is not strategically important to the defense of Israel. He is a modern political leader who relies on advanced weaponry to defend Israel, but bases territorial claims on the biblical history of the land of Israel.[16] The difficulty in understanding Begin is nowhere more apparent than when considering his political rhetoric. While Begin has been acclaimed as one of Israel's most effective political persuaders, many of his speeches confound such claims.

For example, he often makes emotional statements about the holocaust which seem designed to anger his audience. Begin's brutal attack on Helmut Schmidt, chancellor of West Germany, for his service with the German army in the Second World War, could hardly improve Israel's relations with West Germany.[17] Begin

4

also embarrassed many supporters of Israel with his speech at the Peace Treaty Signing Ceremony in Washington. In his speech at the ceremony, Anwar Sadat removed two paragraphs that pointedly referred to the rights of the Palestinian people.[18] Sadat wanted to avoid any comments that might threaten the agreement. By contrast, Begin made several statements that could only offend the Arab world and the West. Suzanne Weaver of the Wall Street Journal summarized the reaction to Begin's speech:

> Begin produced acute discomfort in some parts of the audience when he said what many did not wish to hear at the moment, that this portion of peace for his country had been bought only with the blood of its soldiers and that in the past, when Jews had no armies of their own, the good offices of the West had not been used to save them from Hitler's ovens or Stalin's prisons.[19]

At a ceremony designed as a celebration of peace, Begin introduced the only discordant notes.

In addition, Begin defends current Israeli policies by citing events in the biblical past. An American president who endorsed a policy because George Washington had once supported that position would be treated as a fool. Yet, Begin often refers to the biblical history of Israel almost as if it had happened yesterday. Unlike the Labor party,[20] he sees the biblical history of Israel as directly relevant to the problems facing Israel today. In his speech to the Knesset during Sadat's visit to Jerusalem, Begin responded to Sadat's claim that the land of Israel belonged to the Arab people by downplaying the importance of recent history and referring to the biblical past:

> The President [Sadat] mentioned the Balfour Declaration. No, sir, we took no foreign land. We returned to our Homeland. The bond between our People and this Land is eternal. It was created at the dawn of human history. It was never severed. In this Land we established our civilization; here our prophets spoke these holy words you

cited this very day; here the Kings of
Judah and Israel prostrated themselves; here we became a nation; here
we established our Kingdom and, when
we were exiled from our country by the
force that was exercised against us,
even when we were far away, we did not
forget this Land, not even for a
single day.[21]

To Sadat, concerned with the last thirty years of
conflict between Egypt and Israel, Begin's biblical
nationalism must have seemed quite odd.

Finally, Begin often makes statements which can
only be characterized as non-strategic. He makes
speeches which he knows will offend his audience. In
the 1940s, Begin equated the British with the Nazis.[22]
He even claimed that the British were worse than the
Nazis because Britain was Hitler's master.[23] Such
statements might have been acceptable in Israel itself
(the Jewish people were understandably angry with the
British for their failure to bomb the railheads to the
death camps), but Begin compared the British to the
Nazis in Irgun releases that were designed for the
United States. These statements could only strike
many Americans as offensive. The British built no
death camps in Palestine, and they fought Hitler for
six long years. Even today, Begin often makes statements which, like this characterization of the British, seem designed to offend his audience. In December 1981, Begin responded to U.S. criticism of the
Israeli annexation of the Golan Heights by complaining
that the U.S. attacks were motivated by anti-Semitism.
He compared U.S. policy dealing with Israel to the
Spanish Inquisition.[24] While U.S. foreign policy may
have tilted toward the Arab world in recent years, the
characterization of Israel's last remaining real
friend as anti-Semitic seems ill-advised.

During the 1982 Israeli invasion of Lebanon,
Begin made a similar statement. When members of the
Senate Foreign Relations Committee asked him a number
of very tough questions about the invasion of Lebanon,
Begin responded bitterly. Newsweek reported that
"Begin . . . seemed to resent even the mention of U.S.
support for Israel. He came to Washington, he said,
'representing a sovereign state, and I don't come with
my hand outstretched for aid.' The U.S. Senate, he
said, 'could keep its money.'" When Senator Paul

6

Tsongas tried to establish some rapport with Begin by making reference to the brutal treatment that his Greek ancestors had received at the hands of the Turks, "Begin rebuffed the gesture. 'Do you want to compare holocausts?' he snapped." After Begin left the committee, the Israeli ambassador was forced to apologize to a number of U.S. senators.[25] Begin's comments to the Senate Foreign Relations Committee are typical. Although he is by all accounts a brilliant speaker, he often makes statements which are not well-adapted to persuading his immediate audience.

The Solution

The explanation behind Begin's apparently irrational rhetorical and political choices is that he does not view the world from the same sort of ideological perspective as do most political leaders. Begin's speeches and policies are not shaped by general ideological principles and self-interest. Instead, he sees the world through a myth. His mythic perspective on the holocaust and redemption shapes his world view, his political policies, and his rhetoric.

In order to understand how a mythic approach to Begin's rhetoric might explain the apparent inconsistencies in Begin's rhetoric and policies, consider briefly the characteristics of myths. My purpose here is not to define myth exhaustively, but to tailor a stipulative definition of its essential formal and functional characteristics to the task of explaining Begin's rhetoric.

The term myth comes from the Greek word mythos meaning story or plot. Myths are, first and foremost, stories. As Robertson writes, "A myth is a story told or an oft-told story referred to by a label or allusion. . . ."[26] While a myth is a story, it is also a way of looking at the world. The story told in a myth functions as a world view, a lens through which reality is seen. The vision of reality produced by a myth is accepted as true. In Malinowski's terms, myths function as "a reality lived."[27] As a lived reality, myths serve as moral paradigms defining good and bad behavior and structuring society. The characters in myths serve as "models of what should and should not, could and could not be attempted."[28] In sum, the myth serves as a structuring agent which explains some portion of the world. Theodore Gaster writes in relation

7

to Old Testament mythology that "the essential thing
about them [the myths and stories of the Old Testa-
ment] is that they are paradigms of the continuing
human situation. . . ."[29] Consequently, the common
definition of myth as a false story is inaccurate.
The model of the world in a myth may be either true or
false, but the vision of reality contained in it will
be viewed as true by those who accept the myth.   In
that way, myths can be distinguished from other literature which tells of the action of great heroes in
the distant past. Those works may possess the general
form of myth, but, unless they are accepted as an
accurate vision of reality, they do not function as
myths.

     As paradigms or models of the world, myths serve
a number of social functions. In primitive societies,
myths serve the functions that science and history
perform in modern societies.[30]   They describe the
natural environment and retell tribal history.   However, myths continue to serve crucial social functions
in modern societies. They provide the basic models
that support a society. Bennet writes: "The basic
models of society are called myths. . . ."[31] Malinowski makes the same point in his study of Melanesian
society. He writes: "It [myth] expresses, enhances,
and codifies belief; it safeguards and enforces
morality; it vouches for the efficiency of ritual and
contains practical rules for the guidance of man."[32]
Thus, myth explains the development of the society and
justifies the practical restrictions and moral rules
which organize it.[33]

     Humans also turn to myths to deal with moral
problems. Gardner writes: "Myths are designed to
deal with problems of human existence which seem
insoluble; they embody and express such dilemmas in a
coherently structured form and so serve to render them
intelligible."[34]   Science is an excellent tool for
measuring or explaining natural phenomena, but it is
not equipped to identify the good. Frye argues that
only in myth can ultimate questions of value be confronted: "Myth, in short, is the only possible language of concern, just as science, with its appeal to
evidence, accurate measurement, and rational deduction
is the only possible language of detachment."[35] Myths
are used to deal with problems that must be solved but
to which there is no rational solution. Larue cites
the story of Job as an example of the capacity of myth
to confront fundamental human problems.[36]

8

The formal structure of myth is adapted to the fulfillment of its social function. Because myths are stories, they can deal with problems that cannot be treated in discursive terms. Robertson writes:

> Very often, the problem being "solved" by a myth is a contradiction or a paradox, something which is beyond the power of reason or rational logic to resolve. But the telling of the story, or the recreation of a vivid and familiar image which is part of a myth, carries with it--for those who are accustomed to a myth, those who believe it--a satisfying sense that the contradiction has been resolved, the elements of the paradox have been reconciled. Dramatic retelling provides catharsis, as Aristotle pointed out about tragedy, which the audience--the participants in the myth-- take to be an explanation, a structured understanding of the original problem.37

Moreover, stories are not judged by the same logical standards applied to other symbolic forms. One consequence is that two inconsistent mythic descriptions of the same event may both be accepted as true.38 Myth is not illogical. Rather, it possesses a psychologic distinct from the logic of discursive reasoning.39 The logical structure of myth gives the storyteller great flexibility in confronting a problem.

The functions of myth in structuring society and resolving social problems are tied to four characteristics of mythic form. First, the main characters of myth are always larger than life. They are great heroes or villains whose story encapsulates the social problem facing a society. The characters in myth must be heroic because characters with less stature could not solve social problems or fulfill a modeling function. But, while mythic characters are larger than life, there is no single type of mythic hero. Some characters in myth are gods, others are heroes with special powers, and still others are simply great humans. Some critics argue that gods are the characters found in myth, while other types of heroes are found in sagas and legends. This view is not useful. The definition of myth as a type of story in which the

9

characters are heroic is not arbitrary but is derived from the function of myth. Since the social function of myth can be fulfilled by stories which tell of great humans who are not gods, any definition of the specific type of hero found in "true" myth should be avoided. It can be said only that the type of hero found in a particular myth depends upon the culture in which the myth is told and the needs of the story. As a general rule, the more difficult the problem faced in a myth, the greater the hero must be in order to deal with that problem.

The second defining characteristic of mythic form is occurrence outside normal historical time. Truly heroic events do not occur in the present. Thus, stories about such events must be shifted forward or backward in time. In general, myths tell of the actions of great heroes at either the beginning or end of some epoch or culture. As Altizer writes: "The mythical occurrence, as such, exists apart from all that is chronologically temporal. It lies either at the beginning or at the end of time."[40]

Myths occur outside of historical time not only because truly heroic events do not occur in the modern era, but also because, as Eliade argues, there is special power associated with beginnings and endings.[41] In addition, Eliade claims that the "perfection of beginnings . . . [is] movable."[42] That is, "it [myth] can now signify not only the perfection of the beginnings in the mythical past but also the perfection that is to come in the future, after this world is destroyed."[43] Thus, myths may draw upon the elemental power associated with either the beginning or end of the universe. Moreover, the beginning or ending of any human act posseses in diluted form the special power which is associated with the beginning or end of the universe. Eliade writes: "The idea implicit in this belief [the special power of origins] is that it is the first manifestation of a thing that is significant and valid, not its successive epiphanies."[44] Thus, a myth may retell the story of actual historical events at the beginning or end of a society. Through that story, the symbolic power associated with beginnings or endings is tapped. Eliade comments:

This prestige of the "origin" has also survived in the societies of Europe. When an innovation was to be made, it

10

was conceived, or presented, as a return to the origin. The Reformation began the return to the Bible and dreamed of recovering the experience of the primitive Church, or even of the earliest Christian communities. The French Revolution had its paradigmatic models in the Romans and the Spartans. The inspirers and leaders of the first successful radical revolution in Europe, which marked not merely the end of a regime but the end of a historical cycle, thought of themselves as restoring the ancient virtues praised by Livy and Plutarch.[45]

In the United States, a mythology telling the story of the founding of the nation and the settlement of the continent has developed. These stories tell of the great strength that was present in the heroes who created America. Because those heroes were present at the birth of the nation, they are presumed to possess a special greatness. As MacKenzie writes:

> By dramatizing, say, the arrival of the Pilgrim Fathers at Plymouth Rock, or, on the local level, the founding of some particular settlement or city, modern Americans renew contact with the sources of their history, affirm their unity with the pioneers, perform a ritual that reinforces patriotism and civic pride.[46]

In summary, myths tell the story of events which occur outside of normal historical time at the beginning or end of the universe, a culture, a nation, or a political system. Because myths occur at the time of perfect beginnings or transcendent endings, they allow humans to tap the special power associated with such events. They "transform historical time (Historie) into sacred time (Geschichte)."[47] Moreover, modern humans can tap the power present in creations and endings via myth. Through its retelling, the power of the myth can be transferred to the present generation: "any human act whatever acquires effectiveness to the extent to which it exactly repeats an act performed at the beginning of time by a god, a hero or an ancestor."[48]

11

The third formal characteristic of myth, also
tied to its function, is geography. Myths usually
occur either outside of the normal world or in a place
in the real world that possesses some special symbolic
power. In either case, the geographic locale of the
story adds force and credibility. Truly heroic events
do not occur in average places but in heaven or hell
or in a sacred location. The paradigm case for an
earthly place with special power is Jerusalem. Childs
writes:

> The main characteristics in mythical
> thinking about space are clearly pres-
> ent [in Jerusalem]. Zion has a quali-
> ty of holiness which sets it apart
> from all other "common" space. More-
> over, Zion as a copy of the heavenly
> reality is pictured in terms of the
> human body. The world functions as an
> organism with Zion as its navel.
> Finally there is an identification of
> Zion with Eden.[49]

Finally, mythic images are universal symbols. A
number of mythologists have noted that essentially the
same symbols and stories are found in myths throughout
the world.[50] Some have explained this similarity
through a theory of diffusion. Jung points to the
collective unconscious as the repository of mythic
archetypes upon which all humans draw.[51] A simpler
explanation focuses on mythic function. In this view,
similar images and themes are part of the common world
in which all humans live. Consequently, common themes
and images serve important mythic functions, regardless of the culture. Heroes are born of virgins
because such a birth is a mark of special power.
Northrop Frye writes:

> I do not mean by this phrase [univer-
> sal symbols] that there is any arche-
> typal code book which has been memo-
> rized by all human societies without
> exception. I mean that some symbols
> are images of things common to all
> men, and therefore have a communicable
> power which is potentially unlimited.
> Such symbols include those of food and
> drink, of the quest or journey, of
> light and darkness and of sexual ful-

fillment, which would take the form of
marriage.[52]

In sum, myths are stories about great heroes who
operate outside of historical time, usually at the
time of the creation or end of a culture, epoch, or
the universe. They ordinarily occur either outside
the real world, in heaven or hell or in a real place
with special symbolic power. And the images and
themes found in myth are drawn from universal human
experience. These characteristics are essential
attributes of the form of myth, necessary to fulfilling its function.

Given the crucial functions of myth in modern
societies, one would expect to find a good deal of
mythic rhetoric. If it is myth that provides the
structure for society, and if it is myth that answers
the basic problems facing a society, then it would
seem that many rhetors would draw upon the power of
myth. Yet, there is relatively little rhetoric that
is mythic in form and content.

Rhetorically, myth may be used as a strategic
device to persuade an audience to accept a position,
or it may function as an all-encompassing world view.
Many politicians use myth as a strategic device to
appeal to the American people. They draw upon the
popular mythology associated with the founding of
America in order to gain partisan political advantage-
Such strategic use of myth may be used to great effect
and is found in many rhetorical acts.

However, in some instances, a rhetor presents a
myth, not as a persuasive device to support a conclusion, but as a way of encompassing a problem. In that
situation, the rhetoric does not draw upon a culture's
myths but presents a new myth or recreates an old
myth.[53] Such a myth functions as a new world view or
model for the society. At the close of the Roman
Empire, Christianity functioned as such an all-
encompassing myth. It challenged pre-existing Roman
mythology by providing a world view justifying a new
social order and promising a transcendent future
through the resurrection of Christ. The myth answered
the needs of Roman society and was widely accepted. A
new myth regenerates or redefines the models structuring society. In such cases, the myth may possess
great persuasive power. For example, much of the
appeal of fascism and communism can be traced to the

13

mythic dimensions of these movements. They answered the needs of many people for a new social order and a transcendent purpose that could make life meaningful.[54] Frye notes the power of such all-encompassing myths to change a society drastically: "Those who have most effectively challenged the attitudes of society--Rousseau, Freud, Marx--are those who changed its mythology."[55]

While strategic use of myth as a rhetorical device is fairly common, rhetorical acts in which a myth functions as a world view are quite rare. The explanation for the failure of more rhetors to build such all-encompassing myths is relatively simple. Rhetors, like everyone else in a society, are taught the myths of that society, and, like most people, simply accept them. In addition, for a new mythic view such as Marxism or fascism to be accepted, the preexisting myths of the society must fail to meet the problems facing the society. If a society's myths are functioning, a new mythology will not be credible.

In other words, myths may be used as strategic devices to make a speech or essay more persuasive. In this sense, a reference to myth may be added to a speech or essay in the same way that additional evidence can be added to make an argument stronger. Alternatively, a rhetorical act may itself take the form of myth and function as a new world view. Here, the myth is not a strategic device, but a paradigm for describing and evaluating the world. Frye makes a similar point when he distinguishes between the symbols and archetypes which make up individual works of literature and the anagogic phase of literature. In the anagogic phase, archetypes and symbols are not strategic devices, but form "a self-contained literary universe."[56] The anagogic literary phase is most often found in relation to "scripture or apocalyptic revelation"[57] because such literature provides the all-encompassing vision that defines a society. Myth as world view operates in the anagogic phase. It provides a way of seeing and evaluating the world and, thus, structures human experience. While myth as strategy is much more common than myth as world view, those myths which function as total visions of the human universe are particularly important. Myth as world view shapes society; it produces a quasi-religious fervor. It was myth as world view that energized the two great totalitarian movements of the twentieth century. And it is myth as world view to

14

which one must turn for an explanation of Begin's rhetoric.

The inexplicable elements in Begin's ideology and rhetoric may be explained by treating him as a myth-maker in the anagogic sense. His inability to adapt to a variety of audiences may reflect the myth which shapes the world which he sees. In the same way, his constant references to the biblical history may be explained by a mythic view of the lived reality of Israel's biblical history. Begin's apparently non-strategic statements may be explicated in a similar fashion. The reality of his myth may forbid compromise, even with Israel's most important ally. This argument cannot be developed here, but must be deferred to later chapters where I consider the rhetoric of the Irgun in the 1940s and the rhetoric of the Begin government. At this point, it is enough to say that if Begin views the world through myth, this may explain paradoxical aspects of his policies and statements.

A description of Begin as a mythmaker might also explain the political role which Begin has played in Israeli politics. For many years, Begin has aroused an almost religious fervor among his supporters. Segal wrote of the 1966 convention of Begin's political party: "for some people membership in Herut serves some profound psychological needs: and not just as an instrument for political action. Time and again the assembly took on the appearance of a mass revival rally where the faithful renew their loyalty by unquestioning reaffirmation of faith."[58] The delegates to the convention treated Begin as a great hero: "The style at conventions has remained the same to this day, many speakers referring to Mr. Begin as 'my commander' and he in turn calling delegates 'my children.'"[59] The members of the successor party to Herut, the Likud coalition, still treat Begin as an almost Messianic figure. In 1980, Philip Gilion wrote that Likud is in agreement about only one thing, "the near divinity of Menachem Begin."[60] An aide to Begin and one of his biographers, Harry Hurwitz, compared Begin to Bar Kochba and Judas Maccabeus.[61] Such treatment of Begin seems out of place in a secular, democratic, liberal state. But if Begin is a myth-maker in the anagogic sense, then such treatment is understandable.

Scope of the Study

The subject of this study is the rhetoric of Menachem Begin. The key to his rhetoric lies in the period when he commanded the Irgun against the British. Begin has stated again and again that the most important event in his life was his service as commander of the Irgun. Even after his election as Prime Minister of Israel, Begin continued to take that position. In the 1977 edition of The Revolt, Begin explained:

In the full recognition of the facts I say unhesitatingly: with all the grave responsibility that goes with this post in the State of Israel, it was a higher task to lead the fighting patriots in that unequal struggle, under the heaviest odds possible, of the few against the many. Why do I still feel this way? The answer is clear. When a man fights for freedom with an incessant risk of his life, he identifies himself completely with the very essence of liberty. Such identification seldom comes more than once in a lifetime. It is in a spirit of continued dedication to such a meaning of liberty that I present to the reader, whether Jew or Gentile, the new edition of The Revolt.[62]

Begin's recurrent references to the Irgun also suggest that his later rhetoric is deeply influenced by his prior rhetorical action. This view is supported by the comment of Wolf Blitzer of the Jerusalem Post that anyone wanting to understand Begin should first read The Revolt.[63] Consequently, the first work considered in this study is The Revolt. It is Begin's memoir of the most important period in his life and is often cited by biographers for what it reveals about Begin. The Revolt is a disjointed combination of excerpts from speeches, descriptions of Irgun actions, and didactic lectures defending Irgun policies. If Begin's rhetoric is shaped by myth, The Revolt should reveal his world view. However, it does not necessarily follow that if The Revolt is informed by a myth, the rhetoric of the Irgun, during the fight against the British, was similarly inspired. In order to test whether

16

the Irgun's revolt was shaped by myth, I consider a number of speeches and essays written by Begin while he commanded the Irgun. Initially, I focus on four representative works of Irgun rhetoric: Irgun Zvai Leumi, "A Message From the Commander-in-Chief of the Irgun to the Diaspora," September 1946; Irgun Zvai Leumi, "From Kishenev to Acre: On the Sixth Anniversary of the Death of David Raziel," May 30, 1947; Irgun Zvai Leumi, "The Ten Martyrs Under Cursed Britain Compared to 10 Martyrs Under Rome," July 30, 1947; Menachem Beigin [sic], "The First Prerequisite of Freedom is Complete Victory," May 15, 1948.[64] However, even if these works were energized by the same mythic view found in The Revolt, this would not prove that Begin's contemporary rhetoric is inspired by myth. In order to test this question, I focus on Begin's rhetoric as prime minister of Israel. The three works which I analyze--Begin's speech to the Knesset during Sadat's visit to Jerusalem, his speech at the signing of the Egyptian-Israeli peace treaty, and his statement following U.S. criticism of Israeli annexation of the Golan Heights--are particularly important.[65] They treat crucial issues in Israeli-United States relations and the peace negotiations with Egypt. If these crucial works do not evince the same mythic dimension, that would be strong evidence of a major change in Begin's rhetoric. By contrast, if The Revolt, representative works of Irgun rhetoric, and his most important modern rhetorical acts are all shaped by the same mythic world view this is strong support for characterizing Begin's rhetoric as a whole as mythic.

Although the primary sources for this study are The Revolt and selected speeches and essays by Begin, other sources were also consulted. In order to understand the situation Begin faced while commander of the Irgun, I reviewed the available secondary material on Begin and the Irgun. Aside from the four biographies already cited, the most valuable work is J. Bowyer Bell's brilliant Terror Out of Zion. I also examined representative secondary works on the founding of the state of Israel, Zionism, modern Judaism, the holocaust, the peace negotiations between Egypt and Israel, and myth.[66]

17

Justification

One justification for a study of Begin's rhetoric is the absence of critical literature on that subject. While a number of scholars have focused on Begin's life and the role of the Irgun in forcing the British to leave Palestine, no significant analysis of his rhetoric has yet been done. Until recently, most of the biographical and historical work on Begin's life accepted the view that Begin was simply a brutal terrorist. Following his participation in the Government of National Unity from 1967-1970, historians began to reevaluate him. Unfortunately, this research has not included detailed analysis of his rhetoric. Bell's history of the Irgun mentions the symbolic importance of Irgun tactics and quotes extensively from Begin's speeches and essays, but Bell does not consider rhetoric an object worthy of study in itself. Begin's major biographers all quote him and pay tribute to his rhetorical skill, but they do not analyze his rhetoric in any depth,[67] nor have the memoirs of various Irgun leaders systematically analyzed Begin's speeches and writings.

Moreover, Begin's rhetoric has not been scrutinized by rhetorical critics.[68] Two recent essays treating the relation between rhetoric and the Middle East conflict point to the potential value of such an analysis. Heisey describes the general characteristics of Arab and Israeli rhetoric and suggests changes which must be made in that rhetoric if peace is to come to the region.[69] Seibold considers the rhetoric of the Jewish Defense League,[70] and notes that the J.D.L. cites the Irgun as an example of the type of defense organization that Jews should form. He also considers the psychological importance of the holocaust as it affects the J.D.L. However, neither essay focuses on Begin directly.

One of Begin's speeches has received some analysis. Frank compares the speeches that Begin, Carter, and Sadat presented at the ceremony for the signing of the Egyptian-Israeli peace treaty and concludes that, unlike Carter and Sadat, Begin failed to adapt to the rhetorical situation present at the peace treaty signing ceremony.[71] In a second essay, Frank describes the development of the Israeli peace movement and discusses Begin's role in the peace process.[72] Frank's work points to the importance of Begin's rhetoric, but does not exhaust its study.

One recent work treats the myth underlying the ideology of the revisionist Zionist movement. Raël Jean Isaac characterizes the myth of the revisionist movement with the phrase, "Malchut Yisrael" [the Kingdom of Israel].[73] She also describes the development of the movement's ideology.[74] Her work is quite useful, but it does not contain any detailed analysis of Begin's rhetoric.

The final hurdle to be surmounted in justifying this study involves translation. The key question is whether the English translations of The Revolt and of Begin's speeches and essays are adequate for analysis. One commentator believes that the translation of The Revolt is quite bad. In his review of The Revolt in The Middle East Journal, Teller writes: "The English translation of the book is deplorable. At times it degenerates into ridiculous jargon. The story of the Irgun's underground campaign against the British could make absorbing reading had the book been better edited."[75]

While the translation of The Revolt is no doubt imperfect, there are good reasons to believe that it is adequate for this study. The English version of The Revolt is addressed explicitly to an English speaking audience. In the introduction, Begin addresses "a special message to the British reader" (p. xi). Clearly, Begin intended the book to be read in English by readers who lacked Hebrew. In addition, Begin himself supervised the translation and editing of the book. In the editor's preface, Martin Greenberg explains Begin's role in the editing process: "In the actual translation, Mr. Samuel Katz, working with the author, cut out a good deal of matter of a more limited and local interest"[76] (p. viii). The editing process described by Greenberg may explain why Teller found the translation difficult to follow. However, given Begin's participation in the translation, there is every reason to believe that the translation accurately reflects his views. Further, the translator, Samuel Katz, was a member of the Irgun, head of the Irgun's English department, and a close friend of Begin.

Finally, a number of reviewers and secondary sources have validated the translation of The Revolt directly or indirectly by writing of the usefulness of the work. In a review of The Revolt, S. Benaron of the Jerusalem Post characterizes the translation as "excellent."[77] As I noted earlier, Wolf Blitzer of the Jerusalem Post admonishes the U.S. public to read The Revolt in order to understand Begin. In their reviews of The Revolt, both Choice and the Library Journal note the value of the book as a primary source.[78] In addition, The Revolt is often cited as a primary source by experts on terrorism. In a bibliographic note on the study of underground organizations in Palestine, J. Bowyer Bell comments: "Fortunately, some of the most interesting or important works are in English: Begin's The Revolt. . . ."[79] While The Revolt is a difficult book, there is reason to believe that Katz's translation accurately reflects Begin's rhetoric.

Fortunately, there is little problem with translations of the other primary sources. The speeches and essays from the 1940s come from the Irgun's own English language periodicals. Those periodicals were designed to be read in English, not Hebrew, in order to generate American support for the Irgun. Begin's recent speeches also pose few problems of translation. Without exception, all of the recent speeches which I cite were presented in English or translated by the Israeli government for distribution in the United States.

Plan of the Study

Chapter Two, "The Myth of Return in Zionism and Jewish History," describes the treatment of "return" in Zionism and traditional Judaism. The myth of the Irgun can be understood only in the context of prior and competing Jewish mythologies. The Jewish people lived through several cycles of exile and return before they were finally expelled from Palestine following the revolt against Rome. One response to the problems of living in dispersion was a myth of return to Palestine. After describing the traditional myth of exile and return, I explain how the Zionist myth redefined the concept of "return" in order to deal with the threats of assimilation and anti-Semitism.

In Chapter Three, "Menachem Begin and the Holocaust: The Inevitability of a Mythic Response," I briefly sketch the historical situation that led Begin to attack the British in Palestine and the psychological and moral problem created for Zionism by the holocaust. I draw upon the work of theologians and of the writer Elie Wiesel in order to explain how the holocaust pushed Begin toward myth. Finally, I argue that the other Jewish mythologies could not adequately respond to the moral problems raised by the holocaust.

In Chapter Four, "Menachem Begin and The Revolt: The Myth of Holocaust and Return," I begin building the case that Begin's rhetoric is mythic by arguing that The Revolt takes the form of a rhetorical myth. It fulfills the functions typically served by myth and possesses the typical form of myth. In building this argument, I draw a parallel between The Revolt and heroic myth as described by Joseph Campbell in his classic work, The Hero With a Thousand Faces, and then sketch the solution the Irgun's myth offers to the moral problem of the holocaust.

In Chapter Five, "Only Thus: The Myth of the Irgun," I consider whether the mythic pattern present in The Revolt is representative of the rhetoric of the Irgun during their conflict with the British. In order to test this question, I examine four representative examples of Irgun rhetoric. I conclude that Irgun rhetoric was shaped by the same myth found in The Revolt.

In Chapter Six, "Begin's Modern Rhetoric: The Holocaust and the Myth of Return," I complete the argument that Begin's rhetoric is mythic by considering whether Begin's rhetoric as prime minister of Israel is shaped by the same mythic pattern found in the rhretoric of the Irgun. I argue that most of the mythic characteristics found in The Revolt and the rhetoric of the Irgun are present in Begin's rhetoric in the 1980s. Two of his most important speeches--the speech to the Knesset during Sadat's visit to Jerusalem and the speech at the signing of the Israeli-Egyptian peace treaty--draw upon the myth of return which is found in Irgun rhetoric. Begin's statement to the United States after the annexation of the Golan Heights also shows signs of being influenced by that same myth. Based on this evidence, I argue that Menachem Begin's rhetoric from the 1940s to the present day has been dominated by the myth of holocaust and redemption through return.

In Chapter Seven, "The Social Implications of Menachem Begin's Myth of Return," I argue that an understanding of Begin's mythic world view illuminates Begin's career. A number of commentators have characterized the policies of the Israeli government under Prime Minister Begin as confusing and contradictory. An understanding of the myth which dominates Begin's life eliminates much of that confusion. After explaining the influence of myth on Begin's ideology, I consider whether the myth of return solved the problems created by the holocaust.

In Chapter Eight, "The Value of a Mythic Approach to Criticism," I consider the implications of this study for mythic criticism as a method of rhetorical criticism. I argue that there is no single theory which adequately explains all varieties of myth and that Lévi-Strauss's structuralist method has limited value. Finally, I argue that the critic can discover the appropriate theory or method of explaining and evaluating a myth only by moving inductively from the characteristics of the individual myth to the proper theory or method of criticism.

Notes

[1] Revisionist Zionism is a conservative movement in Zionism. In the 1920s and 1930s, when labor Zionists were calling for a self-governing Jewish home in Palestine, revisionists, led by Vladimir Jabotinsky, advocated the creation of a Jewish state in Palestine. They believed that the Jews could survive in the world of power politics only by creating their own state complete with an army. For a more detailed description of revisionism and Jabotinsky see chapter three.

[2] See J. Bowyer Bell, Terror Out of Zion: Irgun Zvai Leumi, LEHI, and the Palestinian Underground, 1929-1949 (New York: Avon, 1977). Bell argues that the Irgun played an important role in forcing the British out of Palestine (p. viii). He later notes that by whipping (p. 231) and hanging (pp. 299-300) British soldiers in retaliation for similar acts, the Irgun humiliated the British. See also Nichols Bethel, The Palestine Triangle: The Struggle for the Holy Land 1935-1948 (New York: Putnam, 1979), p. 356; Eitan Haber, Menachem Begin: The Legend and the Man (New York: Delacorte, 1978), p. 191, cites the opinion of the last commander of the Palestine police that it was the Irgun which forced the British out of Palestine. Note that either Menahem or Menachem is considered correct as a rendering of Begin's first name.

[3] The Jewish Agency was the organization of the Jewish community which served a number of governmental functions in health care, immigration, and so on. The Haganah (defense) organization was the official self-defense organization of the Jewish community.

[4] See Harry Hurwitz, Menachem Begin (Johannesburg, South Africa: Jewish Herald, 1977), pp. 56-57, where Hurwitz reports that Begin puts so much stress on his service as commander of the Irgun that at a meeting honoring the memory of Vladimir Jabotinsky he asked to be introduced first as the former commander of the Irgun and only then as prime minister of Israel.

[5] As I use it here, rhetoric includes all public symbolic acts aimed at persuading an audience to take some action: "Rhetoric is the study of all the processes by which people influence each other through symbols. . . ." Karlyn Kohrs Campbell, The Rhetorical Act (Belmont, CA: Wadsworth, 1982), p. 7.

[6] Campbell notes that a photograph may in some situations be rhetorical, The Rhetorical Act, p. 7.

[7] Bell, p. 134.

[8] Frank Gervasi, The Life and Times of Menahem Begin: Rebel to Statesman (New York: Putnam, 1979), p. 182.

[9] Menachem Begin, The Revolt, trans. Samuel Katz (New York: Nash, 1972), p. 52. Further references to The Revolt will be made in the text.

[10] Hurwitz, p. 143.

[11] Haber, p. 99.

[12] Haber, p. 47.

[13] Gertrude Hirschler and Lester S. Eckman, Menahem Begin: From Freedom Fighter to Statesman (New York: Shengold, 1979), p. 19.

[14] Gervasi, p. 21.

[15] Hurwitz, p. 147.

[16] See Frederick Kempe, "House Divided: Israel's War Costs Include an Increase in Internal Discord," Wall Street Journal, 12 July 1982, p. 11.

[17] For a description of Begin's attack on Schmidt, see William Claiborne, "Begin Rules out Deal on Missiles, Assails Schmidt," Washington Post, 7 May 1981, p. A27.

[18] See Bernard Gwertzman, "Peace Treaty Signed by Egypt and Israel," New York Times, 27 March 1979, p. A10.

[19] Suzanne Weaver, "Somber Gladness Pervades Carter's Party for Peace," Wall Street Journal, 30 March 1979, p. 14. Also see Thomas W. Lippman, "Egypt Greets Peace Treaty With Mix of Joy, Indifference," Washington Post, 27 March 1979, p. A12. Anthony Lewis argues that many of Begin's speeches produce this effect. See Anthony Lewis, "Why the Palestinians Feel Left Out," Kansas City Times, 2 October 1979, p. 12a.

[20] It should be noted that far more than most nations, important elements of Israeli life are influenced by ancient history. Traditional Jewish laws are enforced by the Israeli state and religious parties are represented in the Knesset.

[21] Menachem Begin, "Text of Address by Mr. Menahem Begin, Prime Minister of the State of Israel, At a Special Session of the Knesset," Israel Information Centre, 20 November 1977, p. 5.

[22] See Irgun Zvai Leumi, "Irgun Offers Plan of Action," The Answer, 29 October 1947, p. 6.

[23] Menachem Beigin [sic], "The First Prerequisite of Freedom is Complete Victory," The Answer, 28 May 1948, p. 4.

[24] Begin's statement is reprinted in "Israel Hits Back After U.S. Sanctions," The Jerusalem Post International Edition, 20–26 December 1981, p. 2.

[25] All of the references to the Senate Foreign Relations Committee discussion are from John Lindsay, "A 'Lively' Discussion," Newsweek, 5 July 1982, p. 38.

[26] James Oliver Robertson, American Myth, American Reality (New York: Hill and Wang, 1980), p. 6.

[27] Bronislaw Malinowski, Magic, Science and Religion (Garden City, NY: Anchor Doubleday, 1954), p. 100. Also see Mircea Eliade, "Myth in the Nineteenth and Twentieth Centuries," in Dictionary of the History of Ideas, 1973 ed., vol. 3, p. 314.

[28] Gerald A. Larue, Ancient Myth and Modern Man (Englewood Cliffs, NJ: Prentice Hall, 1975), p. 67.

[29] Theodore Gaster, Myth, Legend and Custom in the Old Testament (New York: Harper and Row, 1969), p. xxxiv.

[30] See Gaster, p. xxxv; Reinhold Niebuhr, "The Truth in Myths," in Faith and Politics, ed. Ronald H. Stone (New York: George Braziller, 1968), p. 25.

[31] W. Lance Bennet, "Myth, Ritual, and Political Control," Journal of Communications, 30 (1980), p. 170.

[32] Malinowski, p. 101.

[33] Malinowski, p. 101.

[34] Howard Gardner, The Quest for Mind: Piaget, Lévi-Strauss, and the Structuralist Movement, 2nd ed. (Chicago: University of Chicago Press, 1981), p. 148.

[35] Northrop Frye, "Literature and Myth," in Relations of Literary Study: Essays on Interdisciplinary Contributions, ed. James Thorpe (New York: MLA, 1967), pp. 40–41.

[36] Larue, p. 142.

37 Robertson, p. 6. Also see Albert Cook, Myth and Language (Bloomington: Indiana University Press, 1980), pp. 2-4.

38 See Melville J. Herskovitts and Frances S. Herskovitts, Dahomean Narrative: A Cross Cultural Analysis (Evanston: Northwestern University Press, 1958), p. 18.

39 For one view of this psychological logic see Ernst Cassirer, Mythical Thought, vol. 2 of The Philosophy of Symbolic Forms, trans. Ralph Manheim (New Haven: Yale University Press, 1955).

40 J. J. Altizer, Oriental Mysticism and Biblical Eschatology (Philadelphia: Westminster Press, 1966), p. 69.

41 Mircea Eliade, Myth and Reality, trans. Willard R. Trask (New York: Harper, 1963), pp. 21-53, especially p. 34.

42 Eliade, Myth and Reality, p. 6.

43 Eliade, Myth and Reality, p. 75.

44 Eliade, Myth and Reality, p. 34.

45 Eliade, Myth and Reality, p. 182.

46 R.A.F. MacKenzie, Faith and History in the Old Testament (Minneapolis: University of Minnesota Press, 1963), pp. 65-66.

47 Eliade is cited by Altizer, p. 69.

48 Mircea Eliade, The Myth of the Eternal Return or, Cosmos and History, trans. Willard R. Trask (Princeton: Princeton University Press, 1954), p. 22.

49 Brevard S. Childs, Myth and Reality in the Old Testament, 2nd ed. (London: SCM Press, 1962), pp. 89-90.

50 See for instance Clyde Kluckhohn, "Recurrent Themes in Myth and Mythmaking," in Myth and Mythmaking, ed. Henry A. Murray (Boston: Beacon Press, 1968), p. 46.

51 See C. G. Jung and C. Kerenyi, Essays on a Science of Mythology (New York: Pantheon, 1949).

52 Northrup Frye, Anatomy of Criticism: Four Essays (Princeton: Princeton University Press, 1957), p. 118. Also see Shirley Park Lowry, Familiar Mysteries: The Truth in Myth (New York: Oxford University Press, 1982), p. 30.

26

[53] The rhetor either creates a totally new mythology or draws upon an earlier myth which had been rejected in the society.

[54] See Henry Hatfield, "The Myth of Nazism," in Myth and Mythmaking, pp. 199-219; Louis J. Halle, "Marx's Religious Drama," Encounter, 25, no. 4 (October 1965), pp. 29-37.

[55] Frye, "Literature and Myth," p. 41.

[56] Frye, Anatomy of Criticism, p. 118.

[57] Frye, Anatomy of Criticism, p. 120.

[58] Mark Segal, "Herut Brings Down the Roof," Jerusalem Post, 8 July 1966, Inter-Documentation Company microfiche. No page number was included on the microfiche.

[59] Segal, "Herut Brings Down the Roof."

[60] Philip Gilion, "The Feud in Labour," Jerusalem Post International Edition, 23-29 November 1980, p. 11.

[61] See Hurwitz, p. 38.

[62] Menachem Begin, "Preface to the Revised Edition," in The Revolt, trans. Samuel Katz (New York: Dell, 1977), p. 14. The 1977 edition of The Revolt is exactly the same as the original edition except for a new introduction and preface by the author.

[63] See Wolf Blitzer, "Responsibility in the Middle East," New York Times Book Review, 29 January 1978, p. 9.

[64] See Irgun Zvai Leumi, "A Message From the Commander-in-Chief of the Irgun to the Diaspora," The Answer, September 1946, pp. 11-12; Irgun Zvai Leumi, "From Kishenev to Acre: On the Sixth Anniversary of the Death of David Raziel," The Answer, 30 May 1947, p. 6; Irgun Zvai Leumi, "The Ten Martyrs Under Cursed Britain Compared to 10 Martyrs Under Rome," The Answer, 15 August 1947, p. 6; Menachem Beigin [sic], "The First Prerequisite of Freedom Is Complete Victory," pp. 4-5. Although Begin wrote essentially all of the Irgun rhetoric, the authorship of the first three works is not identified in the text of the works. Consequently, I have listed the author as the Irgun. In all likelihood they were written by Begin. Begin was the commander of the Irgun in September 1946.

[65] For the address during Sadat's visit to Jerusalem see Begin, "Text of Addresses by Mr. Menahem Begin, Prime Minister of the State of Israel, At a Special Session of the Knesset." The

27

peace treaty speech is found in Menahem Begin, "Prime Minister Begin's Speech at the Signing of the Peace Treaty with Egypt," 20 March 1979, State of Israel Government Printing Office. Begin's statement on the Golan is reprinted in "Israel Hits Back after U.S. Sanctions," pp. 1-2.

66 For the works considered, see the bibliography.

67 Begin's rhetoric has received no significant attention in either the popular press or political science journals. Even those commentators who mention Begin's rhetoric fail to analyze it in any depth. See for instances Amos Perlmutter, "Begin's Rhetoric and Sharon's Tactics," Foreign Affairs, 62 (1982), pp. 67-83.

68 The most detailed analysis of rhetoric in any work on Begin is found in a reprint of an essay by Begin on Jabotinsky's rhetoric. See Hurwitz, pp. 47-48.

69 D. Ray Heisey, "The Rhetoric of the Arab-Israeli Conflict," Quarterly Journal of Speech, 56 (1970), pp. 12-21.

70 David Seibold, "Jewish Defense League: The Rhetoric of Resistance," Today's Speech, 21 (1973), pp. 39-48.

71 David A. Frank, "In Celebration of Peace: A Rhetorical Analysis of the Three Speeches Delivered at the Middle East Ceremony of Peace 26 March 1979," paper presented at the Speech Communication Association Convention, Anaheim, California, 13 November 1981.

72 David A. Frank, "'Shalom Ashshav'--Rituals of the Israeli Peace Movement," Communication Monographs, 48 (1981), pp. 165-181.

73 Raël Jean Isaac, Party and Politics in Israel: Three Visions of a Jewish State (New York: Longman, 1981), p. 135.

74 Isaac, pp. 135-161.

75 Judd L. Teller, "The Revolt: Story of the Irgun," The Middle East Journal, 6 (1952), p. 361.

76 Begin was fluent in English at the time he wrote The Revolt. See Robert St. John, Shalom Means Peace (Garden City, NY: Doubleday, 1950), p. 173; Jorge Garcia Grandados, The Birth of Israel: The Drama As I Saw It (New York: Knopf, 1948), p. 155. Today, Begin often gives public speeches in English.

[77] S. Benaron, "Passionate Account of I.Z.L.'s Exploits," Jerusalem Post, 22 April 1965, Inter-Documentation microfiche. The microfiche does not list page numbers.

[78] "Begin, Menahem," Choice, 15 (June 1978), p. 603; "Begin," Library Journal, 76 (October 15, 1951), p. 1704. Both reviews are brief.

[79] Bell, pp. 444-445.

CHAPTER II

THE MYTH OF RETURN IN ZIONISM AND JEWISH HISTORY

The myth which Menachem Begin created in response
to the holocaust can be understood only in the context
of pre-existing Jewish mythologies, for Begin's revisionist myth grew out of a more general Zionist myth,
itself created in the nineteenth century in answer to
continuing anti-Semitism in even the most enlightened
areas of Europe. This Zionist myth prophesied the
redemption of the Jewish people and the creation of a
perfect society on earth through the establishment of
a Jewish state in Palestine. The Zionist myth, in
turn, can be understood only in the context of traditional Jewish love of Zion. Throughout nineteen centuries of exile, Jews prayed for their return to
Zion. Although Jewish life was shaped by many factors, the tie to ancient Israel and a myth explaining
the exile and promising an eventual return were continuing forces influencing that life. In developig
their mythology, Zionist leaders emphasized the
Israel-centered aspects of Jewish tradition and
ignored many other aspects of their history.[1] They
projected back on Jewish history a pre-modern myth of
exile and return as the dominating force in Jewish
life. Thus, Begin's mythic response to the holocaust
arose out of two related Jewish myths: 1) A traditional Jewish myth of exile and return created both by
traditional religious Jews and by Zionist leaders who
interpreted all Jewish history in Israel centered
terms,[2] and 2) a modern Zionist myth which called for
the redemption of the Jewish people through return to
Zion. In order to understand Begin's myth of holocaust and redemption through return, it is necessary
to consider these two prior mythologies.

In the view of both modern Zionists and many
traditional Jews, a cyclical pattern of exile and
return is at the very core of Jewish existence.[3] All
Jewish history is interpreted as reflecting this
cycle. Beginning with the covenant of Abraham, the
Jewish people have claimed the land of Zion by right
of eternal grant from God.[4] Three times in their long
history they have been exiled from that land. The
first cycle began when Joseph, one of the sons of
Jacob, the last of the patriarchs, was sold into

slavery in Egypt. Joseph eventually rose to high office within Egypt, and when famine struck the Jews in Canaan, he persuaded the Pharaoh to accept them into Egypt. Thus began the first exile from the land of Israel, an exile that came to an end when Moses, aided by God, led the Jews from Egypt to Sinai. The Hebrew God first hardened the heart of the Pharaoh that he might be destroyed utterly, and then provided the Jews with miraculous assistance in the form of plagues to effect their release. After many years in the desert following the escape from Egypt, in which time God gave the ten commandments to Moses, the Jews returned from Sinai to Israel.

There followed a long period of life in the land of Israel. This was the time of the Judges, of Saul, David, and Solomon, and of two Jewish states, Israel and Judah. The northern state, Israel, which occupied Samaria, was destroyed by the Assyrians in 772 BCE. The southern state, Judah, including Jerusalem, survived for another century. In about 600 BCE, a king of Judah, Jehoiakim, withheld tribute from the king of Babylon, Nebuchadnezzar. Nebuchadnezzar then invaded Judah and in 598 BCE captured Jerusalem. Jehoiakim and 10,000 hostages were taken into exile. Eight years later, Zedekiah, who had been placed on the throne by the Babylonians, revolted. The Jews held out for four years, but in 586 BCE on the ninth of Ab, Jerusalem fell, and the temple was destroyed. Nearly fifty years passed before some Israelites were to return to Jerusalem. In 538 BCE, the Persian king Cyrus, who had conquered the Babylonian empire, allowed them to begin work rebuilding the temple. The first group returned from Babylon to Palestine in that year and the temple was completely rebuilt seventy-one years after its destruction.

Israel then went through a long period of independence or autonomous rule under the protectorship of some other power in the area. The greatest threat to the Jewish people came in 168 BCE when Antiochus IV of the Seleucid empire (a successor state to the empire of Alexander) ordered the Jews to give up their religion. At the small village of Modiin, a local leader, named Mattathias, and his five sons refused to allow their altar to be fouled and killed the Greek soldiers who had been sent to enforce the decree. This spark set off the Maccabean revolt. Mattathias's third son, Judas, led the revolt against Greek rule over Zion. By 165 BCE, the Maccabean revolt had captured Jerusalem and cleansed the temple. The victory is celebrated every year at Hannukah. The Hasmonean dynasty that was born in the Maccabean revolt lasted until 63 BCE.

The third great cycle of exile and return began in 66 CE when the Zealots revolted against Rome. For a time the revolt was successful, but in 70 CE, again on the ninth of Ab, Jerusalem fell and the temple was destroyed. The Zealot garrison at the mountain fortress of Masada held out until Passover in 73 CE, but, faced with superior Roman forces, the defenders elected to commit suicide rather than be captured. The long exile of the Jewish people from Palestine, which was to last nearly 1900 years, had begun. One last attempt was made to re-establish a Jewish state in Palestine. Some sixty years after the temple had been destroyed, the emperor Hadrian ordered a new temple honoring Jupiter to be built on the temple mount in Jerusalem. Viewing Hadrian's plan as an offense against God, the Jewish people led by Simon Bar Kochba revolted against the Romans. For a time Bar Kochba's revolt was quite successful, and many Jews thought he might be the Messiah. The greatest religious leader of the age, Rabbi Akiba, referred to Bar Kochba as "the Messianic king."[5] However, Rome was too strong, and Bar Kochba was gradually pushed back until finally Jerusalem fell. Bar Kochba made his last stand at Bethar, a fortified village southwest of Jerusalem. According to tradition, it fell on the ninth of Ab in 135 CE. There would not be a Jewish state in Palestine for over 1800 years.

For nearly nineteen centuries, the Jewish people lived in foreign lands. Steeped in the Zionist tradition, some modern Jewish historians argue that the same cycle of exile and return was often repeated in miniature during this period. The Jews were accepted in a country only to be forced to leave and begin again elsewhere:

> The rhythm of exile and return is one that persists throughout the traditional history of the Hebrews and the Jews. . . . The Jews were habituated to looking back at a repeating pattern of promise, fulfillment, transgression, punishment, and pardon, a cyclical granting and withdrawal of the gifts of territory and sovereignty,

33

and of concomitant lament and thanksgiving.[6]

During the centuries of exile, the Jewish people maintained an independent culture while living within foreign nations. The myth of exile and return explained
both why the Jews lived in exile from Zion and how
they might return to the land of Israel. The two
halves of the myth justified Jewish life in the
Diaspora and described the redemption which was to
come. According to the myth, the Jews lived in exile
from the land of Israel because they had sinned:
"Exile is also a penalty that the Jews brought upon
themselves and continue to suffer 'because of our many
sins.'"[7] However, it was not merely the sins of the
Jewish people which maintained the exile through the
centuries. If it had been only the sins of the Jews
that needed to be cleansed prior to return, the Jews
would have returned to Zion long ago. The first exile
from Palestine, in Egypt, lasted four or five hundred
years. The exile to Babylon lasted only fifty years.
Why then did the third exile of the Jewish people from
Palestine continue for so many centuries? The myth
answered this question by pointing to the status of
the Jews as the chosen people of God. The Jews were
being tested because they had been chosen. "Exile is
a penance for which the Jews were singled out precisely because they are the 'Chosen people.'"[8] The Jews
had taken upon themselves the sins of the world and
would return to Zion only after they had been thoroughly tested by God:

> The doctrine of the "suffering ser-
> vant" was invoked and expanded, that
> the people of Israel in the mysterious
> will of God was bearing not only its
> own sins but the sins of others. The
> Exile was a time of testing, a pro-
> longed trial, like God's trial of
> Abraham. The task of the people was
> to remain faithful and to remember
> Zion.[9]

While exile was a horror that the Jews must endure, it
was also an honor. They lived in exile because they
had been chosen by God.

The exile was bearable for the Jewish people
because they knew that some day they would return to
Zion. Over the centuries, they built an idealized

picture of the land of Israel which gave their lives
meaning. The land of Israel was the Holy Land on
which all their hopes rested. Hertzberg quotes from
the Talmudic literature to show the unbreakable link
between the land of Israel and the Jewish people:

> Living in the Land of Israel equals in
> import the performance of all the com-
> mandments of the Torah. Rabbi Zeira
> said: "Even the conversation of those
> who live in the Land of Israel is
> Torah." Ten measures of wisdom came
> into the world. The Land of Israel
> took nine, and the rest of the world
> took one.[10]

In the view of nineteenth and twentieth century Zionists, the vision of a return to a redeemed land of
Israel was at the core of Judaism. Rabbi Abraham
Isaac Kook's expression of love for Zion is typical of
this perspective:

> Eretz Yisrael is not something apart
> from the soul of the Jewish people; it
> is no mere national possession, serv-
> ing as a means of unifying our people
> and buttressing its material, or even
> its spiritual survival. Eretz Yisrael
> is part of the very essence of our
> nationhood; it is bound organically to
> its very life and inner being. Human
> reason, even at its most sublime, can-
> not begin to understand the unique
> holiness of Eretz Yisrael; it cannot
> stir the depths of love for the land
> that are dormant within our people.[11]

A second aspect of the return was a millenial
vision of the perfect age which would come once the
Jews had come back to Palestine. The return of the
Jews to Zion would signal the Messianic age:

> The restoration of the Jews to their
> ancestral Land, when it occurred,
> would be a matter of extraordinary and
> universal significance auguring or
> even instituting a millenial situation
> in which something like the harmony
> between man and his Creator that had

35

obtained before the Fall would be restored.[12]

Maimonides believed it would be the Messiah who personally re-established the Kingdom of Israel:

> The annointed King [the Messiah] will in time arise and establish the kingdom of David in its former position and in the dominion it originally had. He will build up the sanctuary and gather the scattered of Israel. In his day, the laws will become what they were in olden time. . . .[13]

The exile could be suffered because it would someday end with the coming of the Messiah.

One reason that most Jews made no effort to return to Zion during the centuries of exile was their belief that the Kingdom of Israel would be recreated and the exiles ingathered, either through the actions of the Messiah or as a sign of the beginning of the Messianic age.[14] They felt that to fight through political means for a return to Zion would be to deny the special mission of the Jewish people in cleansing the world of sin. Indeed, to press for an early return to Zion was almost sacrilegious. The Messiah would not come through political action. For this reason, many traditional Jews opposed Zionism.[15] For example, in July 1897, a group of rabbis attacked the First Zionist Congress: "The efforts of so-called Zionists to found a Jewish national state in Palestine contradict the Messianic promises of Judaism as contained in the Holy Writ and in later religious sources."[16] The Zionist myth's re-interpretation of the Israel centered aspects of traditional Judaism was unacceptable to many traditional Jews.

However, the myth of exile and return promised more than the future redemption of Israel. It also provided structure for the daily life of the Jewish people. According to both Zionists and traditionalists who opposed Zionism, the rhythm of daily life in the Diaspora was shaped to some degree by the rituals and festivals commemorating the myth of exile and return. These rituals celebrated the pattern of life in Zion. Steinberg writes:

Similarly the consciousness of Palestine pervades every phase of his [the Jew's] religious life. The Scripture he reads, the prayers he recites, the rabbinic literature he studies are full of allusions to it. And as for Jewish rites and observances, having been fashioned in the Holy Land, they reflect their native scene. Like other faiths Judaism takes cognizance of the cycle of the seasons. But the calendar it follows is Palestinian in form and inspiration. Passover marks the ripening of the first grain, Pentecost the garnering of the first fruits, Tabernacles the final ingathering--all as they occur in the Holy Land.[17]

The rituals of Judaism maintained the tie to Palestine even when the events which those rituals recalled were not relevant to life in the Diaspora. Vital notes that Jewish rituals preserved,

almost to absurdity, the sense of a vital tie to an actual living land: the prayers for rain delivered regularly in even the wettest parts of Europe; the annual harvest festival (Shauveot); the close study of the body of land law and of the law governing the practice of agriculture which are integral parts of the Talmud, and more generally, the repetition, in a great variety of verbal forms in every service of prayer, of the fundamental belief that the people of Israel had been granted a land and that the present (Exilic) condition was temporary and would come to its appointed end.[18]

In reality, the lives of the Jewish people were not totally shaped by rituals drawn from their history in Israel, but in the view of Zionists and their traditionalist opponents, the rituals of the Jewish religion reaffirmed the relevance of Jewish history to the present generation. For example, one section of the Passover service reads, "In every generation, one ought to regard himself as though he had personally come out of Egypt."[19] Through ritual, the Jewish people maintained a tie to the biblical past. As Trepp notes, "For Jews history is an eternal present."[20] The myth of exile and return not only promised the Jewish people future redemption through a Messianic return to Israel, but also structured their lives, in the meantime, around a series of symbolic returns to Zion.

The myth of exile and return was present throughout the nineteen centuries of exile as one aspect of Jewish life. However, it did not dominate all aspects of that life, nor was it the only Jewish mythology. The view that the myth of exile and return served as a total vision of Jewish life was largely the creation of nineteenth and twentieth century Zionist leaders and their opponents. This myth served the purpose of the Zionist because it emphasized the long standing tie of the Jewish people to Israel. At the same time, for traditionalists it justified the rejection of Zionism; the Messiah would not come through political means.

While Zionism drew upon the traditional Jewish love of Zion, it was the twin threats to Jewish existence of assimilation and anti-Semitism[21] which first energized the movement. In the eighteenth and nineteenth centuries, laws restricting Jewish life in several nations in Western Europe were gradually liberalized. The new freedom threatened traditional Jewish culture by making assimilation a tempting alternative. During periods when the Jews were hounded and legally restricted, assimilation was a relatively small problem. While some Jews did convert to Christianity, legal restrictions limited the problem. However, after those limits were removed, it became easier for Jews to slide away from their faith and culture. Thus, the liberalization of Western society opened the gates which made assimilation possible. Max Nordau argued that assimilation threatened Jewish identity: "He [the Jew] has lost his home in the ghetto. . . ."[22]

In addition to the danger of assimilation, the liberalization of laws restricting Jewish life created expectations[23] that were then shattered by vicious outbreaks of anti-Semitism. Jews in earlier centuries had grown to expect persecution, but by the late nineteenth century, the Jews of Western Europe thought that the bad old days had been left behind. For this

38

reason, the Dreyfus affair and the pogroms in Russia
had such an influence on Herzl and others. For many
Jews, the hope that they would be allowed to live in
an enlightened world was suddenly snuffed out. In
addition, the Jews of Eastern Europe suffered increasingly violent persecution. The threats of assimilation and an increasing anti-Semitic backlash created
the needs which led to the Zionist movement. As
Walter Laqueur explains: "It [Zionism] became a psychological necessity for central European intellectu-
als, who realized that emancipation of Jews had trig-
gered off a powerful reaction and who then found the
road to full emancipation barred by strong hostile
forces."[24]

The Zionist movement confronted the problems
facing Jewish society by creating a new mythology, at
the core of which was a return to Zion. As Hertzberg
writes, "Modern Zionism was nurtured in the soil of
the religious doctrines about the Holy Land and the
return to it."[25] While the Zionist movement drew upon
the love for Zion found in traditional Judaism, it
called for a radically different "return" than that
described in the myth of exile and return. The Zionists re-defined the "return" in political terms. The
Jews would not wait for the Messiah or hide behind
their rituals, but would build a new nation in the
ancient land of Israel.

While the Zionist movement drew upon the love of
Zion inculcated in the Jewish people over nineteen
centuries of exile, the concept of a "return" to Zion
was not in any logical sense essential to the movement. To those political Zionists whose aim was to
create a state where the Jews could live as all other
peoples of the world lived, there was no necessity
that the state be placed in Palestine. The labor
Zionist dream of creating a perfect society on earth
could have been actualized outside of Palestine.
Moreover, for the majority of the Zionists who were
"predominantly secular, even atheistic,"[26] a focus on
return to Zion would seem to have been paradoxical.
Despite these factors, the symbol which best defined
the Zionist movement was "return." The strength of
return as a symbol, even for secular Zionists, is
obvious in the Sixth Zionist Congress's treatment of a
possible British offer of Uganda as a homeland for the
Jewish people. It took all of Herzl's prestige to
persuade a small majority of delegates at the Congress
to study the possibility of accepting Uganda as a

temporary sanctuary, prior to an eventual return to Palestine.[27]

Aside from the love of the land of Israel, the myth created by the dominant wing of Zionism, the labor Zionists led by Weizmann and Ben-Gurion, was quite different than the Messianic myth of exile and return. The Messianic aim of traditional Judaism was redefined to represent not the coming of a great Jewish hero to earth, but the achievement on earth of a perfect society. Hertzberg writes:

> What marks modern Zionism as a fresh beginning in Jewish history is that its ultimate values derive from the general milieu. The Messiah is now identified with the dream of an age of individual liberty, national freedom, and economic and social justice--e.g., with the progressive faith of the nineteenth century.[28]

The perfect society, to be created in Palestine, would be based on equality and hard work in a socialist framework. Through the Kibbutz and the Histadrut (an organization of Jewish workers),[29] the Jewish people would "make the desert bloom."[30] Heavily influenced by the writings of David Gordon, who believed in the redemptive power of work,[31] the leaders of labor Zionism believed that hard work in an egalitarian framework could create the preconditions for the perfect society. This "socially 'redeemed' society"[32] would gradually develop into the "ideal state,"[33] and through this ideal state the Jews would serve as modern social prophets. They would lead the people of the world to a better society fulfilling the principles of equality, hard work, and social justice.[34] Raël Jean Isaac summarizes the myth of the labor Zionists.

> The second vision, that which was to be the dominant perspective among those who came as pioneers to Palestine and assumed political leadership of the Yishuv, as the Jewish community of Palestine was known, was of a Jewish Palestine in which there would live an ideal society of men. As David Ben-Gurion, the man who became the chief representative of this

40

vision, put it: "My goal, long before I became Prime Minister, was the creation of a model society which could become, in the language of the Bible, a light unto the nations." This vision involved a synthesis of Jewish nationalism with the blueprints for a perfect society in vogue in nineteenth-century Eastern and Central Europe. The Jewish state would be built upon Jewish labor, and the individual Jew would be redeemed through work at the same time the Jewish people were restored to a normal national existence and could take their proper place among the nations.[35]

The myth of labor Zionism responded to the problems created by the threats of increased anti-Semitism and assimilation. It countered the danger of assimilation by redefining the role of the Jews as the chosen people of God who were to lead the world to a better society, just as the Jews had once led the world to reject human sacrifice. The Zionist myth responded to anti-Semitism by calling for a physical return to Palestine where the Jewish people could escape from the anti-Semites of the world. In addition to these components, the myth of the labor Zionists drew upon the liberal ideals of the age. Their myth described the perfect society of humans working together in freedom and equality.

Like the myth of exile and return, the myth of labor Zionism called for a return to Zion in order that Israel might again serve as "a light unto the nations." But in labor Zionism, as compared to traditional Judaism, the relation of the return and the Messianic age to come was inverted. The labor Zionists called for a literal return to the land of Israel so that a perfect society could be created on earth. In the myth of labor Zionism, the "return" is literal, while the Messianic age, which follows that return, is symbolic. In the secular socialistic view of Ben-Gurion, there would never be a Messianic age in any literal sense. Rather, through a return to Zion, the Jewish people could create a society that would serve as an example to the nations of the world.

The concept of return is at the core of both the myth of exile and return and the myth of labor Zion-

41

ism. There is a bond between the Jewish people and the land of Israel that has been reinforced over the last three thousand years. That tie is so strong that even secular Zionists who no longer believe in God remain committed to Zion as the only possible homeland of the Jewish people.

In the succeeding chapters, I argue that both the traditional myth of exile and return and the labor myth of making the desert bloom were ill-adapted to resolving the enormous moral problems created by the holocaust. As a consequence, when news of the holocaust reached Israel, a new myth was needed. It was then that Menachem Begin drew upon the writings of Vladimir Zeev Jabotinsky and created the myth of holocaust and redemption through return which dominates his view of the world to this day.

[1] I am indebted to S. Daniel Breslauer for the insight that the myth of "exile and return" was not the dominant force in Jewish life throughout the exile. Rather, the view that the myth dominated all aspects of Jewish life represents an interpretation of the exile by nineteenth and twentieth century Zionist leaders. For the argument that the utopian elements in modern Jewish thought reinterpreted the past to conform to their views see Gershom G. Scholem, The Messianic Idea in Judaism: And Other Essays on Jewish Spirituality (New York: Schocken, 1971), p. 4.

[2] Of course the myth of exile and return was not the only myth found in traditional Judaism. For an analysis of a number of mythical elements in Jewish thought see Gershom G. Scholem, Major Trends in Jewish Mysticism (New York: Schocken, 1941).

[3] The view of Jewish life contained in the myth of exile and return is not a fully accurate historical description of Jewish existence. Rather it represents a projection back on that history of a mythic perspective. For the argument that Jewish life was not totally shaped by love of Zion, but was heavily influenced by the pattern of daily life in each country with a significant Jewish population see Ben Zion Dinur, Israel and the Diaspora (Philadelphia: Jewish Publication Society, 1969), pp. 7-8. Dinur argues that the desire for return to Zion was one major force that influenced Jewish life, pp. 58-63.

[4] For representative works describing the cycles of Jewish history in the myth of exile and return see H. H. Ben-Sassoon, ed., A History of the Jewish People (Cambridge: Harvard University Press, 1976); Leonard Johnston, A History of the Jewish People (Westport, CT: Greenwood, 1949); Werner Keller, Diaspora: The Post-Biblical History of the Jews, trans. Richard and Clara Winston (New York: Harcourt, Brace, and World, 1966).

[5] Rabbi Akiba is cited in Keller, p. 67.

[6] David Vital, The Origins of Zionism (Oxford: Oxford University Press, 1975), pp. 4-5.

[7] Ben Halpern, The Idea of a Jewish State (Cambridge: Harvard University Press, 1961), p. 67.

[8] Halpern, p. 66.

[9] Arthur Hertzberg, Judaism (New York: George Braziller, 1962), pp. 154-155.

10 Hertzberg, Judaism, p. 151. This quotation illustrates how modern Zionists have emphasized the Israel centered aspects of Jewish life and ignored other aspects of Jewish culture that were not shaped by love of Zion. For example, Dinur writes on p. 8, "The success of this struggle [to take root outside of Zion] was obviously bound to weaken the link between the nation and its own land. Evidence of this can be found in Jehudah Halevi's well-known admission, in his Cuzari, that the repetition by the Jews of his time of such expressions as 'Bow down to His holy mountain,' 'Bow down to His footstool' and 'Who restoreth His Presence to Zion' and the like are 'mere twittering, since we do not think about what is said in these and other passages.'" Similarly, Breslauer writes that "traditionally the symbol of God provided by locus of Jewish hopes and ethical ideals with Zion as a tangential concern. . . ." See S. Daniel Breslauer, The Ecumenical Perspective and the Modernization of the Jewish Religion (Missoula, Montana: Scholars Press, 1978), p. 106.

11 Kook is quoted by Hertzberg, Judaism, p. 175. Also see Roland B. Gittelsohn, The Modern Meaning of Judaism (Cleveland: Collins, 1978), p. 196.

12 Vital, pp. 3-4.

13 Maimonides is quoted in Hertzberg, Judaism, pp. 218-219. The brackets and ellipsis are in the original quotation.

14 See Shlomo Avineri, The Making of Modern Zionism: The Intellectual Origins of the Jewish State (New York: Basic Books, 1981), p. 4.

15 See Vital, p. 4; Raël Jean Isaac, Party and Politics in Israel: Three Visions of a Jewish State (New York: Longmans, 1980), pp. 2-3.

16 The rabbis are quoted in Halpern, p. 144. Also see Moshe Menuhin, The Decadence of Judaism in Our Time (Beirut: The Institute for Palestine Studies, 1969), p. 22.

17 Milton Steinberg, Basic Judaism (New York: Harcourt Brace Jovanovich, 1947), p. 97.

18 Vital, p. 5. This view clearly represents an interpretation of Jewish culture. There are many aspects of that culture which were not tied to Zion. For the argument that much Jewish culture was not shaped by love of Zion see Dinur, pp. 7-8.

19 The Passover service is cited in Efraim M. Rozenweig, We Jews: Invitation to Dialogue (New York: Hawthorn Books, 1977), p. 42.

44

[20] Leo Trepp, The Complete Book of Jewish Observance (New York: Behrman House, 1980), p. 169.

[21] See Walter Laqueur, A History of Zionism (New York: Schocken, 1976), p. 590.

[22] Max Nordau, "Speech to the First Zionist Congress," in Arthur Hertzberg, The Zionist Idea (New York: Atheneum, 1959), p. 239.

[23] See Avineri, p. 7.

[24] Laqueur, p. 59.

[25] Hertzberg, Judaism, p. 172.

[26] Boas Evron, "The Demise of Zionism?" New Outlook, 23, no. 4 (November-December 1980), p. 30.

[27] Laqueur, pp. 125-129.

[28] Hertzberg, The Zionist Idea, p. 18.

[29] See Isaac, pp. 92-94.

[30] This phrase symbolizes the myth of labor Zionism. See Arthur Hertzberg, "Begin and the Jews," New York Review of Books, 18 February 1982, p. 12.

[31] Isaac, p. 91.

[32] Isaac, p. 92.

[33] Isaac, p. 91.

[34] Isaac, p. 91.

[35] Isaac, p. 3. Also see Avineri, p. 97.

CHAPTER III

MENACHEM BEGIN AND THE HOLOCAUST:
THE INEVITABILITY OF A MYTHIC RESPONSE

Humans build myths because discursive symbolic forms are not adequate to serve their needs.[1] Myth is well fitted to transcending reality, but not to the give and take of daily life. Put differently, myths function as a reality lived.[2] Such living realities are not created in response to trivial problems.[3]

It is the thesis of this chapter that Menachem Begin raised the banner of revolt against the British and built a myth of "return" to ancient greatness in response to the holocaust. To support my claim, I shall explain how Begin's life has been dominated by the holocaust and argue that the holocaust is the paradigmatic case of a problem which cannot be confronted through any means other than myth. Drawing upon the work of the three most important theologians who have studied the holocaust--Richard Rubenstein, Emil Fackenheim, and Eliezer Berkovits--I conclude that the holocaust defies rational explanation and demands a mythic response.

Begin and the Irgun

The life of Menachem Begin and the actions of the Irgun Zvai Leumi,[4] the underground organization which he led against the British, are not the focus of this study. However, some knowledge of crucial events in his life is needed to understand his response to the holocaust.

Menachem Begin was born in Brest Litovsk, Poland on August 16, 1913.[5] He grew up in one of the most virulently anti-Semitic areas in all Europe and participated in Zionist activities from an early age. Begin was prepared for the revolt against the British through his experience in Betar, the youth organization of the revisionist wing of the Zionist movement. There, Begin learned minimal martial skills and fell under the influence of the head of the revisionist movement, Vladimir Zeev Jabotinsky.[6]

Jabotinsky believed that the Jewish people lived in a time of crisis. Pointing to events in Hitler's Germany, in Poland, and throughout Eastern Europe, he argued that European Jewry faced a catastrophe of unimaginable proportions. As Isaac and Isaac argue, "Jabotinsky had an almost physical sense of the approaching doom of European Jews."[7] In 1935, at the Founding Conference of the New Zionist Organization, he said: "We apparently live on the threshold of the last portal to hell, on the eve of the final holocaust in the global ghetto."[8] In his testimony to the Royal Commission on Palestine in 1937, Jabotinsky described the coming catastrophe as a "social earthquake"[9] and claimed that the Jewish people were already living in a "Jewish Hell."[10] Then, in prophetic words, he argued that the Jewish people needed to leave Europe immediately:

> I assure you that you face here today
> in the Jewish people with its demands,
> an Oliver Twist who has, unfortunate-
> ly, no concessions to make. What can
> be the concessions? We have got to
> save millions, many millions. I do
> not know whether it is a question of
> rehousing one-third of the Jewish
> race, half of the Jewish race, or a
> quarter of the Jewish race; I do not
> know; but it is a question of mil-
> lions.[11]

Almost alone of all the Zionist leaders, he saw the catastrophe which threatened European Jewry. The slogan which he repeated throughout Eastern Europe from the early 1930s until his death, "Liquidate the diaspora or the diaspora will liquidate you,"[12] was proved tragically accurate in the death camps of Nazi Germany.

In answer to the catastrophe facing European Jewry, Jabotinsky called upon the Jews to put aside their passivity and take up arms. In his view, the fate of the Jewish people depended upon their ability to defend themselves: "As with other nations also with us our national future depends on arming oneself, and life compels us again to put forth the demand for defense, self defense at the center of our political struggle."[13] Jabotinsky not only called for the Jews to take up arms, but actively led the first steps in that direction. He was one of the founders of the

Zion Mule Brigade which fought in the first World War. He also founded both the Haganah (Defense force, later the semi-official defense organization of the Jewish community in Palestine) and the Irgun Zvai Leumi. In addition, through Betar, thousands of Jewish youths were given some military training.

While Jabotinsky believed in the importance of military training, he also realized that by itself such training would not save the Jewish people. Nineteen centuries of dispersion had, in his view, sapped the courage of the Jewish people. Through Betar, Jabotinsky tried to teach Jewish youth not only martial skills, but also pride in themselves. His demand that Jews be treated with absolute equality[14] had a profound influence on Begin.[15]

Jabotinsky also used Betar to teach Jewish youth the value of Hadar, a Hebrew concept which means nobility of spirit and strength of will. As Laqueur explains: "It [Hadar] implied outward beauty, respect, self-esteem, politeness and loyalty; it covered cleanliness and tact and quiet speech; it meant in brief, to be a gentleman."[16] Jabotinsky combined the call for nobility with speeches and writings which reminded the Jewish people of Eastern Europe of their heroic past. Jabotinsky's biographer, Schectman, notes:

> He [Jabotinsky] told the youth that they--the poor, persecuted, miserable, underprivileged boys and girls of the Jewish ghettos in Poland, Rumania, Lithuania--were the heirs to the Kingdom of David, to the spiritual values of the prophets and to the proud, heroic tradition of the Maccabees and Bar Kochba.[17]

Here, Jabotinsky drew upon the stories of Old Testament heroes in order to rekindle Jewish pride and courage. Laqueur writes that: "He [Jabotinsky] wanted to give fresh hope to a generation which was near despair, and he believed that this could be done only by invoking myths--blood and iron and the kingdom of Israel (Malhut Israel)."[18] In his novel Prelude to Delilah, Jabotinsky spoke through the character Samson to tell the Jewish people that if they were to survive, they must get "iron."[19] But even more than arms, Jabotinsky believed that the Jewish people needed

49

models of courage and pride who could be imitated by
the Jewish youth. Through his fiction, his references
to ancient Israel, and his personal example, Jabotinsky tried to provide those models.

Finally, Jabotinsky believed that the Jewish
people must have a state of their own in order to survive. Unlike other Zionist leaders, who in the 1930s
called for a Jewish home, not a state, in Palestine,
Jabotinsky demanded that the British first establish a
Jewish state in all of Palestine and then leave.
Jabotinsky knew that the establishment of a Jewish
state would result in conflict between Jews and Arabs,
but he believed that the great need of the Jewish
people must take precedence over Arab rights.[20]

While Begin drew many of his ideas from the works
of liberal politicians, particularly Garibaldi, no
person had more influence on the development of his
thought than Jabotinsky. For Begin, as for many other
Eastern European Jews, Jabotinsky served as a prophetic figure who pointed the way to the salvation of
the Jewish people. In 1944 when he took over the command of the Irgun, Begin based his program largely on
Jabotinsky's ideology. Moreover, the ideology of the
political parties that grew out of the Irgun (first
Herut, and later Gahal and the Likud coalition) was
heavily influenced by Jabotinsky.[21] Begin's continuing
admiration for Jabotinsky is obvious in his references
to Jabotinsky as his "teacher." As Haber explains:
"For . . . [Begin] the writings that Jabotinsky left
behind him rank with the volumes that describe Moses
leading the Children of Israel to the Promised
Land."[22]

While Jabotinsky heavily influenced Begin, Begin
is not merely Jabotinsky's disciple. Jabotinsky's
ideology was much more flexible than the ideology
Begin was to develop. For example, in the 1930s
Jabotinsky worked with the government of Poland,
despite its anti-Semitic policies because he believed
that he might persuade the Polish government to aid
Jewish emigration to Palestine.[23] In a similar circumstance in the 1950s, Begin bitterly opposed accepting war reparations from Germany, despite Israel's
need for the money.[24] Another difference between
their views is that Jabotinsky, unlike Begin, put
great faith in the British administration of the
Palestine mandate.[25] Moreover, Jabotinsky was willing
to accept a Jewish state which would not possess the

50

full powers of a normal nation: "As long as it [the Jewish state] is a local self government, and as long as there is a Jewish majority in the country,"[26] any state was acceptable. Begin would never have accepted such a limited state. Finally, Jabotinsky, unlike Begin, had grave doubts about the value of military force as a means of forcing the British to recognize a Jewish state.[27]

Begin's ideology was heavily influenced by Jabotinsky, but, in a number of areas, Begin's views were and are harsher and less flexible than those of Jabotinsky. This difference was already apparent in 1938:

> When after the Munich Agreement in 1938 at a public meeting Menachem Begin insisted that it was impossible any longer to have faith in the conscience of the world, Jabotinsky replied that if he had stopped believing in this, he had better drown himself in the Vistula.[28]

This incident illustrates the differences between Begin and Jabotinsky. Jabotinsky foresaw the holocaust and fought to prevent it. But for Jabotinsky there was always the hope that it could be avoided. He still had faith in the British. By 1938, that hope was gone for Begin and it was the holocaust that was largely responsible for the more radical aspects of Begin's ideology.

Begin's main contact with Jabotinsky occurred in Betar. In that organization, Begin rose rapidly through the hierarchy until he became the commander of its largest national organization—the Polish chapter. In 1939 Begin lost contact with Jabotinsky when he and his wife were carried through the outer reaches of the whirlwind of the holocaust to safety. In September 1939, Begin and his wife attempted to flee Nazi-occupied Europe, but were able to make it only as far as Vilna in Russian-occupied Poland. There, Begin was picked up by the Russian secret police and eventually convicted of serving as an agent of Great Britain and of committing other anti-Soviet acts. He was sentenced to eight years in prison. After serving a little over one year in Soviet prisons and work camps, he was released to join the free Polish army of General Anders in its fight against the Nazis. Here, fortune smiled upon Begin. He was assigned to a unit in Anders' army which moved to Palestine. There, he requested a leave of absence and joined the underground.

In Palestine, Begin found the Irgun in a state of disorganization following the death of its commander, David Raziel, who had been killed leading a commando operation for the British into Syria. Within a short period after arriving in Palestine, Begin became commander of the Irgun and drastically changed the Irgun's policy from cooperation to conflict with the British. The proximate cause of this change in policy was the holocaust.

Beginning in late 1942, the details of the death camps gradually became known in Palestine.[29] With the knowledge that the Jewish people were being systematically massacred came an overpowering need to do something, anything, to fight the Nazis. And yet the British did not seem to care about the holocaust. They prevented the Jewish population of Palestine from taking any effective action to relieve their fellow Jews. They denied requests for immigration permits and actually sent ships back to Hitler's Europe. They refused to set up any significant Jewish army and failed to bomb the death camps. In light of these failings, Begin and the Irgun decided to act. If they could not fight the Germans directly, they could at least fight the British who seemed to be aiding the Germans.

Consequently, in February of 1944, the "revolt" against British rule over Palestine was proclaimed. The proclamation of revolt ended with a clear statement that it was the holocaust which required military action:

> We shall fearlessly draw conclusions. There is no longer any armistice between the Jewish people and the British Administration in the Land of Israel which hands our brothers over to Hitler. Our people is at war with this regime, a war to the end. This will demand many and heavy sacrifices, but we enter it with the knowledge that we are being faithful to our brothers who have been and are being slaughtered. It is for their sake

that we fight, to their dying testimony that we remain loyal.[30]

The holocaust continued to energize the revolt through
four long years of struggle with the British. In an
Irgun message addressed to the Labour government of
Britain in July 1945, Begin noted the role of the
holocaust in motivating their action:

> This experience, which has cost the
> Jewish people six million lives,
> teaches us that only a war of libera-
> tion, independent and real, will set
> in motion political and international
> factors and bring redemption to our
> enslaved and decimated people.[31]

Several years later, Begin reflected upon the revolt
and identified the holocaust as the decisive motive:

> In January 1944 we got the first news
> from Europe about the mass extermina-
> tions in German concentration camps.
> Then we knew that if we didn't fight
> back everything was lost. So we
> issued a declaration that there was no
> more truce between the Jewish youth of
> Palestine and the British.[32]

Although the primary enemy in the "revolt" was the
British administration of Palestine, the Irgun faced
two other opponents as well: Arabs who wanted to
limit Jewish immigration or who threatened the Jewish
population of Palestine, and the official Jewish
organizations, such as the Jewish Agency and the
Haganah, who opposed conflict with the British. While
the Irgun was quite successful in fighting the British
and somewhat successful against their Arab foes, in
the contest with other Jewish organizations, they
ultimately failed.

From February 1944 through the spring of 1948,
when the British finally left Palestine, Begin led the
Irgun in their underground war against the British.
He realized that the Irgun could not defeat the
British militarily. Only a few score full-time Irgun
fighters were arrayed against up to 100,000 British
troops in Palestine. Moreover, Begin was unwilling to
take any action which might impede the British war
effort against the Nazis. Consequently, he forbade

53

attacks on British military installations prior to the end of the war.[33] In addition, in any major military confrontation with the British, thousands of innocent Jews would inevitably perish. A direct military approach was out.

Begin's strategic response to this situation was brilliant. He focused the Irgun's raids on British prestige.

> We decided to attack the British at
> their most vulnerable point, the place
> it would hurt the most, their pres-
> tige. Our tactics were not to try to
> kill off the hundred thousand British
> soldiers in Palestine, but to take
> such actions as would demonstrate to
> them that they could no longer rule
> here.[34]

Begin's men blew up the immigration offices which symbolized British regulations, preventing Jews from escaping from Hitler's Europe. They raided British banks, stole weapons, and after the end of the war in Europe, blew up British planes. They destroyed the British headquarters in Palestine and staged one of the largest prison breaks in history. Each operation had an immediate military objective, but each also served the long-term objective of destroying British prestige. For example, in 1944, the Irgun threatened to create a major disturbance at the Wailing Wall if the British interfered with worship. The Irgun had no intention of staging a battle because of the civilians who would be killed, but hoped to scare the British into retreating. When the British backed down, the Irgun won a major propaganda victory.[35] In another instance, the Irgun responded to British flogging of Irgun soldiers by flogging several British officers. The British were then intimidated into banning flog-ging and "became the laughing stock of the world press."[36] By striking at British prestige, the Irgun made it almost impossible for the British to govern in Palestine. The British could have crushed a purely military revolt quite easily, but did not know how to defend themselves from the attacks on their prestige.

Begin's second major tactic was to rely on the power of the word. Begin believed that through rhe-toric he could win over the Jewish population to his side. Consequently, he focused his personal energy on

preparing newspapers, radio broadcasts, pamphlets, and so on.[37] In this material, Begin made a particular point of telling the truth. In one case, he proposed to his aides that the Irgun report that a confiscation operation had netted fourteen guns. When his aides pointed out that fourteen guns was hardly an impressive total, he refused to change the story on the grounds that the Irgun's credibility was its most important asset.[38]

Finally, Begin set strict rules which the Irgun followed in its battle against the British. He required soldiers of the Irgun to wear arm bands in lieu of uniforms, avoid operations which could kill innocent civilians, and send warnings of upcoming operations whenever possible. Further, the Irgun eschewed personal assassination as a method of fighting the British.[39] Begin felt that these limitations on the conflict were ethically required and would make the revolt more palatable to those who questioned the ethics of violent methods.

The rhetorical dimension of these strategies should be obvious. The Irgun attacked the prestige of the British because a frontal assault on their power was not possible. At the same time, Jews in Palestine could be proud of the successful yet ethical action of the Irgun. Unlike most underground organizations, the Irgun was not a purely terrorist group. They did not attack innocent women and children and they sent warnings to protect civilians who might be hurt in an operation. This combination of tactics was designed to create Hebrew pride while making the British look foolish. In other words, the Irgun aimed at defeating the British symbolically, not militarily. They would make Palestine ungovernable and make the British feel that they had lost. The Irgun, under Begin's command, fought a rhetorical war. In this context, Begin's emphasis upon propaganda is understandable.

The Irgun was also involved in a struggle with the official Jewish organizations to convince them to fight for a state. Here, Begin used all his persuasive skills to convince the Haganah and other organizations to join in the revolt. They responded by trying to crush the Irgun. Despite this response, Begin forbade use of force against other Jews.[40] He feared that the revolt against the British could become a civil war among Zionist groups. Therefore, when Ben-Gurion ordered the Haganah to inform on and even kidnap Irgun members, Begin refused to allow any retaliation. In 1948, this order was put to a severe test. Troops under the orders of Prime Minister Ben-Gurion blew up the Irgun weapons ship, Altalena, and several members of the Irgun were killed. The country was on the verge of civil war and Ben-Gurion claimed that the Irgun had planned a coup to topple the government. There is no longer any doubt that Ben-Gurion was wrong. The Irgun planned no coup.[41] However, at the time, Ben-Gurion's version of the Altalena affair was widely believed.[42] Despite the injustice of the charges and the demands of many members of the Irgun for vengeance, Begin refused to allow any retaliation.

The unsuccessful battle to convince the Jewish organizations to fight the British was conducted with the same rhetorical weapons as the battle against the British. Again, the Irgun relied upon their operations to convince the official Jewish organizations that the British could not win. They used their propaganda to spread this message. By refusing to kill civilians and, most of all, by refusing to fight against their fellow Jews, Begin and the Irgun tried to prove the moral worth of their cause.

In the contest with the Arabs, Begin adopted a different approach. Here he was less concerned with prestige; rather, he meant to deter Arab gangs from attacking Jewish settlements. He also intended to terrify the Arabs into acquiescing in the development of a Jewish state. As a consequence, the Irgun adopted a policy of retaliation. When Arabs killed Jews, the Irgun retaliated. The Irgun attempted to kill those responsible for the attacks, but carried out raids when they knew that innocents would be killed. The war against the Arabs was fought by different rules than the war against the British. For example, the Irgun threw bombs into crowds of Arabs, some of whom were completely innocent.[43] The massacre at Dir Yassin[44] should be understood in this light. The Irgun attacked the Arab village of Dir Yassin in the spring of 1948 because the village commanded a key approach to the city of Jerusalem. In the ensuing battle, more than two hundred Arabs, mainly women and children were killed. There is little question that the Irgun did not intend to kill the innocent civilians.[45] All observers agree that the Irgun attempted to warn the villagers of the attack, but the vehicle carrying the loudspeaker fell into a ditch and was not able to deliver the warning effectively. It was not

Irgun policy to murder civilians. The massacre occurred because the Irgun was unable to capture the village through direct assault and so used high explosives to blow the village up, house by house. In this process, innocent people were killed. From the perspective of the Irgun, this loss of life was unfortunate, but unavoidable.

The Irgun used a different military strategy against the Arabs than against the British because their goal in fighting the Arabs was different from their goal in fighting the British. They wanted to destroy the prestige of Britain and force the British to leave. Killing the innocent dependents of British troops could not further that aim. It could only inflame both the British troops and world opinion. Therefore, the Irgun took every possible precaution to protect people. By contrast, the Irgun's goal in fighting the Arabs was to convince them that there was no advantage in fighting against the Jews. The Arabs must be taught not to attack Jewish settlers. Since the parties responsible for an Arab attack could not always be located, the Irgun must guarantee that someone was punished for the attack. If innocent people were killed, that was too bad, but someone had to pay. The approach of the Irgun in responding to Arab violence is still present in current policies of the Israeli Defense Force responding to PLO terrorism.

The purpose of this study is not to evaluate the success of the Irgun revolt. However, it is worth noting that for a number of years historians paid very little attention to the role of the underground organizations in the fight for Israeli independence.[46] Recently, a number of scholars have concluded that the Irgun at least hastened the British departure from Palestine and may have been the proximate cause of the British decision to turn the question of Palestine over to the United Nations.[47] In the case of the Arabs, the Irgun was somewhat less successful. In the short term, the operations of the Irgun which scared many Arabs into fleeing Palestine aided the state of Israel. In the long term, these same operations helped create the Palestinian refugee problem which haunts Israel to this day. In addition, Dir Yassin became a symbol unifying Arab opposition to Israel.

In the struggle with other Jewish organizations, the Irgun was almost totally unsuccessful. Except for a period of joint resistance between November 1945 and

September 1946, the Irgun and the official Jewish organizations did not cooperate. In the aftermath of the Altalena episode, many were convinced, erroneously, that Begin was a neo-Fascist who had intended to take over the government. Largely because of Labor party hatred of the Irgun, Begin and Herut (the party which he formed when the Irgun was dissolved) remained outside the mainstream of Israeli politics for almost twenty years. Prime Minister Ben-Gurion routinely called upon all parties, except Herut and the Communists, to join him in a coalition government.[48] Another indication of the antipathy of Labor for Begin can be found in Ben-Gurion's refusal to acknowledge his existence. In the Knesset, Ben-Gurion often referred to Begin as "the man sitting next to Dr. Bader."[49] Once Ben-Gurion even compared Begin to Hitler.[50] For almost twenty years Begin lived as a political outcast in his own nation. While a minority of the population idolized him, the majority rejected his political leadership and his party. Only in 1967 was Herut accepted as a partner in the Government of National Unity, and only in 1977 was Likud (the coalition which contains Herut) able to win an election and form a government.

During this entire period and to this day, the dominant force motivating Begin has been the holocaust. If his training in Betar prepared him to lead the Irgun, and his years as commander of the Irgun constituted a revolt against the British directly and against the holocaust indirectly, then the years since have been the years of sanctification. Begin has dedicated and continues to dedicate his life to making certain that there can never be another holocaust.

The influence of the holocaust upon Begin is obvious in his writings and public speeches, and in the issues he has emphasized since the creation of the Israeli state. Since 1948, Begin's primary interests have been national defense and foreign policy. These interests can be traced to concern over the holocaust. In 1952, he threatened the Ben-Gurion government with civil war if it accepted war reparations from Germany. Begin believed that Israel's desperate financial straits could not justify any dealing with the Nazi murderers. Haber reported Begin's speech outside the Knesset:

There is no sacrifice we will not make. We will be killed rather than

58

let this come about. This will be a
war for life or death. A Jewish government that negotiates with Germany
can no longer be a Jewish government.
. . . There is no German who did not
kill our fathers. Every German is a
Nazi. Every German is a murderer.
Anenauer is a murderer. . . . This
will not be a short or cold war.
Maybe we will go hungry for want of
bread. Maybe we will again part from
our families. Maybe we will go to the
gallows. No matter.[51]

Begin's addresses on the West German reparations issue
illustrate the dominance of the holocaust in his view
of the world. There is no question that it was in the
immediate economic interest of Israel to accept the
German aid, but Begin rejected that aid because he saw
it as somehow absolving the German people of their
guilt.

Through the years, Begin has seen many issues as
related to the holocaust and his speeches have been
filled with references to it. In November 1961, he
blamed the holocaust upon the Zionist leadership who,
he claimed, had not paid adequate attention to
Jabotinsky's warnings.[52] In 1965 he bitterly fought
against recognition of Germany arguing: "Can anyone
deny that the Nazis of yesterday constitute the Germany of today? . . . It is up to us not to normalize
relations, before the eyes of the world, between the
exterminated and the exterminators."[53] He viewed Arab
mobilization prior to the June 1967 war as threatening
another holocaust[54] and argued that any compromise in
returning land to the Arab states could create a
situation in which Israeli children might be murdered
as 1.5 million children had been murdered in the death
camps.[55] His recent statements and actions show the
same concern for the holocaust. He justified the 1981
air raid upon an Iraqi reactor as aimed at preventing
another holocaust: "'There won't be another Holocaust
in history,' he [Begin] said at a crowded news conference. 'Never again, never again.'"[56] When Chancellor
Helmut Schmidt of West Germany attacked Israeli policies on the West Bank and argued that the PLO should
be included in the peace process, Begin saw this
statement through the lens of the holocaust. He
responded by criticizing Schmidt for serving Hitler
and then described the death of his family in the

death camps.[57] In the same vein, Begin attacked Willy Brandt for giving aid to what Begin believes is a modern day Nazi organization, the PLO:

> He [Willy Brandt] went to the Warsaw Ghetto, knelt down and asked forgiveness, forgiveness and absolution from the Jewish People and its progeny, slaughtered by his nation during the reign of the National Socialists . . . [ellipsis in original] Mr. Willy Brandt must know, that should the base murderer's organization [the PLO] triumph, an organization whose like has no precedent since the days of the Nazis, that he, Mr. Willy Brandt would again kneel and ask forgiveness and indulgence for himself and his people.[58]

Concern with the holocaust is manifested in other ways as well. To this day Begin refuses to speak German or ride in a German automobile.[59] In a recent interview, Begin explained the influence of the holocaust on his life:

> So I think I finished saying that the holocaust lives within me. It is the prime mover of all that we have done in our generation; for instance, our fight for liberation is a result of the recognition that we, in our time, must create conditions so that never again will the Jew be defenseless. Our scourge was the defenselessness of the Jewish people. And that defenselessness which became helplessness was the real provocation for the murderers. They say that they can do to the Jew anything they want to. A cruel man is a coward. If he sees that there is no resistance that there is no danger to him, then he doesn't know any limits. . . . It lives within me. And I live within it. And I will live with it until the last day of my life. . . .[60]

The holocaust is, in Begin's view, the seminal event of our time which all peoples must confront. He characterizes this age in the history of the state of

Israel with the phrase, "From the holocaust to redemption."[61]

The claim that Begin's view of the world is dominated by the holocaust is hardly unique. Any number of journalists have made this point.[62] However, while many commentators have noted the influence of the holocaust on Begin, the import of this influence has not been recognized. Some simply argue that Begin is paranoid about the holocaust or misuses the holocaust in his speeches.[63] Others see Begin's concern over the holocaust as a tactical problem which must be overcome in the peace negotiations with the Arabs.[64] These commentators do not recognize that for Begin and for many Israelis, the holocaust is the crucial moral event of our time.[65] Moreover, they do not understand Begin because they fail to see that the holocaust pushed Begin into developing a myth of return. It is the myth he created in response to the holocaust which continues to dominate his life. In the following section, I shall show that Jewish theologians and writers agree that the holocaust requires a mythic response. And in subsequent chapters, I shall argue that Begin's world view is just such a mythic reaction.

Myth and the Holocaust

The holocaust poses three questions which cannot be satisfactorily answered through any means other than myth. The first great moral question raised is: Where was humanity? While Hitler systematically murdered six million Jews, the rest of the world did essentially nothing. There is no longer any question that the Allies knew about the holocaust and chose not to intervene. Arthur D. Morse among others has documented the failure of the Allies to take actions which could have saved many Jewish lives.[66] They could have bombed the railheads leading to the death camps or the death camps themselves. The missions would have been difficult, but longer raids were carried out. At the very least, they could have broadcast over the BBC the details of the holocaust and threatened to take severe actions against anyone involved. Such a threat might have saved thousands of lives.[67] There was no easy way for the Allies to stop the death camps from operating, but they could have made the attempt. Bauer argues that thousands of Jews could have been saved if the Allies had continued negotiations with Himmler's representatives over the possibility of trading trucks

for Jewish lives. They would not have had to make the
deal. The very act of negotiating with the Germans
might have delayed German actions and saved many
lives.[68] The Allies did nothing, according to Bauer,
because they were ambivalent about whether they wanted
the Jews to survive.[69] Berkovits even argues that the
Germans counted on Allied anti-Semitism to aid them in
carrying out the "final solution":

> M. D. Weissmandel, in Min Hamezar,
> tells how the Germans and their accom-
> plices in Czechoslovakia and Hungary
> were wont to joke: The safest way to
> get vital military transports to the
> front was to put some Jews in them and
> write in large letters. "This is a
> Jew transport to an extermination
> camp." Thus it was sure not to be
> molested by the Allies.[70]

The failure of the Allies to do everything possible to
stop the holocaust calls the nature of Western civilization into question. What kind of civilization could
allow the murder of six million fellow humans? Eliezer
Berkovits puts it this way: "The Western claims that
they represent an ethical civilization also perished
in the death camps and crematoria. . . . Either something new will emerge from the ashes, or mankind is
approaching its ultimate cataclysm. Auschwitz is like
a final warning to the human race."[71] Emil Fackenheim
makes the same point, "For Planet Auschwitz murdered,
along with men, women, and children, the idea of Man
itself."[72]

Jews must come to grips with a Western civilization which did not care enough to attempt military
operations when more than six million lives were at
stake. Perhaps more important for the Jewish people,
the failure of the West to act against the death camps
raises the question, Could it happen again? In light
of the indifference to Jewish life manifested in Western reaction to the holocaust, Israelis must wonder
whether the promises of the United States and of other
powers to protect them against Arab or Soviet aggression will be honored if such aggression occurs.
Berkovits argues that we still live in the holocaust
world:

> If at all possible, the world con-
> science is sicker today than it was

during the Nazi era, because it is
still more hypocritical. . . . Essentially, this is still the holocaust
world. What happened then, may happen
again, anywhere and everywhere. It is
no less conceivable today than it was
in the twenties in Germany. On the
contrary! In the meantime mankind has
become even more desensitized to the
spectacle of inhumanity and barbarism.
The disintegration of value standards
has been proceeding apace.[73]

The second problem raised by the holocaust is:
Where was God? For religious Jews who believe that
God acts in history and that the Messiah will come
when the Jewish people most need him, the holocaust
poses insuperable difficulties. If God acts in history, why did he not act to stop Hitler? Where was
the Messiah at Auschwitz? A. B. Yehoshua summaries
the religious difficulty created by the holocaust:

> The Holocaust was the final and con-
> clusive proof that there is not and
> never was a God in heaven. How can
> any theological belief that speaks of
> Divine Providence, of reward and pun-
> ishment, of divine grace, be main-
> tained after the slaughter of a mil-
> lion children in the concentration
> camps? What meaning can religious sin
> have, given the Nazis' total nondis-
> crimination between the righteous and
> the evil, between those who observed
> the commandments and those who denied
> God's existence? And what remains of
> the uniqueness of the Jewish people,
> for did not the Gypsies suffer a simi-
> lar fate? If someone doubted the
> existence of God prior to the Holo-
> caust, the Holocaust provided him with
> final confirmation of his doubts.[74]

The Jewish people had been nourished for over two
thousand years on stories describing God's intervention to save his chosen people in Egypt. Why, then,
in this greatest of all threats to the Jews, did he
remain silent?

63

Finally, the holocaust raises a horrible question about the Jewish people themselves. Why, when Hitler began liquidating the ghettoes, did they not fight back? Why did so many Jews calmly dig their own graves and wait to be shot? Raul Hilberg argues in his masterful work, The Destruction of European Jews, that Jewish passivity aided Hitler in carrying out the final solution.[75] While other scholars, notably Dawidowicz and Bauer,[76] disagree, the question Why did we not resist? has haunted Jews since the holocaust. As Moshe Kahn argues, "The question that Jews have been in the habit of asking about the Holocaust is: Why did we go as sheep to the slaughter?"[77] The reaction to death camp survivors in Israel illustrates the guilt which many Israelis feel: "The disdain with which the Palestinian Jewish youth treated the first survivors of the concentration camps is an indication of the hostility toward the victim role. They were called sabon (sheep), and this term became synonomous with cowardice and weakness."[78]

In addition, many death camp survivors felt guilt because of their very survival. They asked themselves why they deserved to live when their fellows had perished. Berkovits explains:

> For some time after their liberation many a survivor walked about with a guilty conscience for not having died with all his loved ones, with the rest of his people. As one of them, for instance, wrote: "I would like to do penance for the sin of survival, or of having returned to life."[79]

The three great moral problems raised by the holocaust defy rational solution. There is no adequate explanation for the holocaust. There is no way to give meaning to its horror. As Rosenfeld and Greenberg argue: "Without exception, those of us who bring ourselves to reflect on the Holocaust are met by the most wrenching of paradoxes: the events must be recorded and remembered, yet language, our primary medium, fails us when we most need it."[80] It is not the magnitude of the holocaust alone which makes it an incomprehensible event; it is also the manner in which the Jewish people were slaughtered. Throughout the centuries, Jews had been slaughtered in bloody pogroms, but the holocaust was not simply a pogrom on a larger scale. It was not organized by uneducated barbarians, but by the leaders of one of the most civilized nations on earth. Moreover, it was not anti-Semitism alone, but the combination of anti-Semitism with bureaucratic efficiency and modern science that made the death camps possible. In earlier centuries, when anti-Semites murdered Jews, the killing ended when the anger of the anti-Semites had been satisfied. In the holocaust, apparently normal Germans continued killing Jews until the end of the war, not because of overpowering hatred, but because it was their job. German efficiency was applied to the job of killing Jews, just as it might have been applied to designing a new car. The holocaust revealed the capacity for evil in all humans. At Auschwitz and Buchenwald, apparently normal Germans killed millions of Jews. While the German people pretended that the camps did not exist, the Jews were systematically and horribly slaughtered. Those who were fit were forced to work until they died. Those who could not work were marched into the showers and scientifically gassed or used in horrible medical experiments. Even their remains were put to use. Jewish skin was made into lampshades, Jewish fat into soap. Throughout this horror, the civilized world stood by and did little or nothing, and for the most part, the Jews themselves passively accepted their fate. The violent passion of a pogrom can be understood, but not the systematic slaughter of an entire people. The inadequacy of reason for comprehending the holocaust is made clear in a passage from Elie Wiesel's autobiographical novel of the holocaust, <u>Night</u>:

> Another prisoner came up to us:
> "Satisfied?"
> "Yes," someone replied.
> "Poor devils, you're going to the crematory."
> He seemed to be telling the truth. Not far from us, flames were leaping up from a ditch, gigantic flames. They were burning something. A lorry drew up at the pit and delivered its load--little children. Babies! Yes, I saw it--saw it with my own eyes . . . those children in the flames. (Is it surprising that I could not sleep after that? Sleep had fled from my eyes.)

So this was where we were going. A
little farther on was another and
larger ditch for adults.
I pinched my face. Was I still
alive? Was I awake? I could not
believe it. How could it be possible
for them to burn people, children, and
for the world to keep silent? No,
none of this could be true. It was my
nightmare. . . . Soon I should wake
with a start, my heart pounding, and
find myself back in the bedroom of my
childhood, among my books. . . .
My forehead was bathed in cold
sweat. But I told him [his father]
that I did not believe that they could
burn people in our age, that humanity
would never tolerate it. . . .
"Humanity? Humanity is not concerned with us. Today anything is
allowed. Anything is possible, even
these crematoria."[81]

The evil which Wiesel witnessed in his first moments
at Auschwitz cannot be rationally comprehended, but it
must be faced. It still dominates life in Israel[82]
and raises questions which must be answered if life is
to have meaning.

The only possible answer is myth. Humans have
used myths throughout the ages to solve problems which
defied solution by other means, for through myth
inherently inconsistent positions can be reconciled.
As long as the story told in the myth is itself internally consistent, the world view projected in that
myth may contain many truths. The holocaust is a
paradigmatic case of a problem demanding mythic
response. Therefore, it is not surprising that the
three most important contemporary Jewish theologians
who have focused on the holocaust, Eliezer Berkovits,
Richard Rubenstein, and Emil Fackenheim,[83] all find
reason an inadequate tool for confronting it, and that
each ends by creating a mythic response to it.

Richard Rubenstein argues that Jewish theology
must measure itself against its ability to answer the
problems raised by the holocaust and then goes on to
compare the holocaust to a "psychological and religious time bomb which has yet to explode fully in the
midst of Jewish religious life."[84] For Rubenstein,

66

humanity and God must share guilt for the holocaust. He argues that all German society participated in the extermination process and even blames the German church for failing to act.[85] Nor can the rest of the world be exempted from the guilt. They did nothing while millions of Jews were killed. Given the response of the world to the holocaust, Rubenstein argues that Israelis must learn to trust nothing but their own will and determination.[86] Rubenstein does not exempt the Jewish people from responsibility for the holocaust; the Jewish community prevented resistance and, thus, unwittingly aided Hitler.[87] Finally, Rubenstein holds God directly responsible for the death camps. There is no heavenly purpose which could have justified them.[88] If God exists and failed to intervene, then God must be a sadist: "I must sadly conclude that the God they affirm [Wiesel, Rakover, and Fackenheim] is by their own description--a willful cosmic sadist who repays the love offered by his tortured believers with criminally obscene punishments."[89] Rubenstein rejects this alternative and, therefore, rejects the existence of an historical God. God as a cosmic force may or may not exist, but there is no omnipotent God who acts in history and is concerned with his people.[80]

Rubenstein reasons fearlessly from his premises to conclude that high technology combined with an all-powerful state created the death camps.[91] Consequently, the Jewish people can find meaningful life only by protecting themselves from the power of the state. The only answer to the holocaust comes from recognizing that there is no God and finding meaning in the protection of the Jewish people. Through these actions the Jewish people may find peace:

> After the death camps, life in and of itself, lived and enjoyed in its own terms without any superordinate values or special theological relationships becomes important for Jews. One cannot go through the experience of having life called so devastatingly and radically into question without experiencing a heightened sense of its value, unrelated to any special categories of meaning which transcend its actual experience. This distrust of superordinate ideologies is increased immeasurably because of our knowledge

of the role such ideologies played in
the creation of the death camps. Life
need have no metahistorical meanings
to be worthwhile.[92]

Rubenstein hopes that the love of life for its own
sake can be expressed in an Israel "come forth from
the ashes," filled with vitality and "assuring the
future of their progeny in the wasteland of human
existence we call the twentieth century."[93]

Rubenstein's answer, on its face, is logical and
consistent and certainly not mythic. It was an evil
world, Jewish passivity, and trust in a God that
doesn't exist which caused the holocaust. It would
seem that he has faced the holocaust and developed an
answer--however unpleasant--thus denying that myth is
the only language which can confront the holocaust.
However, Rubenstein's answer is not very satisfying.
He tells us that the whole world, Jews included, was
responsible for the holocaust and that there is no God
to redeem the world from its sin. Although he writes
of this demystified world as if it could be an exhila-
rating place, there is little room left for happiness
or purpose. There are no ultimate values; there is no
God; and the Jews can trust no one in the world, themselves included.

Rubenstein recognizes that the universe he has
described does not fill the needs of Jews in the post-
holocaust era. He explicitly argues that the Jews
need to retain their myths and rituals in order to
fulfill their need for purpose.

In all ages religion has addressed
itself through myth and ritual to such
questions as "What is my origin? What
is my destiny? How can I be cleansed
of my guilt? What are the meaning and
purpose of life?" These are questions
of ultimate concern. The fact that
myth and religious symbols no longer
are regarded as true at the manifest
level is entirely irrelevant to their
central function, which is to give
profound expression to our feelings at
the decisive times and crises of our
life.[94]

Humans can find meaning in the post-holocaust universe by recalling the myths and rituals which have provided that meaning for centuries:

> Myth and ritual are the domains in which we express and project our unconscious feelings concerning the dilemmas of existence. They are indispensible vehicles of expression in an institution in which the decisive moments of existence are to be shared and celebrated at both the conscious and unconscious levels.[95]

Rubenstein's rationalistic explanation of the holocaust and its moral implications finally compels a return to myth as the only means of providing meaning for the Jewish people. This defense of myth is clearly inconsistent with his other writings about the holocaust. Although he does not believe the myths are true, Rubenstein sees them as a necessary part of the response to the horror of the holocaust.

Emil Fackenheim asks essentially the same questions as Rubenstein, but comes to very different answers. Like Rubenstein, Fackenheim sees the holocaust as the most important event of our time and argues that it is still with us. He sees no sign that the world cares more now than it did during the 1930s and 1940s.[96] He also recognizes that the holocaust left terrible psychological scars on the Jewish people and points to the guilt Jews feel.[97] Like Rubenstein, he argues that the old concept of a God of Progress breaks up on the shoals of the holocaust.

> After these dread events, occurring in the heart of the modern, enlightened, technological world, can one still believe in the God who is necessary Progress any more than the God who manifests His power in the form of a superintending Providence? It seems that anyone who today still seeks the Divine at all must totally contradict the ancient Midrash and turn away from history in his search for God—whether to Eternity above history, to nature below it, or to an individualistic inwardness divorced from it.[98]

69

Fackenheim sees the same three problems as growing out of the holocaust. We live in a world which did little to save the six million. It could happen again. Moreover, the Jewish people are filled with guilt. Finally, like Rubenstein, he denies that belief in a historical God of Progress is credible after the holocaust. Worst of all, there is no rational answer to these problems: "This [Auschwitz] is the rock on which through all eternity all rational explanations will crash and break apart. . . ."[99] No moral lesson is evident in it: "No meaning or purpose will ever be found in the event and one does not glorify God by associating his will with it."[100]

Fackenheim argues that although there can never be a rational answer to the problems raised by the holocaust, "to seek a response is inescapable."[101] His response is mythic. In the Jewish tradition, there are 613 commandments defining the proper life for Jews; Fackenheim proposes a 614th:

> If the 614th commandment is binding upon the authentic Jew, then we are, first, commanded to survive as Jews, lest the Jewish people perish. We are commanded, second, to remember in our very guts and bones the martyrs of the Holocaust, lest their memory perish. We are forbidden, thirdly, to deny or despair of God, however much we may have to contend with him or with belief in him, lest Judaism perish. We are forbidden, finally, to despair of the world as the place which is to become the kingdom of God, lest we help to make it a meaningless place in which God is dead or irrelevant and everything is permitted. To abandon any of these imperatives, in response to Hitler's victory at Auschwitz, would be to hand him yet other posthumous victories.[102]

In other essays, his response to the holocaust is expressed in what he calls the Commanding Voice of Auschwitz, which is a modern equivalent of the revelation at Sinai: "Jewish opposition to Auschwitz cannot be grasped in terms of humanly created ideals but only as an imposed commandment. And the Jewish secularist, no less than the believer, is absolutely singled out by a Voice as truly other than man-made ideals--an imperative as truly given as was the voice of Sinai."[103] The Commanding Voice orders all Jews to tell the tale of Auschwitz, lest it be forgotten.[104] It orders them to survive at all costs: "The Commanding Voice of Auschwitz singles Jews out; Jewish survival is a commandment which brooks no compromise. It was this Voice which was heard by the Jews of Israel in May and June 1976 when they refused to lie down and be slaughtered."[105] The Commanding Voice also orders Jews not to despair of the world. Fackenheim writes: "Two possibilities are equally ruled out: To despair of the world on account of Auschwitz, abandoning the age-old Jewish identification with poor and persecuted humanity; and to abuse such identification as a means of flight from Jewish destiny."[106] Finally, the Commanding Voice orders Jews not to despair of God. The religious Jew is commanded to continue his or her faith, and the secular Jew is forbidden to use Auschwitz against that faith.[107] Hitler must not be granted any additional victories.

Fackenheim's mythic response to the holocaust is not limited to the Commanding Voice and the 614th commandment. He sees remythologizing "in evidence in Jewish life on every side"[108] and quotes stories of the death camps which were created to deal with the holocaust. He concludes "On Faith in the Secular World" by arguing that a meaningful response to the holocaust must come from the stories about that event:

> Is there an authentic Jewish enduring
> of the contradictions of present Jew-
> ish existence? Is it giving rise to a
> quest, to a listening, indeed, to an
> interrogating of God which, born of
> faith, may itself bespeak a Presence
> while as yet no voice is heard? Per-
> haps one must look to philosophers or
> even theologians. Perhaps one must
> look to a novelist whose heaven-
> storming shatters conventions and
> literary forms.[109]

He then quotes from three of Elie Wiesel's novels which deal with the holocaust.[110] Here, Fackenheim treats Wiesel's novels and stories as a mythology answering the questions raised by the holocaust. Fackenheim also draws upon myth when he quotes from new Midrashim (Jewish folklore) which have arisen out

71

of the holocaust in order to deal with the horrors of the event.[111]

Eliezer Berkovits identifies the same problems flowing from the holocaust as do Fackenheim and Rubenstein. After summarizing the historical evidence indicating that the West did not act against the death camps because of anti-Semitism, he concludes that "in it [the holocaust], Western civilization lost its every claim to dignity and respect."[112] While he argues that revolt against the Germans was impossible, he also recognizes that many Jews feel guilt because of their failure to resist.[113] Finally, he also recognizes that the holocaust shattered the faith of some Jews.[114] Although Berkovits points to the same three problems--Why didn't the world act? Why didn't God act? Why didn't the Jews act?--he comes up with very different solutions to these problems than do Fackenheim or Rubenstein.

Berkovits applies a traditional Jewish theological perspective to the holocaust. Initially, he argues that the people of the world did not act because they did not care about the Jews. Thus, Jews must learn never to depend upon the aid of others. Berkovits writes:

> The Jewish response must be the one given by the Jews of Israel in the Six Day War: Never Again! If it is to die, it is better to die with a gun in one's hand than in a concentration camp or gas chamber. Resist! Resist! It must be incorporated in the very core of Jewish education until it produces an instinctive reaction of resistance to any attack.[115]

He then denies that Jews should feel guilt over a passive response to the holocaust. They did not fight back against the Germans because they had no chance to fight.[116] And finally, he argues that God did not act, because God could not act. God's grant of free will to all humans denied him the power to act:

> If man is to be, God must be long-suffering with him; he must suffer man. This is the inescapable paradox of divine providence. While God tolerates the sinner, he must abandon the

victim; while he shows forebearance
with the wicked, he must turn a deaf
ear to the anguished cries of the violated. This is the ultimate tragedy
of existence: God's very mercy and
forebearance, his very love for man,
necessitates the abandonment of some
men to a fate that they may well experience as divine indifference to
justice and human suffering.[117]

On the surface, Berkovits's traditional answer to the
problems raised by Auschwitz appears to be reasonable
and leading away from myth.

A closer look reveals that, like Fackenheim and
Rubenstein, Berkovits's response to the holocaust
depends upon myth. Berkovits's answer to the religious problems raised by the holocaust is the answer
proposed by traditional Judaism. He says that God did
not act in the holocaust, because God grants humans
free will. Yet this answer quickly leads to the position of Rubenstein. If God grants humans free will,
then God cannot act in history and God is removed from
the world. Berkovits is unwilling to accept this conclusion. Consequently, he interprets the holocaust in
mythic terms. He argues that while God is powerless
to act in history, God's very powerlessness was
responsible for the defeat of Nazi Germany:

> Nothing could be further from the
> truth than the mad suspicion of a Jew-
> ish conspiracy against Germany. Yet,
> the fear was real; more real than any
> fear human beings have of superior
> material or political forces that may
> be arrayed against them. It was a
> metaphysical fear of the true mystery
> of God's "powerless" presence in his-
> tory as "revealed" in the continued
> survival of Israel. It was well-
> justified fear. For the presence of
> the "powerless" God in history indeed
> spelled the doom of the Nazi-German
> rebellion against all universal human
> values from the very beginning.[118]

In Jewish history, God acts, but without "manifest
divine intervention"[119] to protect Israel. Berkovits
explains: "Because of Israel the Jew knows that

73

history is messianism, that God's guidance--however impenetrably wrapt in mystery--is never absent in the life of the nations."[120] One example of this action came in the Six Day War when God aided Israel and prevented its destruction.[121] God acts in history through hidden means to protect the Jews, and in the end, the Jews will be rewarded for their faith:

> Yet all this does not exonerate God for all the suffering of the innocent in history. God is responsible for having created a world in which man is free to make history. There must be a dimension beyond history in which all suffering finds its redemption through God. This is essential to the faith of a Jew. The Jew does not doubt God's presence, though he is unable to set limits to the duration and intensity of his absence. This is no justification for the ways or providence, but its acceptance. It is not a willingness to forgive the unheard cries of millions, but a trust that in God the tragedy of man finds its transformation.[122]

Like Rubenstein, Berkovits first seeks a purely rational theological explanation for the holocaust and then retreats to myth. The Jews survived the holocaust because God's powerless presence guided them. Israel survived as a nation and won the Six Day War because of God's secret actions. And there will someday be a dimension beyond history in which the Jews will be rewarded for their suffering. Berkovits does not tell a story, but in every other way he builds a myth. He draws upon the traditional stories of the Bible and depicts an all-powerful, all-loving God who intervenes in secret ways in order to protect the Jewish people while guaranteeing human free will.

The work of Berkovits, Rubenstein, and Fackenheim is compelling evidence of the necessity for a mythic response to the holocaust. The three greatest philosopher/theologians to confront the holocaust all sought a rational answer to it, but could not find one. They then moved to the level of myth, because it is only through myth that the holocaust can be confronted.

74

Other theologians and philosophers who have considered the holocaust also use the language of myth. Hans Jonas closes his essay, "The Concept of God After Auschwitz," by proposing a myth.[123] Friedlander concludes his collection of essays and stories about the holocaust with "A Parable" about the prophet Elijah and the six million.[124] More evidence of the need for myth in confronting the holocaust is found in the work of the writer Elie Wiesel. Wiesel, who influenced Rubenstein, Fackenheim, and Berkovits,[125] is essentially a mythmaker. Because he believes that it will never be possible to solve the religious problems created by Auschwitz in rational terms,[126] Wiesel responds through stories.[127] It is appropriate to treat these stories as myths. Wiesel refers to his work as a mythology[128] and explains his novel Dawn as filling the need for the "dream" and "legend" which all humans require to survive.[129] In addition, many of his stories concern mythological heroes. In Night, Wiesel describes the murder of the Messiah at Auschwitz.[130] He also tells the story of the return of the prophet Elijah during the holocaust.[131] The cantata, Ani Maamin, tells the story of how the patriarchs of ancient Israel negotiated with God in order to save the Jews from Hitler's Germany.[132]

Wiesel uses his novels to consider systematically possible answers to the holocaust. In Night, he confronts the radical despair of Rubenstein. In Dawn, he considers Begin's "revolt" as a response.[133] Berenbaum argues that in these works, Wiesel creates a new covenant to replace the original covenant between God and humanity. The new covenant is not between God and the Jews but between the Jews and their past:

> Wiesel partially resolves this dilemma
> by suggesting an additional covenant
> forged at Auschwitz. This covenant is
> no longer between humanity and God or
> God and Israel, but rather between
> Israel and its memories of pain and
> death, God and meaning. The covenant
> cannot be between God and Israel for
> God has proved an unreliable partner
> in the covenantal bondedness, there-
> fore, if we are to continue as Jews,
> our self-affirmation must be based on
> our choice to remain Jews and to
> assume the past of Jewish history as
> our own and as in some way implicated

in our future. This self-affirmation
is a covenant with the past of Israel,
with its pain, its overwhelming experience of death and its memories of
God and of a world infused with meaning.[134]

In this view, Wiesel's mythology functions as a new
revelation which responds to the holocaust.[135]

The holocaust is the moral event of the twentieth
century. Philosophers and poets feel the need for new
mythology to encompass it. The evil of the Nazis, the
lack of concern of the Allies, and the failure of the
Jewish people to fight back all lead to despair. How
can humans live in a world where people commit such
monstrous acts? Moreover, God's failure to intervene
destroyed the faith of countless Jews. The guilt,
doubt, fear, and horror which the holocaust created
can never be explained away or transcended. No purpose could justify such horror. But Fackenheim is
right; the guilt, doubt, and horror must be confronted, and the only possible language in which they can
be confronted is myth. Moreover, the holocaust
demanded a new mythology. The traditional myth of
exile and return and the myth of labor Zionism each
fulfilled important needs. The myth of exile and
return responded to the problems created by exile and
dispersion. The myth of labor Zionism responded to
the problems raised by anti-Semitism and assimilation. Neither myth could deal adequately with the
problems created by the holocaust.

The myth of exile and return explained why God
had not ended the exile from Palestine. According to
the myth, the Jews were being tested and when they
proved themselves worthy, the Messiah would come and
lead them to Zion. God had not deserted them, but
would save the Jewish people as he had saved them in
Egypt and Babylon. The holocaust made nonsense of
this explanation. If God had been testing the Jewish
people, then their passive response to Hitler proved
their loyalty to God. The myth of exile and return
explained why God would let some of his people be
persecuted. That persecution was necessary to bring
the Messiah into the world. The myth could not
explain why God allowed six million of his people to
be slaughtered. As Richard Rubenstein argues, a God
who would allow six million of his chosen people to
die, as part of a test of their worthiness, can only

76

be labeled a "cosmic sadist." Moreover, traditional
Jews had always believed that the Messiah would come
in the hour of the greatest need of the Jewish people.
Jews at Auschwitz prayed that the death camps would
force the Messiah to come. But the Messiah did not
come. The myth of exile and return provided no satisfactory answer to the question: Where was God at
Auschwitz?

Nor did the myth of traditional Judaism answer
the other great moral problems raised by the holocaust. The answer provided in the myth exacerbated
the problem of Jewish guilt. The myth taught Jews
that passivity and weakness were the proper roles for
Jews who were being tested by God. But those very
qualities helped make the death camps possible. In
addition, the traditional myth provided no answer to
how the Jews could go on living under conditions that
permitted six million Jews to be slaughtered. The
myth concerned the spiritual development of the Jewish
people and the need to protect them from isolated
outbreaks of anti-Semitism. The passive response
advocated in the myth was not appropriate for the
dangers of living in the holocaust world.

The labor Zionist myth of a perfect society on
earth also failed to deal with the holocaust adequately. The labor mythology was aimed at "making the
desert bloom" in a perfect society based on Jewish
labor in an egalitarian framework. The problem of
Jewish guilt and the difficulty of surviving in the
holocaust world were absolutely foreign to it. To
many who accept the labor myth, the question of how
faith in God could be maintained after the death camps
was no problem at all. They ceased to believe in God
long before the holocaust.

The inapplicability of the labor mythology to the
problems raised by the death camps helps explain why
the holocaust was never the overriding issue to Ben-
Gurion that it was to Begin. Ben-Gurion's speeches
and writings from the 1944-1948 period contain references to the holocaust, but they are fewer and without
the emotional intensity of Begin's references during
that period.[136] Similarly, Ben-Gurion may have felt
that it was appropriate to accept war reparations from
Germany in the 1950s because his ultimate goal was to
make the desert bloom and create a perfect society.
By contrast, to Begin, whose ultimate goal was fighting the holocaust, the idea of accepting money from

77

the Germans, even if that money was desperately needed, was obscene.

The holocaust raised problems for the Jewish
people that had to be confronted if life was to go
on. As the work of Fackenheim, Rubenstein, Berkovits,
and Wiesel has made clear, those problems could be
confronted only in myth. However, neither the traditional Diaspora myth of exile and return nor the myth
of a perfect society could deal satisfactorily with
those horrors. A new mythology was needed. Begin's
myth of holocaust and redemption through return is
that mythology.

Notes

[1] Discursive form is logical and linear. It moves directly from evidence to a conclusion. See Suzanne Langer, Philosophy in a New Key (New York: New American Library, 1951), p. 77.

[2] Myths create models through which people view the world. They also function as prescriptive devices identifying good and bad behavior. The term "reality lived" is drawn from the work of Bronislaw Malinowski. He described the manner in which myth shaped Melanesian culture. See Bronislaw Malinowski, Magic, Science and Religion (Garden City, NY: Doubleday, 1948), p. 100.

[3] For a similar view see Charles D. Laughlin and Christopher D. Stephens, "Symbolism, Canalization and P Structures," in Symbol as Sense: New Approaches to the Analysis of Meaning, ed. Mary Le Cron Foster and Stanley H. Brandes (New York: Academic Press, 1980), p. 338.

[4] Irgun Zvai Leumi is a Hebrew name which means National Military Organization.

[5] The crucial biographies from which I have taken the details of Begin's life are Eitan Haber, Menahem Begin: The Legend and the Man, trans. Louis Williams (New York: Delacorte, 1978); Gertrude Hirschler and Lester Eckman, Menahem Begin: From Freedom Fighter to Statesman (New York: Shengold, 1979); Frank Gervasi, The Life and Times of Menahem Begin: Rebel to Statesman (New York: Putnam, 1979); Harry Hurwitz, Menachem Begin (Johannesburg: The Jewish Hearald, 1977). The most important work on the Irgun is J. Bowyer Bell, Terror Out of Zion: Irgun Zvai Leumi, LEHI, and the Palestine Underground, 1929-1949 (New York: Avon, 1977).

[6] In addition to Jabotinsky, a number of other Zionist leaders defended positions similar to the position which Begin was to develop. The writings of Berdichevski and Klatzkin are particularly important. For a sample of their work see Arthur Hertzberg, The Zionist Idea: A Historical Analysis and Reader (New York: Antheneum, 1977), pp. 290-302, 314-327. There is no direct evidence that their work significantly influenced Begin.

[7] Erich and Raël Jean Isaac, "The Impact of Jabotinsky on Likud's Policies," Middle East Review, 10, no. 1 (Fall 1977), p. 43.

[8] Isaac and Isaac, p. 43.

[9] Vladimir Jabotinsky, "Evidence Submitted to the Palestine Royal Commission (1937)," in The Zionist Idea, p. 560.

[10] Jabotinsky, p. 560.

[11] Jabotinsky, p. 561; also see Walter Laqueur, A History of Zionism (New York: Schocken, 1976), p. 372.

[12] Isaac and Isaac, p. 32.

[13] Raël Jean Isaac, Party and Politics in Israel: Three Visions of a Jewish State (New York: Longmans, 1981), p. 139.

[14] Isaac, Party and Politics in Israel, p. 138.

[15] Haber, pp. 28-29.

[16] Laqueur, p. 360.

[17] Joseph B. Schechtman, Fighter and Prophet: The Vladimir Jabotinsky Story The Last Years (New York: Thomas Yoseloff, 1961), p. 411.

[18] Laqueur, p. 360.

[19] Jabotinsky is cited in Schechtman, p. 533.

[20] Jabotinsky, pp. 562, 569.

[21] Isaac and Isaac, p. 37.

[22] Haber, p. 26.

[23] Isaac and Isaac, p. 35.

[24] Isaac and Isaac, pp. 44-45.

[25] Laqueur, p. 350.

[26] Jabotinsky is quoted in Ben Halpern, The Idea of the Jewish State (Cambridge: Harvard University Press, 1961), p. 206.

[27] Isaac and Isaac, p. 34.

[28] Isaac and Isaac, p. 35.

[29] See for instance, "Tale of One Death Camp," Palestine Post, 16 February 1944, p. 1.

[30] The Irgun statement of "revolt" is quoted in Chapters in the History of Jewish Underground Activities (Tel Aviv: National Labor Federation in Israel, n.d.), p. 66.

[31] Irgun Zvai Leumi, "We Shall Give the Labour Government a Chance to Keep Its Word," in The Hebrew Struggle for National Liberation, submitted to the United Nations Special Committee on Palestine, 1947, p. 55. The Irgun statement was originally made in July 1945.

[32] Begin is quoted in Robert St. John, Shalom Means Peace (Garden City, NY: Doubleday, 1950), p. 175.

[33] Haber, p. 98.

[34] Begin is quoted in St. John, p. 175.

[35] See Hirschler and Eckman, p. 91.

[36] Hirschler and Eckman, p. 129.

[37] See Bell, pp. 146-147; Haber, pp. 99, 195-196.

[38] See Bell, p. 150.

[39] See Thurston Clarke, By Blood and Fire: The Attack on the King David Hotel (New York: Putnam, 1981), p. 100; Arthur Koestler, Promise and Fulfillment: Palestine 1917-1949 (New York: The Macmillan Company, 1949), p. 253; Bell, p. 442.

[40] See Koestler, Promise and Fulfillment, pp. 91-92.

[41] For the story of the Altalena see Myra Avrech, "The Captain of the 'Altalena' Tells His Story," Jewish World, September 1956, pp. 14-16; Hirschler and Eckman, pp. 165-184; Haber, pp. 217-225; Bell, pp. 400-411.

[42] For a typical argument that the Irgun brought in the Altalena as part of an attack on the Ben-Gurion Government see Harry Sacher, Israel: The Establishment of a State (Westport, CT: Hyperion, 1952), pp. 193-194.

[43] The Irgun set off bombs in crowds of Arab civilians. See Sam People Bewer, "Irgun Bombs Kill 15 Arabs; 3 of 5 Attackers Are Slain," New York Times, 8 January 1948, pp. 1, 19; Bell, pp. 335-337; Clark, p. 257.

[44] For the clearest defense of the argument that the Irgun massacred Arabs at Dir Yassin, see Jacques de Reyneir, "Deir

Yasin," in <u>Who is Menahem Begin</u> (Beirut: Institute for Palestine Studies, 1977), pp. 16-20.

[45] For good descriptions of Dir Yassin see Bell, pp. 369-372; Haber, p. 209.

[46] Two examples of historical works which gave relatively little attention to the Irgun are Larry Collins and Dominique Lapiere, <u>O Jerusalem</u> (New York: Simon and Schuster, 1972); Dan Kurzman, <u>Genesis 1948: The First Arab-Israeli War</u> (New York: World, 1970).

[47] See for instance Nicholas Bethell, <u>The Palestine Triangle: The Struggle for the Holy Land, 1935-1948</u> (New York: Putnam, 1979), p. 356; Clarke, p. 257; Haber, p. 191; an interview by John F. Sims with J. Bowyer Bell in <u>South African Jewish Times</u>, 1 June 1977, p. 1.

[48] Haber, p. 239.

[49] Bader was Herut's economic specialist. See Haber, p. 239.

[50] Haber, p. 255.

[51] Haber, p. 234.

[52] "Begin Charges Zionist Abandoned European Jews," <u>Jerusalem Post</u>, indistinct date, apparently 13 November 1961, Inter-Documentation Company microfiche, n. page.

[53] Haber, pp. 237-238.

[54] Menachem Begin, "The Inheritance of Our Fathers," <u>The Jewish Herald</u>, 28 March 1972, p. 12.

[55] Menahem Begin, "Why We Must Stand Fast," <u>The American Zionist</u>, January 1971, pp. 10, 11.

[56] Begin is quoted in David K. Shipler, "Begin Defends Raid, Pledges to Thwart a New 'Holocaust,'" <u>New York Times</u>, 10 June 1981, p. 1.

[57] For a description of Begin's speech see William Claiborne, "Begin Rules out Deal on Missiles, Assails Schmidt," <u>Washington Post</u>, 7 May 1981, p. A27.

[58] Menachem Begin, "Statement by Prime Minister Begin in the Knesset, 7/9/79, Following the Visit by the Leader of the P.L.O. to Austria," Embassy of Israel, 10 July 1979, excerpts, p. 3.

[59] See Gervasi, p. 39; "Sounding Off With a Vengeance," Time, 18 May 1981, p. 37.

[60] Begin is quoted in Eric Breindel, "The Many Wars of Menachem Begin," Rolling Stone, 3 November 1977, p. 87.

[61] Menachem Begin, "From the Perspective of a Generation," in The Revolt, rev. ed. (New York: Dell, 1977), p. 18.

[62] See for instance Meir Merhav, "The Constancy of Menahem Begin," Jerusalem Post International Edition, 23 August 1977, p. 7; Ezer Weizman, The Battle For Peace (New York: Bantam, 1981), p. 135; Hurwitz, p. 10; John Brecher et al., "A Roadblock to Peace?" Newsweek, 14 September 1981, p. 39.

[63] See for instance Richard Cohen, "Holocaust Is Trivialized for Political Purposes," Washington Post, 29 June 1980, p. B1; Yehuda Bauer, "Jewish Masochism," Jerusalem Post International Edition, 15-21 June 1980, p. 13.

[64] For articles which raise the question whether Begin can make peace given his view of the holocaust, see Raymond Carroll et al., "Why Begin Is Tough," Newsweek, 30 January 1978, p. 42; Merhav, p. 7.

[65] See Jacques Derogy, The Untold History of Israel (New York: Grove, 1978), p. 175; Uri Avnery, Israel Without Zionists: A Plea for Peace in the Middle East (New York: The Macmillan Company, 1968), p. 92.

[66] One of the most famous analyses of the lack of concern of the West during the holocaust is Arthur D. Morse, While Six Million Died: A Chronicle of American Apathy (New York: Random House, 1968). Although the argument is more complete in Morse and others, it is present in less well-documented form in the submission of the Irgun to the United Nations Special Committee on Palestine. See Irgun Zvai Leumi, Memorandum to the United Nations Special Committee on Palestine, presented to the United Nations Special Committee on Palestine, 1947, pp. 20-23.

[67] See Alexander Donat, "Jewish Resistance," in Out of the Whirlwind: A Reader of Holocaust Literature, ed. Albert H. Friedlander (New York: Schocken, 1976), pp. 53-54.

[68] See Yehuda Bauer, The Holocaust in Historical Perspective (Seattle: University of Washington Press, 1978), p. 154.

[69] Yehuda Bauer, The Jewish Emergence from Powerlessness (Toronto: University of Toronto Press, 1979), p. 25.

70 Eliezer Berkovits, Faith After the Holocaust (New York: Ktav, 1973), p. 11.

71 Berkovits, p. 36.

72 Emil Fackenheim, The Jewish Return into History: Reflections in the Age of Auschwitz and a New Jerusalem (New York: Schocken, 1978), pp. 270-271.

73 Berkovits, p. 163.

74 A. B. Yehoshua, Between Right and Right, trans. by Arnold Schwartz (Garden City, NY: Doubleday, 1981), p. 7.

75 Raul Hilberg, The Destruction of the European Jews (New York: Harper, 1961). A similar argument is developed in Bruno Bettelheim, The Informed Heart: Autonomy in a Mass Age (New York: Avon, 1960).

76 See Lucy S. Dawidowicz, The War Against the Jews 1933-1945 (New York: Bantam, 1975), pp. 463-465; Bauer, The Jewish Emergence, pp. 27-33.

77 Moshe Kahn, "Thoughts on the Holocaust," Jerusalem Post International Edition, 5 October 1978, p. 21.

78 Constance A. Katzenstein, "Israel--The Jewish Response to Feelings of Helplessness," New Outlook, 22, no. 7 (October 1979), p. 32; also see Arthur Herzberg, "It Is Not Because of the Masada Zealots That the People of Israel Lives," New Outlook, 22, no. 2 (March 1979), p. 45.

79 Berkovits, p. 35.

80 Alvin H. Rosenfeld and Irving Greenberg, "Introduction" in Confronting the Holocaust: The Impact of Elie Wiesel, ed. Alvin H. Rosenfeld and Irving Greenberg (Bloomington: Indiana University Press, 1978), p. xi; also see Yehoshua, p. 5.

81 Elie Wiesel, Night, trans. Stella Rodway (New York: Avon, 1958), pp. 42-43.

82 See for instance, Jay Y. Gonen, A Psychohistory of Zionism (New York: New American Library, 1975), pp. 154-155.

83 See Michael Berenbaum, The Vision of the Void: Theological Reflections on the Works of Elie Wiesel (Middletown, CT: Wesleyan University Press, 1979), p. 152.

[84] Richard L. Rubenstein, After Auschwitz: Radical Theology and Contemporary Judaism (Indianapolis: Bobbs-Merrill, 1966), p. 223.

[85] Richard L. Rubenstein, The Cunning of History: The Holocaust and the American Future (New York: Harper, 1975), pp. 4-5.

[86] William E. Kaufman cites Rubenstein in Contemporary Jewish Philosophies (New York: Reconstructionism Press, 1976), p. 87.

[87] Rubenstein, Cunning, pp. 69-72.

[88] Rubenstein, After Auschwitz, p. 153.

[89] Richard L. Rubenstein, "God as Cosmic Sadist: In Reply to Emil Fackenheim," Christian Century, 29 July 1970, p. 922.

[90] Rubenstein, After Auschwitz, pp. 46, 153, 238.

[91] Rubenstein, Cunning, p. 91.

[92] Rubenstein, After Auschwitz, p. 69.

[93] Rubenstein, "God as Cosmic Sadist," p. 922.

[94] Rubenstein, After Auschwitz, p. 233. In Cunning Rubenstein focuses on explaining how the development of the bureaucratic mentality made the death camps possible. In this work Rubenstein is not concerned with how the Jewish people can answer the moral problems raised by the holocaust. While in Cunning Rubenstein does not argue for a mythic response to the holocaust, nothing in the work contradicts his position in After Auschwitz.

[95] Rubenstein, After Auschwitz, p. 222; also see pp. 196, 239.

[96] Emil Fackenheim, God's Presence in History: Jewish Affirmations and Philosophical Reflections (New York: Harper, 1970), p. 94.

[97] Fackenheim, The Jewish Return, p. 28.

[98] Fackenheim, God's Presence, p. 6.

[99] Fackenheim, The Jewish Return, p. 29.

[100] Fackenheim, The Jewish Return, p. 280.

[101] Fackenheim, The Jewish Return, p. 281.

[102] Fackenheim, The Jewish Return, p. 23.

[103] Fackenheim, God's Presence, p. 83.

[104] Fackenheim, God's Presence, pp. 85-86.

[105] Fackenheim, God's Presence, p. 86.

[106] Fackenheim, God's Presence, pp. 87-88.

[107] Fackenheim, God's Presence, pp. 88-89.

[108] Fackenheim, The Jewish Return, p. 113.

[109] Emil Fackenheim, "On Faith in the Secular World," in Out of the Whirlwind, p. 512.

[110] Fackenheim, "On Faith in the Secular World," pp. 512-514. The three works of Wiesel's are Night, The Accident, and The Town Beyond the Wall.

[111] Fackenheim, The Jewish Return, pp. 32, 124.

[112] Berkovits, p. 18.

[113] Berkovits, p. 27.

[114] Berkovits, p. 67.

[115] Berkovits, p. 163.

[116] Berkovits, p. 32.

[117] Berkovits, p. 106.

[118] Berkovits, p. 117.

[119] Berkovits, p. 114.

[120] Berkovits, p. 158.

[121] Berkovits, pp. 153, 155.

[122] Berkovits, p. 136.

[123] Hans Jonas, "The Concept of God After Auschwitz," in Out of the Whirlwind, p. 468.

[124] "Epilogue," in Out of the Whirlwind, pp. 535-536.

[125] For example, Berkovits, Fackenheim, and Rubenstein all pay tribute to Wiesel. See Berenbaum, p. 153.

[126] Wiesel is cited in Byron L. Sherwin, "Wiesel's Midrash: The Writings of Elie Wiesel and Their Relationship to Jewish Tradition," in Confronting the Holocaust, p. 13.

[127] Sherwin, p. 119.

[128] Harry James Cargas, In Conversation with Elie Wiesel (New York: Paulist Press, 1976), p. 45.

[129] See Ted L. Estess, Elie Wiesel (New York: Frederick Ungar, 1980), p. 38.

[130] See Wiesel, Night.

[131] See Elie Wiesel, Legends of Our Own Time (New York: Avon, 1968), pp. 47-49.

[132] For a discussion of the cantata, see Berenbaum, pp. 109-117.

[133] Elie Wiesel, Dawn, trans. Frances Fenaye (New York: Avon, 1960).

[134] Berenbaum, p. 127.

[135] For another critic who treats Wiesel as a mythmaker, see Maurice Friedman, "Elie Wiesel: The Job of Auschwitz," in Responses to Elie Wiesel, ed. Harry James Cargas (New York: Peresa, 1978), p. 215; also see Berenbaum, p. 193.

[136] For samples of Ben-Gurion's rhetoric, see David Ben-Gurion, Rebirth and Destiny of Israel, trans. Mordekhai Nurock (New York: The Philosophical Library, 1954). In the speeches from the period of the revolt there are many references to the self-reliant pioneering spirit which is at the center of the labor mythology, but very few references to the holocaust.

CHAPTER IV

MENACHEM BEGIN AND THE REVOLT:
THE MYTH OF HOLOCAUST AND RETURN

Menachem Begin's memoir of his years as commander of the Irgun, The Revolt,[1] has been treated by biographers and historians as a veritable treasure trove of information. According to J. Bowyer Bell, The Revolt is one of the most revealing works on the last years of Britain's Palestine mandate.[2] Wolf Blitzer argues that to understand Begin one should read The Revolt.[3] By contrast, literary critics who have evaluated The Revolt have found it unsatisfying. They characterize it as an over-emotional, unorganized lecture, so poorly written that the drama of the Irgun's struggle is lost.[4]

In a sense, both the biographers and the critics are correct. The Revolt is an immensely revealing work, but it is not a well-written or consistent adventure story or memoir. In another sense, both groups misunderstand the structure of the work. The Revolt is not merely a work of practical political philosophy or a poorly written memoir. It encapsulates a myth, the story of the journey of the Jewish people from holocaust to redemption through return. This myth provides the Jews with ways to deal with theological and psychological problems created by the holocaust.

Heroic Myths of Return

The Revolt is best understood as a heroic journey of return of the type described by Joseph Campbell in The Hero With a Thousand Faces. According to Campbell, all heroic myths follow a single basic pattern:

> The standard path of the mythological adventure of the hero is a magnification of the formula represented in the rites of passage: separation--initiation--return: which might be named the nuclear unit of the monomyth. A hero ventures forth from the world of common day into a region of supernatural wonder: fabulous forces are

there encountered and a decisive victory is won: the hero comes back from
this mysterious adventure with the
power to bestow boons on his fellow
man.[5]

The first stage of the heroic myth--separation--intro-
duces the story and the problem facing the society.
This stage begins with a "call to adventure"[6] in which
the hero is summoned to the journey. The "call to
adventure" states the problem with which the myth
deals and establishes the hero's special credentials.
In the separation section the hero crosses the first
threshold into the land of myth.[7] This step must
occur because myths tell of events which do not occur
in normal time or space.[8]

In the second stage--initiation or trial--the
hero overcomes many obstacles and eventually defeats
the evil adversary.[9] This process serves the two
functions of proving the worthiness of the hero and
symbolically solving the social problems which the
myth confronts. This trial section usually occurs
outside the normal world, often in the underworld,
because truly heroic events do not occur in the real
world. What is essential in this section of the myth
is that the hero be thoroughly tested and emerge victorious. The trials which test the hero always
increase in difficulty until an ultimate test is
reached, a test which, if passed, recovers the lost
boon that the society needs to solve its problems.

In the third stage, the hero returns to the real
world from the land of myth with the boon which symbolically solves the problem facing the society.
Campbell has identified the structure of myths that
call for a return to an earlier state. Here, return
is used in two senses. It is not only the third phase
in the myth, but an essential element giving power to
the myth. The hero solves the problem with which the
myth deals through a return to an earlier more heroic
age:

> The cosmogenic cycle is present with
> astonishing consistency in the sacred
> writings of all the continents, and it
> gives to the adventure of the hero a
> new and interesting turn; for now it
> appears that the perilous journey was
> a labor not of attainment, but of

90

reattainment, not discovery but redis-
covery.[10]

A myth of return responds to a social problem by
calling for a return to a more heroic era in a society's history. The journey from separation through
initiation to return encapsulates the problem facing
the society in the conflict between the hero and the
villain. With the hero's eventual victory, the problem is symbolically solved. The typical three-part
plot of the myth is also tied to its function. In the
separation stage, the hero confronts the problem and
is drawn into the heroic journey. The hero must sepa-
rate himself or herself from the real world in order
to return to the past greatness of the society. In
the trial stage, the hero proves his or her worthiness
to serve as a model by overcoming various obstacles
and, in the process of defeating the evil adversary,
recovers the lost boon which the society needs. The
hero may recover the lost power in order to defeat the
villain or defeat the villain in order to recover that
lost power, but in either case, the final, most difficult trial serves as a climactic battle which symbolizes the society's eventual triumph over the problem
it faces. In the third stage, the hero not only
returns to the real world, but also carries the message of salvation through return. It is only through
return that the society can be saved. The mythmaker
not only tells the story of a return, but also uses
the "return" as a sort of "logical model"[11] to resolve
a social problem.

The Myth of The Revolt

The Revolt tells the story of a journey from the
holocaust to redemption through return. It is a play
in three acts preceded by a prologue stating the problem with which the myth deals and followed by a prayer
closing the myth. The three main acts of the myth
follow the pattern of myths of return as identified by
Campbell.

In the prologue or introduction to The Revolt,
Begin both states the problem and the answer to it
which he will then work out in the 380 pages of his
memoir. Paragraph one summarizes the basic ideology
of the Irgun. The Jews must never forget that they
can protect themselves only through strength and vigi-
lence: "I have written this book primarily for my own

91

people, lest the Jew forget again--as he so disaster-
ously forgot in the past this simple truth: that
there are things more precious than life, and more
horrible than death" (p. xi). In paragraph two, Begin
tells the non-Jewish readers of the book that Jewish
heroes have "arisen" and will never give in to weakness again:

> But I have written this book also for
> Gentiles, lest they be unwilling to
> realise [sic], or all too ready to
> overlook the fact that out of blood
> and strife and tears and ashes a new
> specimen of human being was born, a
> specimen completely unknown to the
> world for over eighteen hundred years,
> "the Fighting Jew." That Jew, whom
> the world considered dead and buried
> never to rise again has arisen. For
> he has learned that "simple truth" of
> life and death, and he will never
> again go down to the sides of the pit
> and vanish from the earth. (p. xi)

Begin then identifies the enemy which must be overcome. That enemy is twofold--the weakness which typi-
fied Jewish leadership during the holocaust and the
uncaring world which stood by while the Jewish people
were destroyed:

> It is axiomatic that those who fight
> have to hate--something or somebody.
> We had to hate first and foremost, the
> horrifying, age-old, inexcusable utter
> defencelessness of our Jewish people,
> wandering through millenia, through a
> cruel world, to the majority of whose
> inhabitants the defencelessness of the
> Jews was a standing invitation to mas-
> sacre them. We had to hate the
> humiliating disgrace of the homeless-
> ness of our people. We had to hate--
> as any nation worthy of the name must
> and always will hate--the rule of the
> foreigner, rule, unjust and unjustifi-
> able per se, foreign rule in the land
> of our ancestors, in our own country.
> We had to hate the barring of the
> gates of our own country to our own
> brethren, trampled and bleeding and

92

                    crying out for help in a world morally
                    deaf. (p. xii)

Begin then affirms the value of the Irgun's underground campaign as a model for dealing with the problems facing the Jewish people. Should the need ever
arise, he would return to the underground (p. xiii).
At this point, the myth of The Revolt can begin.
Begin has stated in capsule form the ideology of the
Irgun, the problem the Irgun confronted, the answer to
that problem, and he has reaffirmed his commitment to
that answer as a model for social action. It is now
time to tell the tale.

        Chapter one of The Revolt, "The Gateway to Free-
dom," functions as the call to adventure. Even the
title of the chapter suggests a journey beyond some
threshold where the true adventure can begin. The
chapter opens by describing Begin's sentencing to
eight years in Soviet work camps. Begin describes his
life in a Russian prison, sessions with an interroga-
tor, and how he survived seven days in solitary con-
finement (pp. 9-10). He has survived the first test.
At the end of the chapter, Begin leaves a Soviet prison to go to a Soviet work camp. At this moment, he
moves past the first threshold into the land of myth.

                    And when the gates of the prison were
                    opened and the car slid out into the
                    deserted street, somebody whispered:
                    "This is the beginning of the journey
                    to Eretz Israel [the land of Israel]."
                    Impracticable faith? Maybe. Yet faith
                    is perhaps stronger than reality;
                    faith itself creates reality. (p. 11)

Begin's mythic journey begins when he hears an uniden-
tified, mysterious voice telling him that he will
arrive in Israel. It can be interpreted as a sign
from God. Such signs are found in many myths. Begin's
concluding comment, that faith creates reality, represents the attitude at the core of all myth. The myth
functions as a "reality lived" that creates a new
reality.

        In the second and third chapters, "The Land of
Our Fathers" and "Au Revoir in Freedom," Begin com-
pletes the separation stage of the myth by moving into
the underground. These two chapters describe Begin's
experiences in Soviet work camps and his journey to

                              93

Israel. One crucial incident occurs in the labor
camps. Begin meets Garin, a former Russian Communist
Party leader. Begin describes how Garin, who had
denied his Jewish heritage, longs for Israel:

> All his life he had served another
> idea, a universalist ideal--fighting
> for it on the barricades, being cap-
> tured and tortured for it by the
> "White Russians." Faithfully serving,
> he had risen and become the Secretary
> of the Central Committee of the Party
> and then Assistant Editor of the
> Party's national daily paper. How far
> was he from Zion! And how far from
> Zion was the place to which fate had
> brought us! And this man, in what he
> thought might be his last hours on
> earth, asked us to sing the song of
> Zion.
> We sang. Had the greenish Pechora
> River ever heard "Hatikvah" before?
> Had the dumbfounded Urki [common
> criminals] ever heard a Hebrew song
> before? From the belly of the boat
> the song burst forth:
> "To return to the land of our
> fathers." (p. 22)

Garin's story demonstrates that no matter how far a
Jew strays from Zion, he or she still needs and longs
for Israel. Garin shows Begin that the will to
"return" to Israel is the key to the problems of the
Jews. If Garin can draw strength from "Hatikvah," a
song about the return to Zion, then the Jewish people
can draw more strength from an actual "return" to
their homeland.

From the boat carrying him to a work camp, Begin
is suddenly released to join the free Polish army of
General Anders. In Anders' army he journeys to Palestine and arrives "home" (p. 25) overcome with joy.
The first stage of the journey is complete. Begin's
arrival in Israel places him on the threshold of the
underworld or, in his case, of the underground. The
final page of chapter three describes the transition
from the separation to the initiation stage of the
myth. When Begin joins the underground he enters the
twentieth century equivalent of the underworld. He
will emerge only when the battle is won. The second

94

stage of the mythic journey has begun: "The brigade I served in was a brigade of Hebrew rebels. It operated on the banks of the Jordan, and built a road to freedom for Israel" (p. 25).

The next three hundred pages describe the trials of the Irgun in building that "road to freedom for Israel." Begin opens this section of The Revolt with several discursive chapters explaining the problem facing the Irgun and the answers it developed. In "Army of the Underground," Begin begins the story of the revolt. He describes the organization and tactical obstacles faced by the Irgun. Begin also briefly tells the story of several operations in which the Irgun confiscated British weapons and explains how the Irgun intimidated the British into allowing free worship at the Wailing Wall (pp. 89-91). In "Overt Undergound" and "A Man With Many Names," he describes the various tactics he used to avoid capture by the British. Organizational problems are the first trial facing Begin and the Irgun.

In chapters nine through twelve, Begin describes the conflict between the Irgun and the Jewish community. The conflict between the Irgun and the Jewish Agency and Haganah symbolizes the conflict between the reborn "Fighting Jew" and the Jewish passivity that Begin hated. Two Irgun posters[12] depict this conflict. One poster shows a young man on his knees begging, "I want to live." The caption reads: "The Submissive Jewish Agency Way." The second poster shows the same young man standing with a submachine gun in his hands saying, "I want to live." The caption reads: "The Fighting Hebrew Resistance Way." These two posters represent the second set of trials. Begin and the Irgun must withstand the attacks of the Jewish Agency and Haganah, while neither giving in to traditional Jewish passivity nor causing a civil war.

In chapters nine and ten of The Revolt, Begin describes the "season" in which the Jewish Agency and Haganah aided the British in their efforts to destroy the Irgun. Despite the cooperation with the British, Begin forbade Irgun retaliation against either Haganah or the Jewish Agency. In this difficult situation, it was the heroism of the Irgun which prevented civil war:

When I recall those days, all the love
of which the human heart is capable

wells up in me for those young underground fighters, unflinching, fearless, moved by a supreme fighting
spirit. They went to concentration
camps, were thrown into dark cellars,
starved, beaten, and maligned yet no
one ever broke his solemn undertaking
not to retaliate on his tormentors. I
saw them in their anguish and I was
tormented with them. But I also saw
them in their greatness and I was
proud. . . . A human "order" [not to
retaliate] would have been of no avail
here. The order came from "somewhere,"
from the depths of Jewish history; and
it was obeyed. We were spared the
catastrophe of catastrophes. And
before many months went by the revolt
embraced the whole people. (pp. 152-
153)

The Irgun had overcome the first obstacle in its battle against Jewish weakness.

In the next two chapters, Begin describes two
more instances in which the Irgun's strength was
tested by the official organizations of the Jewish
community. First, he tells the story of the Irgun
assault upon the Arab village Dir Yassin. In April
1948, the Irgun attacked Dir Yassin in order to con-
solidate the Jewish position outside Jerusalem. In
the firefight which resulted, over two hundred innocent civilians were killed. Despite this loss of
life, Begin's focus in retelling the story is on the
duplicity of the Haganah and the Jewish Agency in
their reaction to the attack. Begin quotes a letter
proving that a Haganah commander had approved the
operation (pp. 162-163) and criticizes Ben-Gurion for
his attacks upon the Irgun (p. 164). He focuses little attention on the Dir Yassin massacre itself. The
story of the assault upon Dir Yassin fits in this section of The Revolt because Begin treats it as a second
trial against the weakness and duplicity of the Jewish
establishment. Again, the Irgun is victorious.
Despite the hypocrisy of the Jewish Agency and the
Haganah, the assault on Dir Yassin caused many Arabs
to flee from Israel and this "helped to carve the way
to our decisive victories on the battlefield"(p. 165).

96

Begin also tells the story of the Altalena. The
Altalena, an arms ship brought in by the Irgun during
a U.N. truce in the 1948 war, was destroyed by order
of Ben-Gurion, who feared an Irgun attempted coup.
Begin accuses the Ben-Gurion government of duplicity
in its negotiations with the Irgun over the Altalena
(pp. 168-170). He also describes the landing of the
Altalena, the firefight which developed when Israeli
Defense Force troops opened fire on the ship, and the
final battle after the Altalena had sailed to Tel Aviv
(pp. 170-176). The government continued firing on the
ship after it had surrendered, and the ship was
destroyed. The Altalena incident stands as the final
test of the Irgun against Jewish weakness. Although
the ship was blown up, the Irgun was not defeated.
Despite the actions of the government, the Irgun did
not retaliate, and civil war was avoided: "And so it
came to pass that there was no fratricidal war in
Israel to destroy the Jewish State before it was properly born. In spite of everything--there was no civil
war!" (p. 176).

    The third trial of the Irgun was the fight
against the British in Palestine. Begin opens chapter
thirteen, "United Resistance," by describing the period from 1945-1946 when the Irgun and the official Jewish organizations fought together against the British.
This section appears immediately after the Irgun's
trial against Jewish weakness to symbolize the Irgun's
victory over that weakness. Begin describes the Irgun
attack on the King David Hotel, the British headquarters in Palestine. His description focuses on the
reaction of the Haganah and Jewish Agency to the
operation. The attack itself is described in only a
few sentences (pp. 218-219). After the attack, the
British responded with tough sanctions against the
Jewish community. In response to those sanctions,
both Haganah and the Jewish Agency gave up the struggle. Only the Irgun continued to fight. Begin
describes the willingness of the Irgun to carry on the
fight, despite the tough British responses, as proof
of the superiority of the Irgun. In the next six
chapters, he tells of the attempts by the British to
crush the Irgun with the whip and the gallows. This
long section describes the crucial test which the
Irgun had to overcome to free Palestine. In order for
the revolt to succeed, the Irgun had to be willing to
sacrifice their lives. The test began when an Irgun
soldier was whipped by the British. The Irgun then
responded by whipping several British officers. That

action forced the British to give up the whip as a form of punishment: "The British government never again whipped anybody, neither Jew nor Arab, in Eretz Israel" (p. 236). After overcoming the test of the whip, the Irgun moved on to the more difficult test of the gallows.

The trial of the gallows began when two Irgun soldiers, Ashbel and Simchon, were sentenced to death by a British court. The Irgun kidnapped six British officers and threatened to execute them if Ashbel and Simchon were killed. The death sentences were annulled (pp. 245-250). Begin then tells the story of Dov Gruner, the greatest hero of the Irgun. While fighting a holding action to allow his comrades to escape, Gruner was captured by the British. He was tried by a British court and eventually sentenced to death. In response, the Irgun again kidnapped British officers and again the British were forced to retreat. The execution was delayed, but the sentence was not annulled (p. 256). Although Gruner waited for months in a death cell, he refused to appeal his conviction because he believed that such an appeal would implicitly recognize the legitimacy of the British regime. The Irgun planned an operation to rescue Gruner, but before it could be attempted, Gruner and three other Irgun soldiers were transferred from a prison in Jerusalem to the Acre fortress, where they were hanged (p. 268). After Gruner was hanged, the Irgun faced their greatest challenge: to destroy the gallows as an instrument of British power.

In "A Bastille Falls," the trial of the gallows is overcome. The chapter begins with the story of one of the great prison breaks in all of history. The Acre fortress was breached by Irgun explosives and many Irgun soldiers escaped as "this second Bastille fell . . ."(p. 278). Despite the success of the prison break, a number of Irgun soldiers were captured and three were eventually hanged for their part in the operation (p. 289). In retaliation the Irgun hanged two British sergeants, and the British never again used the gallows as an instrument of political control. With this victory British power in Palestine was compromised. Begin concludes:

> There is no doubt that had we not retaliated, avenues of gallows would have been set up in Palestine and a foreign power would be ruling in our

98

country to this day. The grim act of
retaliation forced upon us in Nathanya
[where the British sergeants were
killed] not only saved scores of Jewish young men from the gallows but
broke the back of British rule. When
gallows are shattered the regime which
rests on them must inevitably crash.
This was confirmed in unambiguous
terms by none other than the former
chief assistant to the Chief Secretary
of the British Government in Eretz
Israel, Colonel Archer-Cust. In a
lecture to the Royal Empire Society,
he said: "The hanging of the two
British sergeants did more than anything to get us out." (p. 290)

The final trial had been surmounted. The British had
been defeated. They would soon leave Palestine.

The Revolt follows the typical pattern of heroic
myths of return. The hero--in this case the Irgun--
faces more and more difficult obstacles until in a
climactic battle the adversary is defeated. Although
the Irgun faced setbacks, in the end they forced the
British to withdraw from Palestine.

The trials section of The Revolt concludes with
four brief chapters summarizing the message of the
previous chapters. "Meetings in the Underground" and
"Meetings in the Dark" describe the series of meetings
between Begin and the United Nations Special Committee
on Palestine, Arthur Koestler, and a number of other
journalists. This section ends with "The Cross-roads
of History" in which Begin describes the various political maneuvers of the British aimed at keeping control of Palestine. But their manipulations were to no
avail: "On the 15th of May, 1948, the British High
Commissioner boarded a British warship. A guard of
honour presented arms in his honour, and in honour of
the flag as it was lowered. The revolt was victorious" (p. 331).

The final section of The Revolt describes the
return of the Irgun from the underground to the real
world and explains the boon their revolt recovered.
Begin begins by describing the British threat to muti-
late the "homeland" (pp. 333-337). Although chronologically this threat occurred before the state of

99

Israel was proclaimed on 15 May 1948, Begin treats it as part of the battle to protect the state after it had been established and not as part of the revolt to push the British out of Palestine. Begin also describes the negotiations between the Irgun and the official organizations of the Jewish community, regulating the transfer of soldiers from the Irgun to the army of Israel (pp. 344-347).

In chapter twenty-nine Begin describes the Irgun's role in the conquest of the Arab city of Jaffa. The battle of Jaffa is important to the story of The Revolt, not only because it shows the heroism of the Irgun, but also because it marks the transition from the underground to the real world. In this battle, the Irgun successfully attacked Jaffa, the Arab port city near Tel Aviv. Begin begins this story by giving a clear sign that the underground portion of the revolt was coming to an end. At an open Irgun meeting preceding the battle, Begin spoke in public: "Below the courtyard the parade waited--the first open parade, of six hundred Irgun officers and men. The days of partisan attacks were, strictly speaking, no more" (p. 354).[13] The battle of Jaffa is a story of the defeat of the Arab defenders and of how the Irgun broke free of the Jewish Agency and Haganah. When the first day's fighting in Jaffa achieved little, the Jewish Agency referred to the Irgun's attack as "abortive . . . [and] barren" (p. 359). According to Begin, the official organizations of the Jewish community "wanted us to be beaten" (p. 360). Their attitude was "another example of the shameful 'self-hatred' that had plagued us Jews . . ." (p. 360).

The soldiers of the Irgun responded to the challenge with what Begin saw as unsurpassed heroism. Begin writes: "On that tragic morning of April the 28th, 1948, the little band of Irgun fighters on the Jaffa front displayed a brave and lofty grandeur of spirit, unsurpassed, I venture to claim in the whole story of human valour" (p. 361). They won not only because of their courage, but also because "new strength flowed miraculously into muscles which had been utterly worn out" (pp. 365-366). The result was not merely victory, but redemption: "For six months that tower [the mosque in Jaffa] had sniped death into the streets of the city [Tel Aviv]--and now at last redemption had come" (p. 369). And with the conquest of Jaffa, the underground war was over; the war of Hebrew independence had begun (p. 371).

The return section of The Revolt closes with
chapter thirty, "Dawn," a symbol representing day
breaking as the soldiers of the Irgun leave the darkness of the underground and return to the newly established Jewish state. At the beginning of "Dawn,"
Begin ties the birth of the state of Israel to the
myth of return:

> The miracle of Return was accompanied
> by the miracle of Revival. Within a
> generation there developed within the
> Jewish people the strength to take up
> arms, to rise against alien rule, to
> throw off the yoke of oppression. How
> long, how endless were the years of
> exile of humiliation and destruction.
> And how short, in comparison, were the
> years of revival, reinvigoration, and
> armed uprising. History has no paral-
> lel in its records. (p. 372)

The exile of the Irgun and of all the Jews had ended:
"The circle of wanderings was closed and the nation
had returned to the Motherland that bore it" (p. 372).
The boon which the Irgun had recovered was the knowledge that only the strong can be free. Begin then
quotes a portion of his first speech after leaving the
underground. With the conclusion of that speech,
Begin and the Irgun re-emerge into the light of day.
Literally and symbolically dawn had arrived:

> Darkness was about us. Black-out.
> Not a glimmer of light. The darkness
> would continue. Blood would still be
> shed. But beyond the sorrow and the
> darkness the rosy dawn was breaking
> through. We had come forth from
> slavery to freedom. On the morrow the
> sun would shine.
> And Jewish children once more would
> laugh. (p. 377)

And with that first sign of dawn, the first child's
laugh, the revolt of the Irgun and the myth of return
ends.

Begin introduces The Revolt with a prologue set-
ting the stage for the myth to follow. He concludes
with a prayer for those heroes who sacrificed their
lives in the revolt. In "We Bow Our Heads," Begin

101

explains that he has not written a history of the
revolt, but "merely presented a few chapters on the
most important events of the period as they are reflected in personal memories" (pp. 378-379). Yet this
story is prescriptive:

> The history of the revolt and the fact
> of its victory will guide us in the
> unknown future. They will teach us
> never to despair even in conditions of
> enslavement. For a nation, enslaved,
> dispersed, beaten, decimated, on the
> brink of utter destruction, can yet
> arise to rebel against its fate, and
> so come to life again. Few against
> many. The weak against the strong.
> Hounded, isolated, forsaken, aban-
> doned, What of it? No arms? They can
> be acquired--if needs be from the
> enemy. No forces? They can be
> raised. No preparations? The strug-
> gle itself will teach and train.
> Only, man's whole spirit must be
> utterly devoted to his ideal, and he
> must be prepared to give his life for
> it. Perhaps this is the only condi-
> tion. All the rest will come of
> itself. (pp. 379-380)

The Revolt is a myth which serves as a model for
solving the problem of Jewish survival in the age of
Auschwitz. "We Bow Our Heads" is Begin's final prayer
honoring the greatness of the soldiers of the Irgun
who fought for Jewish survival:

> I hope, however, that I may be
> permitted, at the close of these chap-
> ters, to pay my last and special trib-
> ute to the heroes and martyrs of the
> Irgun Zvai Leumi.
> Their life was struggle; their
> death herosim, their sacrifice sacred;
> their memory eternal. (p. 380)

And with this prayer for his soldiers, The Revolt concludes.

The narrative structure of The Revolt moves from
the holocaust to redemption. The story opens in
Poland, where the Germans are annihilating the Jewish

102

people. Begin escapes the Germans only to be imprisoned by the Soviets. After his release and journey to Palestine, Begin enters the underground to fight the holocaust. In the underground battle, the Irgun overcomes increasingly difficult trials until they force the British to leave Palestine. They then must fight for their right to be treated as equals in the new state. With their victory at Jaffa and the establishment of the state of Israel, the victory is complete. The Jewish people have been redeemed. The Revolt begins in the blackest night of the death camps and ends as the light of day breaks on the Jewish people. It is a symbolic journey from the hell of the holocaust to redemption through a return to the land and the virtues of the ancient Hebrew people. Begin describes the journey with the phrase, "From the Holocaust to Redemption."[14]

The Symbolic Structure of the Myth of Return

Earlier, I argued that societies use myths to solve problems that cannot be solved through other means. The myth of The Revolt is no exception to this rule. The myth is organized around a problem, an ultimate goal, and the means to achieve that goal. The problem is the holocaust. The goal is a Jewish state. The means is return to the ancient land of Israel and its values.

The evil against which the Irgun fought was the holocaust. The Irgun launched their revolt only when it became clear that the Germans were annhilating the Jewish people and the British were doing very little to stop them. They fought for the victims of the death camps: "It is for their sake [holocaust victims] that we fight . . ." (p. 43). The horror of the holocaust lay at the core of Irgun mythology. Again and again, Begin refers to the destruction of the Jewish people. Early in The Revolt, he writes:

> Dark night, the darkest of all nights, descended on the Jewish people in Europe. One million five hundred thousand Jewish children were transported in the death trains to the gas-chambers. Millions of men and women were shot, or drowned, or burned, or gassed or buried alive. When man becomes a beast, the Jew ceases to be

regarded as a human being. There is
no room here for self-delusion. (p. 36)

Later, he describes the fate of the family of one of
his friends, a Dr. Arnold: "Arnold's little son was
torn from his mother's arms and murdered in a Nazi
gas-chamber. The mother killed herself. All his
other relatives were shot or gassed by the Germans and
his heart took the blow hardly" (pp. 120-121).

To Begin and the Irgun, the horror of the holocaust was not only that six million Jews were killed,
but also that the world stood by and watched without
helping them. Begin places much of the blame for the
holocaust upon the lack of concern showed for the
Jewish people by the Allies. He claims that Hitler
sent the Jews to the death camps only after discovering that the world did not care about the Jews:

> First, he imprisoned the Jews; and
> noted the world's indifference. Then
> he starved them; and still the world
> did not move. He dug his claws in,
> bared his teeth; the world did not
> even raise an eyebrow. So he went on,
> step by step, until he reached the
> climax of the gas-chambers. Hitler
> had originally prepared poison gas for
> use, if occasion favoured it on the
> warfronts; but though his military
> position grew more desperate from year
> to year, the only people on whom he
> dared use gas was on Jews in the gas-
> chambers. (p. 28; also see p. 361)

While the world did not care if the Jews lived or
died, the British government, according to Begin, was
pleased with the effects of the final solution:

> The average Englishman was probably as
> indifferent to Jewish lives as any
> other non-Jew in the world. But those
> who rule Palestine and the Middle
> East, were not in the least "indiffer-
> ent." They were highly interested in
> achieving the maximum reduction in the
> number of Jews liable to enter the
> land of Israel. (pp. 78-79)

Consequently, the British Foreign Office spared no effort to prevent Jews from escaping Nazi Europe to Palestine (p. 34).

While the world must shoulder the blame for allowing Hitler to build the death camps, Begin placed the ultimate responsibility for the holocaust on the Jewish people themselves. He believed that Jewish weakness both encouraged the Nazis to attack the Jews and allowed the attack to be successful. In a sense, Jewish passivity precipitated the holocaust: "It was on this complete disarmament, as much psychological as physical, that our oppressors calculated" (p. 40). In the introduction to The Revolt, Begin refers to the "age-old inexcusable utter defencelessness" of the Jewish people which "was a standing invitation to massacre . . ." (p. xii). This position leads to the unpleasant conclusion that it was the Jews themselves who caused the holocaust. Begin lends credence to this interpretation when he writes that alone among the world's people, only the Jews did not realize that "the world does not pity the slaughtered. It only respects those who fight" (p. 36). If it is true that the world only respects those who fight, then even the British cannot really be blamed for their failure to aid the Jewish people. Through their passivity, the Jews themselves were responsible for the death camps.

Begin's view that the world did not care about the Jews and that Jewish defenselessness caused the holocaust led him to conclude that the holocaust was not a unique event. Auschwitz had been liberated, but the Jewish people were not safe. As long as they depended for their existence upon the world community, they would never be safe. Consequently, Begin saw continuing threats to the existence of the Jewish people. He interpreted a proposed partition plan as yet another final solution to the Jewish problem (p. 46). For Begin and the Irgun, the threat of holocaust would never end as long as the Jews depended on others for protection.

The holocaust threatened the psychological health as well as the physical existence of the Jews. Throughout The Revolt, there are signs of tremendous guilt about Jewish behavior in Nazi Europe. Again and again, Begin makes bitter comments about the demeaning character of Jewish passivity. He writes of how the Jewish people dug their own graves and waited to be slaughtered (p. 26). They were led "like sheep to the slaughter" (p. 26). In an incredibly bitter passage, he compares the death camps to the Chicago stockyards:

> Just as "the world" does not pity the thousands of cattle led to the slaughter-pens in the Chicago abattoirs, equally it did not pity--or else it got used to--the tens of thousands being taken like sheep to the slaughter in Treblinki. (p. 36)

The bitter tone of these comments reflects Begin's shame that Jews did not fight back. At several points, he explicitly refers to this guilt. In his description of the attack on Jaffa, he refers to the "shameful 'self-hatred'" of the Jewish leadership. Guilt is central in his description of an attempt by the Jewish Agency to stop the revolt: "To surrender would be to incur the double shame: of condoning extermination in Europe and enslavement in our homeland" (p. 150).

In addition to the guilt generated by Jewish passivity in Europe, the Irgun was energized by guilt over their own survival. They asked themselves why they deserved to live when so many Jews were dying in Europe. Begin quotes a statement by Irgun soldier Meir Feinstein:

> How blind you are, British tyrants: Have you not learnt yet whom you are fighting in this struggle, unexampled in human history? Do you believe we are to be frightened to death--we who for years heard the rattle of the trucks that bore our brothers, our parents, the best of our people, to a slaughter which, too, had no precedent in history? We who asked and asked ourselves every day; how are we better than they, than millions of our brothers? In what lies our virtue? For we could have been among and with them in the days of fear and in the moments that came before death.
> To these recurring questions our conscience makes one reply: We were not spared in order to live in slavery and oppression to await some new Treblinki. (p. 42)

The passivity of European Jews as well as the survival of Palestinian Jews created guilt which had to be cleansed. Revolt was necessary to redeem the Jewish people from the holocaust. Without it, "the sun would have set on our people" (p. 39). The revolt was fought against the physical danger of a new holocaust and against guilt created by past Jewish weakness.

The goal of the revolt was redemption. Unlike some traditional Jews, Begin does not write of the redemption of the Jewish people in millenial terms. Although he claims that God aided the Irgun, he does not foresee the coming of the Messiah. Nor does Begin write of a perfect society on earth. Begin's vision of redemption is much simpler. For Begin and the Irgun, redemption means only that the Jewish people will be allowed to live in freedom and safety in their homeland. There is no detailed description of this redemption in The Revolt, because for Begin redemption is equated with ordinary life. The goal of the Irgun is that the Jews be allowed to live ordinary lives without being forced to worry about death camps. The key description of the redeemed world comes at the very conclusion of The Revolt: "On the morrow the sun would shine. And Jewish children once more would laugh" (p. 377). Redemption means only that the Jewish people will be able to live normal lives in their entire homeland (p. 140). There will be no more death camps and no unnatural passivity.

The Revolt tells the story of how the soldiers of the Irgun redeemed the Jewish people through their courage, skill, and capacity for sacrifice. According to Begin, the members of the "Fighting family" (the Irgun) were unparalleled soldiers: "Few have ever equaled them" (p. 323; also see the comments on the battle for Jaffa). Their strength and heroism allowed them to achieve great victories: "There were operations in which the combination of traditional Jewish brains and reborn Jewish heroism performed deeds which bordered on the miraculous" (p. 71). In this and other passages, Begin describes the soldiers of the Irgun in heroic terms. They stood larger than life and possessed all the attributes of mythic heroes.

Proof of the heroic quality of the Irgun is found in their willingness to sacrifice themselves for their people: "Out of our blood will flourish the tree of freedom for our country and the tree of life for our people" (p. 121). Only through such sacrifices could

107

the Jewish people be saved: "For the world knows that
a land is redeemed by blood" (p. 264). Begin quotes a
letter which an Irgun soldier, Simchon, wrote while
waiting in a death cell: "I know what awaits me but I
am sure that my death will bring us one step nearer
victory. By our death and sacrifice we shall set up a
free State for our people which will know how to live
and why it lives" (p. 243).

The skill, heroism, and blood of the soldiers of
the Irgun saved the Jewish people. The strength and
heroism of the Irgun defeated the British (pp. 331,
376) and cleansed the Jewish people of the guilt
created by Jewish passivity: "There are times when
everything in you cries out: your very self-respect
as a human being lies in your resistance to evil. We
fight therefore we are!" (p. 46) Through the fight,
"A new generation grew up which turned its back on
fear. It began to fight instead of to plead" (p.
40). The message of The Revolt is that the Jewish
people may save themselves and find meaning in life.
This lesson of the revolt is not timebound; it protects the state of Israel forever: "If we learn and
remember we shall overcome all our enemies. They will
never succeed in enslaving us again. Never" (p. 380).

However, one question remains: From what source
did the new-found strength of the Jewish people come?
The answer is return. The myth of The Revolt serves
as a "logical model" explaining how, after twenty centuries of dispersion and weakness, the Jewish people
suddenly regained their strength through return to the
greatness and heroism of biblical Israel.

The first component of the Irgun's return is the
land of Israel itself. Throughout The Revolt, Begin
emphasizes the special tie of the Jewish people to
Palestine. The strength of the tie is obvious in his
references to Israel as the "Homeland" and "Motherland" (p. 372) and in his ecstatic reaction when he
reaches Israel (p. 25). Later in The Revolt, he
describes the joy which Jewish soldiers on the
Altalena felt when they reched Israel: "These young
people were overwhelmed with joy when they reached the
shores of their Homeland. I saw many of them kneeling
and kissing the salt, damp sand on the shore. In my
ears I still hear the echo of their joyful cries as
their boats ran on to the beach" (p. 171). The importance of the link between the Jewish people and the
land of Israel is established early in The Revolt when

Begin tells of how his father taught him the difference between going and "returning" to Zion:

> From my early youth I had been taught by my father—who, as I was later told, went to his death at Nazi hands voicing the liturgic declaration of faith in God and signing the Hebrew national anthem, "Hatikvah"—that we Jews were to return to Eretz Israel. Not to "go" or "travel" or "come"—but to return. (p. 3)

This story is also important for the reference to one of the crucial symbols of revolt, Hatikvah. Hatikvah symbolizes the link between the Jewish people and the land of Israel. The song, which calls for a "return to the land of our fathers" (p. 22), is sung whenever soldiers of the Irgun sacrifice their lives for the cause (pp. 243, 255, 264-265, 286, 289). For example, Dov Gruner sings Hatikvah as he is led to the gallows. Thus, Hatikvah links the renewed courage of the Jewish people to the return of Zion. Just as Garin drew energy from the song itself, the Irgun drew energy from the return to the land of Israel. Hatikvah serves as a symbol of the renewed heroism of the Irgun which came from a return to the land of Israel.

The myth of the Irgun draws upon Jewish love for Palestine, but modifies the traditional myth. Begin does not see return to Zion as the ultimate Messianic aim of the Irgun,[15] nor does he treat return in purely ritualistic terms. Rather, return is a means to an end. It is the return of the Jewish people to Palestine which makes possible the redemption of the Jewish people. Through return to Zion, the Jews regain the strength which they lost during two thousand years of dispersion. They draw renewed strength from contact with the land itself:

> The revolt sprang from the earth. The ancient Greek story of Antaeus and the strength he drew from contact with Mother Earth, is a legend. The renewed strength which came to us, and especially to our youth, from contact with the soil of our ancient land, is no legend but a fact. (p. 40)

It was return to Israel which made the resurrection of the Hebrew people possible: "The miracle of Return was accompanied by the miracle of Revival" (p. 372).

The Irgun also returned to the role of ancient Hebrew warriors. Irgun soldiers were reborn Hebrew heroes. They regained the strength the Hebrews had as an ancient people. In the introduction Begin writes of the "Fighting Jew" whom "the world considered dead and buried . . ." (p. xi). In the Irgun's revolt, the "Fighting Jew" has "arisen" (p. xi). It was no coincidence that Irgun soldiers often took the names of Hebrew heroes as their codenames.[16] Symbolically, the revolt transformed them into Hebrew warriors. For example: "[Amitai Paglin] was brought to us by the magnet of our ideal, and little Amitai became Gideon who did such great things for the realization of that ideal and for the life of his people . . ." (p. 72).

Begin emphasizes the tie between the Irgun's revolt and the Maccabean revolt against Greek rule over Palestine. According to Begin, "The revolt against the British did not end as the revolt against the Romans had ended. It is not Messada but Modi'in [the village from which the Maccabean revolt was launched] that symbolizes the Hebrew revolt of our times" (p. 47). In the Irgun's call to arms in 1944, Begin explains that the Irgun's modern revolt would succeed just as earlier Hebrew revolts had succeeded: "They [Irgun soldiers] will not surrender until they have renewed our days as of old, until they have ensured for our people a Homeland, freedom, honour, bread and justice. And if you will give them your aid you will see in our days the Return of Zion and the restoration of Israel" (p. 43). It was from the return to ancient greatness as well as from the return to the land of Israel that the soldiers of the Irgun "renewed" their strength: "When a nation reawakens, its finest sons are prepared to give their lives for its liberation" (p. 290, emphasis added).

The myth of return was the Irgun's answer to the holocaust. The Irgun believed that passivity led to the death camps and created Jewish guilt. The Jewish people could be saved and cleansed of their guilt through strength and sacrifice. Through a return to the land of Israel and to the heroism of the ancient Hebrew patriots, the Jewish people could renew their strength and save themselves. The Revolt tells the story of a heroic journey from the holocaust to redemption. The myth underlying The Revolt provides the key which made that journey possible--return.

The Revolt can best be understood as a myth through which the Jewish people moved from holocaust to redemption through return. Not only does the narrative structure and underlying logic of the work fit this pattern, but other aspects of The Revolt are also mythic. For example, the imagery and style of The Revolt are consonant with the myth of return. The dominant image in the work is blood. It is through the blood of the Irgun, that is, through their capacity for sacrifice that the Jewish people could be saved. Begin writes of the link between blood and Hebrew renewal in his description of the battle of Jaffa:

> Acquiring the arms for the battle had cost blood; the battle itself cost blood; the first breach cost blood; and even the softening-up for which every army paid in sweat alone, cost us blood. The altar of God demanded sacrifices without number. Now we were offering the best of our sons as a Passover-sacrifice in order to ensure that our days should be renewed as of old. (p. 358)

Begin's reference to the Passover-sacrifice is particularly important. According to the Bible, the Jewish people were protected from the plague that killed the first born in Egypt by the sacrifice of the paschal lamb. The Jews placed blood from the perfect lamb on the door posts and lintels of their homes "as a signal to the Destroyer of the first born of Egypt to pass over the homes of the Israelites."[17] According to Begin, the sacrifices of the Irgun saved the new state of Israel from annihilation, just as the sacrifice of the perfect lamb and subsequent sprinkling of its blood on Jewish door posts saved the Jewish people in Egypt.

Begin also writes of how the capacity for sacrifice came from the soil of Palestine and from the blood of the holocaust victims:

> Capacity for sacrifice is the measure of revolt and the father of victory. Only when you are prepared to stand up

111

to Zeus himself in order to bring fire
to humanity can you achieve the fire-
revolution. When you continue to
assert, even when threatened by the
stake, that the earth goes round the
sun, not only are you unconquerable,
but you ensure ultimate victory for
your idea, the idea of truth. In
short, in all history there is no
greater force than the readiness for
self-sacrifice, just as there is no
greater love then the love of freedom. The soil of their country and
the blood of their murdered people
infused the Hebrew rebels with both
that force and love. (p. 41)[18]

Begin draws upon the archetypal symbol of blood[19] to
prove that the soldiers of the Irgun had returned to
the greatness of the ancient Hebrew heroes. This use
of blood as a symbol is particularly appropriate to
the myth of return. In the Old Testament, "Blood is
. . . the life principle."[20]

The oracular persona Begin adopts in The Revolt
also fits the myth of return. Begin's concluding comments about the Altalena affair are in the oracular
mode: "And so it came to pass that there was no fratricidal war in Israel to destroy the Jewish State
before it was properly born. In spite of everything--
there was no civil war" (p. 176). The entire chapter,
"The Cross-roads of History," is written in this
style. It begins:

We must pause here for a moment. We
are on the threshold of a fateful
turning-point in the history of Eretz
Israel. Bevin's obstinate assertion
that he did not see how the U.N. could
deal with the Palestine problem before
September, was no mere unpremeditated
remark. He was manoeuvering. He
wanted to gain time--a year, if possible during which he might establish
contact with the United States and
other Governments. He might also
reach an agreement with the United
States on Eretz Israel, if he had more
time. What is certain is that with
more time available the Arabs could be

112

strengthened immensely both in arms
and in instructors. What then would
have been our situation at the onset
of the invasion? (p. 325)[21]

Here Begin reveals the truth to his followers. He is
the oracle who knows the private thoughts of British
Foreign Minister Bevin. Begin's oracular persona is
consistent with his prophetic role in leading the Jews
back to their ancient strength. Moreover, his persona
is similar to that used by the prophets of ancient
Israel.

A number of reviewers of The Revolt criticized
Begin's style as over-emotional. When viewed as a
myth detailing the movement from holocaust to redemption, the emotional tenor of the work becomes understandable. In addition, Begin often uses biblical
language to retell the story of the Irgun. At several
points, for example, he writes of the Irgun smiting
the British "hip and thigh" (pp. 97, 296). The style
of the speech in "Dawn" is also biblical:

"Remember ye were strangers in the
Land of Egypt"--this supreme rule must
continually light our way in our relations with the strangers within our
gates. "Righteousness, Righteousness
shall thou pursue!" Righteousness
must be the guiding principle in our
relations among ourselves. (p. 375)[22]

He concludes the speech by promising, "And in this
battle we shall break the enemy and bring salvation to
our people, tried in the furnace of persecution,
thirsting only for freedom, for righteousness and for
justice" (p. 377). The formal, biblical style of
Begin's prose is well suited to a myth calling for
return to ancient heroism.

Conclusion

The Revolt functions as a myth confronting the
crucial problems raised by the holocaust. It is a
narrative of the heroic struggles of the Irgun to free
Palestine from the British. The struggle is fought by
the soldiers of the Irgun who are described as great
heroes. The brave, honest, and strong soldiers of the
Irgun have drawn upon the heroism of the ancient

113

Hebrew people. They are modern day Maccabees. Thus, while the revolt occurs in real historical time, it draws strength from the ancient state of Israel. In a sense the Irgun's revolt is a repetition of the Maccabean revolt. The story of The Revolt is also mythic in that it occurs outside of normal geography. The underground in which the Irgun carries on its struggle functions as the modern equivalent of the underworld. In addition, the revolt draws upon the special power associated with the land of Israel. Finally, the myth draws upon the archetypal power of "blood" as a symbol of the Irgun's capacity for sacrifice. The biblical language and oracular persona with which Begin tells the story also fit the form of a myth of return.

The description of The Revolt as a myth goes a long way toward explaining the structure and meaning of the work. For example, the apparently, irrational organization of The Revolt is clarified when the work is viewed as a heroic myth, not history. Begin deals with the Altalena and Dir Yassin incidents in the middle of the book rather than at the end where they fit chronologically, because they are two of the trials against the Jewish establishment. Because these trials are less demanding than those against the British, they must be dealt with prior to the battle against the British. In the battle of Jaffa, the Irgun again confronts the Jewish establishment, but because the battle is part of the return portion of The Revolt, it is described at the end of the work. This also explains why Begin considers the battle of Jaffa after the chapter in which he proclaims the victory of the revolt. The battle of Jaffa is part of the return from the underground portion of The Revolt. Chronologically this makes no sense; the battle of Jaffa took place before the founding of the Israeli state. Mythically it makes good sense. The mythic structure of the work is also the reason why Begin mentions the birth of Israel at the end of both chapters twenty-five and thirty. In the first instance, Begin celebrates the victory of the underground. The Irgun has overcome the final test, the trial of the gallows. In the second case, Begin celebrates the return of the underground to the real world. Although the two chapters describe the same event, they are separated in the story because mythically they serve different functions. The conclusion of chapter twenty-five proclaims the victory of the underground. The conclusion of chapter thirty proclaims the return of the underground to the real world.

114

The Revolt is not simply a memoir of the battle against British rule over Palestine. It is a myth which confronts the holocaust. Through the myth of return the Jewish people can remain free and secure and cleanse themselves of their guilt. Through the myth of return they can reject the weakness which made them easy victims. They must return to the strength and heroism of the ancient Hebrew warriors and to the ancient land of Israel. This return protects the Jewish people and redeems them from their exile. Thus, The Revolt is a symbolic journey from Hell (the holocaust) to Redemption (the birth of the state of Israel) through the return to the land and virtues of ancient Israel.

Notes

[1] Menachem Begin, The Revolt, trans. Samuel Katz (New York: Nash, 1972). All future references to The Revolt will be made in parens. in the text.

[2] J. Bowyer Bell, Terror out of Zion: Irgun Zvai Leumi, LEHI, and the Palestine Underground 1929-1949 (New York: Discus, 1977), pp. 444-445.

[3] Wolf Blitzer, "Responsibility in the Middle East," New York Times Book Review, 29 January 1978, p. 9.

[4] See "Ends and Means," The Times Literary Supplement, 5 October 1951, p. 623; "The Irgun Revolt," The Commonweal, 30 November 1951, pp. 106-107; Judd L. Teller, "The Revolt: Story of the Irgun," The Middle East Journal, 6 (1952), pp. 360-361; Edward Hodgin, "Palestine Sensibility and Sense," The Spectator, 5 October 1951, pp. 448-449.

[5] Joseph Campbell, The Hero With a Thousand Faces (Princeton: Princeton University Press, 1949), p. 30. For a similar view of the basic pattern of heroic myth see Shirley Park Lowry, Familiar Mysteries: The Truth in Myth (New York: Oxford University Press, 1982), p. 91.

[6] Campbell, Hero, p. 58.

[7] Campbell, Hero, pp. 77-89.

[8] While I have applied the essential elements of Campbell's pattern of heroic mythology in this criticism, there is no necessity that the precise pattern of sub-stages identified by Campbell be present in every heroic myth. It is only the general pattern that is tied directly to the function of heroic myths of return.

[9] See Campbell's description of this stage, Hero, pp. 97-192.

[10] Campbell, Hero, p. 39. For an insightful analysis of the function of return in mythology see Mircea Eliade, Myth and Reality, trans. Willard R. Trask (New York: Harper, 1963).

[11] Claude Lévi-Strauss refers to myths as a "logical model capable of overcoming a contradiction. . . ." In Lévi-Strauss's view humans use myths to solve logical problems that cannot be solved through other means. See Claude Lévi-Strauss, ed. Richard

T. DeGeorge and Fernande M. DeGeorge (Garden City, NY: Anchor, 1972), p. 193.

[12] See Thurston Clark, By Blood and Fire: The Attack on the King David Hotel (New York: Putnam, 1981). The picture of the posters is on the page of photographs facing p. 129.

[13] During the underground portion of the revolt, there were only a few score full-time soldiers. By the attack on Jaffa, the Irgun had drastically expanded its fighting force.

[14] See Menachem Begin, "From the Perspective of a Generation," in The Revolt, rev. ed. (New York: Dell, 1977), p. 18.

[15] In the aftermath of the Altalena affair the commanders of another organization, Lohamey Heruth Israel (LEHI) came to Begin and argued that the soldiers of the Irgun and LEHI could break free of the infant state of Israel and establish "Free Judea," an independent city state in Jerusalem. "There could be a Third Temple and a new beginning," Bell, p. 412. Begin rejected this proposal and continued the process of integrating the Irgun into the army of Israel.

[16] See Clarke, p. 24.

[17] Nathan A. Barack, The Jewish Way of Life (Middle Village, NY: Jonathan David, 1975), p. 49. Also see Exodus, 12:3-35. All biblical citations are from the Jerusalem Bible (Garden City, NY: Doubleday, 1966).

[18] Here, Begin refers to stories about Prometheus and Galileo. Prometheus is said to have given fire to humanity against the wishes of Zeus. The story is told that after facing a Catholic tribunal and being forced to recant his support of Copernican astronomy, Galileo said, "But it [the earth] still moves." Note that the references to Prometheus and Galileo treat myth in qualitatively different terms. Unlike Prometheus, Galileo was a real man who was transformed into a hero in myth.

[19] See Lowry, pp. 51-52.

[20] "Blood," in International Standard Bible Encyclopedia, 1979 ed., p. 526. Also see Deuteronomy, 12:33.

[21] The quotation is accurately cited. The editor evidently did not note the text shifts.

[22] This is a reference to Leviticus 19:33-34 where the Bible enjoins the Jewish people to treat strangers fairly: "For you

were once strangers yourself in Egypt," or to a similar reference in Exodus 22:21: "You must not molest the stranger or oppress him, for you lived as strangers in the land of Egypt."

CHAPTER V

ONLY THUS: THE MYTH OF THE IRGUN

If the Irgun's revolt against the British was
energized by a myth, then that myth should permeate
Irgun rhetoric. Of course, the presence of a mythic
world view in The Revolt does not prove that all Irgun
rhetoric was so grounded. The Revolt is a retrospec-
tive memoir of the Irgun which Begin might have
colored with mythical symbols not present in Irgun
rhetoric. Thus, in order to test whether the Irgun's
rhetoric followed the mythic pattern of holocaust and
redemption through return identified in The Revolt, I
shall analyze four works of Irgun rhetoric: "A Message From the Commander-in-Chief of the Irgun to the
Diaspora," September 1946; "From Kishenev to Acre: On
the Sixth Anniversary of the Death of David Raziel,"
May 30, 1947; "The Ten Martyrs Under Cursed Britain
Compared to 10 Martyrs Under Rome," July 30, 1947;
Menachem Beigin [sic], "The First Prerequisite of
Freedom Is Complete Victory," May 15, 1948.[1]

I selected these four works because they are
representative of Irgun rhetoric during the most
crucial period of the revolt. They cover the last
three years of the underground fight when the dimensions of the holocaust were fully known and when the
most bitter fighting occurred. The four works are
also representative in that they are drawn from a
variety of sources and addressed to a variety of audiences. "A Message" was addressed to all Jews outside
Israel, with special emphasis on the Jewish population
of the United States which had come through the war
unscathed and had the financial resources needed by
the Irgun. "From Kishenev to Acre," which honored the
memory of the second Irgun commander, David Raziel,
was addressed primarily to Irgun supporters. It was
originally published in Herut, the Irgun's newspaper
in Palestine. "The Ten Martyrs" was broadcast over
Irgun radio to an audience of Irgun supporters and
other interested listeners in Palestine. Begin's
speech "The First Prerequisite of Freedom" was also
broadcast over Irgun radio, but because it was his
first major public speech after the conclusion of
underground activities, it attracted a wide audience
in Israel.[2] Of the four works of Irgun rhetoric,

119

Begin's address, "The First Prerequisite of Freedom," is particularly important. It was presented on the night after Ben-Gurion had proclaimed Israel's independence and was Begin's first public speech after four years of revolt. In it he sums up the meaning of the revolt and describes his vision of the future Israeli state. If the Irgun's underground war with the British was animated by a mythic vision of return, that vision should be apparent in all of these works.

"A Message From the Commander-in-Chief of the Irgun to the Diaspora."

"A Message" was designed to generate support for the Irgun's revolt from Jews living outside Israel. In order to persuade those Jews, particularly U.S. Jews, to aid the Irgun, Begin attempts to justify the Irgun's attacks on the British. In the first paragraph, he explains that the Irgun's goal is to liberate Palestine in order to save the Jewish people from a future holocaust. The revolt is necessary because the British refused to act while the Nazis murdered six million Jews. After the end of the war, they refused to allow the few holocaust survivors to enter Palestine. Thus, there is no alternative to armed rebellion. In paragraphs five and six, Begin defends the Irgun against those who doubt that it can achieve anything by arguing that victory is inevitable. He claims that the British have no chance of defeating the united Jewish people. Then Begin calls for aid from the Jews of the Diaspora. He proposes an "organized boycott" (7) of British goods as a means of putting pressure on the British and requests help "in manpower, financial means and arms" (8) for the Irgun. Begin concludes his message to the world Jewish community by reaffirming the commitment of the Irgun to fight until victory is achieved. While "A Message" was aimed at procuring support for the Irgun, it was not a typical request for money. The final paragraph illustrates the emotional tenor of the essay: "The hour of redemption is near! Take on strength! Rise to the aid of fighting Zion! Rise to the struggle of the nation!" (11)

The mythic character of Begin's appeal is obvious in his references to the holocaust and the return of Zion. In the first two paragraphs of the message, Begin describes the horror of the holocaust: "From the continent of Europe there came to us the moan of Hebrew blood, the blood of our parents and our broth-

120

ers, the blood of the best of our people and our loved ones" (2). According to Begin, the British government "bears the responsibility for the annihilation of millions of our brethren . . ." (1). Later Begin writes, "Had it not been for British perfidy . . . millions of our brethern would still be alive . . ." (2). In addition, the threat of holocaust did not end with the defeat of the Nazis. When the war ended, the British did not allow the death camp survivors to come to Israel (2). Instead, they established "a network of espionage and anti-Hebrew concentration camps . . . in order to condemn its [the Jewish people's] sons both in the Diaspora and in Zion to extinction, annihilation or eternal enslavement" (3). Against this British policy, the Jewish people have but two choices: "Either to fight and be redeemed or to live in the status quo and be destroyed" (4).

While the British bear responsibility for the holocaust and for other threats to the existence of the Jewish people, it is the Jews themselves who made the holocaust possible. It is Jewish weakness which allowed the Nazis to complete the final solution. Such weakness inevitably equals death: "The life of exile and degradation . . . terminates--as its history in every era indicates--in physical decimation" (6). Moreover, Jewish weakness produces guilt. Begin refers to the life of exile as one of "degradation." One purpose of the revolt is to fight against the guilt produced by Jewish passivity: "We have risen in order to put an end to the curse of dispersion and to the stigma of servility" (1, emphasis added).

To cleanse Jewish guilt and prevent a future holocaust, the Jewish people must regain their strength. Their only chance is "to fight and be redeemed . . ." (4). If that fight is to succeed, there must be no compromise, for compromise is a form of weakness. This is why the Irgun is willing to pay "any price, in order to build it [a homeland] and to make fruitful its fields . . ." (5). The Irgun's greatness is proved by their willingness to fight, regardless of the cost, against the enemies of the Jewish people: "We have sworn that no sacrifice shall be too great and that we shall not put down our weapons nor cease our struggle so long as our nation's historic goal has been attained: the whole of Palestine as a free and independent Hebrew state." (1).

121

One symbol dominates the struggle to return to Zion: blood. Blood symbolizes useless sacrifice resulting from Jewish weakness. Blood also symbolizes the sacrifice which will save the Jewish people. Through the blood shed by reborn heroes of Israel, the Jewish people will be redeemed: "And if his life will be demanded as a sacrifice he will give it with a willing heart, for he knows that from his blood there will grow the tree of life for his people" (10).

Through the strength and heroism and blood of the soldiers of the Irgun, the Jewish people will be redeemed. Four times (in paragraphs four, five, six, and eleven) Begin refers to redemption as the aim of the struggle of the Hewbrew people. He does not mean that the battle of the Irgun will bring the Messianic age. Rather, through this battle, the Jewish people will build a Jewish state in which they can live in freedom and safety. This redeemed Jewish state will contain all of the ancient land of Israel: "We have risen in order to reunite the sections of our land west and east of the Jordan . . ." (1).

The heroic struggle of the Irgun to redeem Israel for the Jewish people is not a story of modern Jewish heroes who overwhelm the British oppressor, but is the story of the rebirth, the rejuvenation of the Jewish people upon their return to Zion. Five times in paragraph one Begin refers to the soldiers of the Irgun as having "risen" in order to free their homeland. They arise out of the heroic Hebrew past. This explains why he refers to Palestine as the "regenerated homeland" (7). The battle of the Irgun is not to create a new homeland, but to recreate an ancient one. Begin writes: "Despite everything, the Hebrew people will of itself cut a path to the land of its fathers, will redeem it and renew its days as of old" (6). The Irgun's story is not new; it is the story of return: "Before our eyes there has taken place the miracle of return to Zion" (9).

The return to Zion transformed the Jews from passive weaklings to incredible heroes: "Thus the entire world learned that a new generation had arisen in Israel, a generation which draws super-human strength from the mother land, hallowed from ancient days with the blood of the brave and the holy . . ." (2). At the end of the message, Begin reaffirms the link between ancient Hebrew heroes and the modern heroes of the Irgun and points to the millions of Jewish martyrs in the holocaust as a source of strength for the Irgun: "From the rivers of blood, from the depths of our people's endless history, there have come the rejuvenated forces which have undertaken that campaign, that will decide our fate for generations" (9).

Begin's rhetoric in "A Message" is shaped by the myth of holocaust and redemption through return. The Jewish people are threatened by death and guilt, both of which come from Jewish weakness. No one in the world can be trusted to aid them. In order to redeem themselves, they must fight without compromise to create a state in all of their ancient homeland. The strength for that struggle can come only from a rejuvenation of the Jewish people through a return to the ancient land of Palestine and to the heroism of the ancient Hebrew warriors.

As a request for aid from the American Jewish community, "A Message" is ill-adapted to achieving its aim. In requesting money from the U.S. Jewish community, Begin would have been well-advised to describe in detail the horrors of British policy in Palestine. In the aftermath of the Second World War, U.S. citizens had great admiration for the British. To the American Jewish community, the claim that Hitler had been aided by the British in his attempt to destroy the Jewish people would be incredible. Begin should have presented examples of British cruelty in order to convince his audience that the British were really mistreating the Jewish people. In addition, Begin should have reassured the American Jewish community that the Irgun was a legitimate military organization fighting to save the Jewish people. Although the means to adapt to the American audience were obvious, Begin used none of them. His rhetoric could only have struck many American Jews as that of a fanatic. Begin did not adapt to his American audience because his mythic view of the world prevented it. He described the British as Nazis because in his myth all threats to the Jewish people are viewed as similar to the holocaust. Begin's 1946 message to the Jewish community in the Diaspora is important because it illustrates the influence of the myth of return upon his rhetoric and world view.

"From Kishenev to Acre: On the Sixth Anniversary of the Death of David Raziel."

On the surface, "From Kishenev to Acre" is an essay commemorating the anniversary of the death of David Raziel, the second commander of the Irgun. Paragraph one makes it clear that Raziel was not merely a Jewish leader. He appeared "in anonymity" but "became immortal." Raziel is praised as the man who "laid the foundation of the Hebrew Army" (2). While others had worked with armed Hebrew groups, "it was David who gave it [the Hebrew army] its bayonets" (3). It was Raziel who changed the tactics of Jewish defense groups from passive defense to attack. After discussing the importance of the army which Raziel helped to create, the essay describes him as a figure whose life serves as a model of Hebrew heroism:

> By his spirit, by his brain; by his acts: and by his personal example. He gave to the people of Israel the type of the Hebrew Soldier. He taught, he fought and led the battle. He knew how to put a load of responsibility-- even the most difficult ones--upon himself and upon others. He believed and inspired belief around himself. He blazed the trail for those who came after him: "Difficulties were created to be overcome; there is no 'impossible.'" (10)

However, "From Kishenev to Acre" is not simply a memorial address. Raziel is treated as more than an important leader. He is a mythic hero who helped lead the Jewish people on their journey from holocaust to redemption.

The meaning of the essay honoring Raziel is encapsulated in the title. Kishenev is the name of a Russian village where, in 1903, over fifty Jews were murdered, and many more were raped or beaten in a pogrom.[3] The horror of Kishenev was not only that many Jews were killed or wounded, but that the Jewish population of the village stood by and did nothing to fight against the attacks. The pogrom at Kishenev became a symbol of Jewish passivity. The Hebrew poet Bialik wrote with great bitterness about that passivity: "The grandsons of the Maccabees--they ran like mice, they hid themselves like bedbugs and died the

death of dogs wherever found."[4]   Kishenev symbolizes
Jewish weakness and death; Acre, by contrast, symbolizes Jewish heroism even in the face of death. Acre
was the prison where members of the Irgun who had been
captured by the British were kept. It was the site
where several members of the Irgun went bravely to the
gallows, and it was at Acre, only a few days before
this essay was published, that the Irgun staged one of
the most brilliant jailbreaks in history. The meaning
of the essay is clear in the title. It tells of David
Raziel's heroic role in the movement from Kishenev to
Acre--that is, from Jewish passivity and .pointless
slaughter to heroism and self-sacrifice for the Jewish
state.

     The evil against which Raziel and the Irgun
fought was Jewish weakness. The Jewish people in
exile had lost their strength. For generations they
had reacted passively to every attack. They began the
"return to our Homeland, as 'protected' Jews . . ."
(4). Instead of armed defense, for many years the
Jewish response to attacks had been "books" and "self
restraint" (4). The result of such weakness was death
and dehumanization. Jewish weakness made pogroms "an
inescapable part of our daily existence" (4), and it
led finally to the holocaust. In paragraph nine, the
Irgun quotes a Yugoslav partisan: "The Jews are
cowards. The Jews are afraid to die, and that is why
they get killed" (9). The Yugoslav partisan, who represents heroism, knew that the Jews were killed
precisely because they were afraid to die.

     The weakness of the Jews not only led to their
slaughter, but also threatened their very humanity.
Jewish passivity created feelings of inadequacy and
guilt. The Irgun writes of this with great bitterness: "For tens of generations, we went among the
peoples with a mark on our foreheads: Hefker" (4).
In Hebrew "Hefker" means "ownerless property." The
Jews were "ownerless property" because they had no
place which belonged to them. They had no homeland in
which to ground their existence. Additionally, the
Irgun's characterization of passive Jews as "ownerless
property" is indicative of the guilt created by passivity. The Irgun quotes the Yogoslav partisan to
reinforce the point that passivity threatens the
humanity of the Jews: "They [the Jews] are not a
people. He who is afraid to die in battle has no
right to exist" (9).

125

If the weakness of the Jewish people came from their status as Hefker, the answer lay in rejection of that role. They must become "owned," that is, they must regain a place which they could call their own. Once grounded in a homeland, they would no longer be ownerless property. Thus, through return to the land of Israel, the Jews would regain their strength.

In "From Kishenev to Acre," Raziel is described as a mythic hero who arose to guide his people back to the strength and honor of their ancient heritage. He realized that the Jews could not be safe until they switched from "passive defense . . . [to] attack. No longer 'self-defense,' but the defense of the nation, in the broad sense, just as other nations understand it" (5). Raziel fulfilled the modeling function of all mythic heroes. He provided the "personal example" which the Jewish people needed (10). Through the shift from passivity to attack, the Jewish people regained their strength and saved themselves. It was Raziel's action which transformed "a slaughtered herd into a fighting nation . . ." (8). Because of him, "we have become a nation. No longer is our history made by foreign hands, by those who have arisen to take us out of slavery and into freedom" (7). The switch from passivity to strength saved the Jewish people, and it cleansed them of their guilt: "Then arose the Hebrew Army, the Army of the revolution bearing the idea of freedom, which erases with burning steel the mark of shame, Hefker . . ." (6). A transformation occurred: "A new epoch is begun. We have taken up arms. We have wiped off the shame of the butcheries" (7). Hebrew weakness vanished: "And today, tens of millions of people in the east and in the west, in the north and in the south, praise and respect the heroic acts of Hebrew men, acts of bravery the like of which are but few in the history of the world" (9). The Jews became modern heroes. A people made up of "terrified persecuted beings [was transformed] into awe-inspiring fighters . . ." (8). The Jews moved from the "death cell in Maidanek to this death cell in Jerusalem [where the soldiers of the Irgun were kept before they were hanged]" (11). By imitating Raziel and following his orders, the Jewish people transformed themselves: "We have become a factor. We have become a nation" (7).

The transformation was possible because Raziel tapped the power that lay within the Jewish people. They regained the strength they had lost during their exile. Raziel's great "idea was not new" (3); he brought an old idea back to life. Moreover, the Hebrew army which Raziel led was not created; it "arose" (6). Raziel tapped the strength which lay in the nation's heroic past: "There are within the nation hidden forces which only appear in days of trial and tragedy, because the source of all our strength is the force of renewal, the force of rejuvenation, that transforms an anonymous soldier into an immortal hero, a weak nation into a strong one, an enslaved people into a free one" (8). In the concluding paragraph, the heroism of the Irgun at Acre and in the death cell in Jerusalem is cited as proof that "the spirit of heroism has returned to Israel" (11, emphasis added).

"From Kishenev to Acre" does not explicitly mention the rebirth of ancient Hebrew leaders in modern Israel, nor does it describe the renewed strength of the Jewish people as flowing directly from the land of Israel. Yet, it clearly follows the basic pattern of the myth of return. "From Kishenev to Acre" describes the heroic journey of the Jewish people from weakness, passivity, guilt, and death to strength, courage, ordinary life, and redemption. It tells the tale of the role of one of the Irgun's heroes, David Raziel, in the heroic journey from weakness and the holocaust to strength and redemption through return.

"The Ten Martyrs Under Cursed Britain Compared to 10 Martyrs Under Rome."

The "Ten Martyrs" was part of a broadcast by the Irgun's radio station, "The Voice of Fighting Zion," on July 30, 1947. In its opening sentence, the short statement links the heroes of the Irgun hanged by the British to the ten martyrs of the Jewish revolt against Rome. It is the Irgun soldiers' sacrifice, their willingness to die for the cause, which establishes or "consummates" the link between the two generations. The two groups of heroes, separated by almost two thousand years, are linked: "Our generation, the same as our forefathers in the days of Rome, has had its ten martyrs" (1).

In paragraph two, the Irgun describes the differences between the two sets of martyrs. While the martyrs of the fight against Rome were great men, "our younger brothers were anonymous, completely unknown men who came from the people and whose names became immortal in the fight and the supreme sacrifice." While the ancient martyrs lived at the end of Hebrew freedom and the beginning of the exile," our young brothers were born into the last generation of enslavement. . . ."

After noting these differences, Irgun radio reaffirms the link between the two groups: "But an unbreakable link of love for the people, love of the homeland and a supreme heroism of the soul exists between these two groups" (3). Thus, the modern heroes of the Irgun serve the same function that the martyrs of Rome served throughout the centuries: "Generations will live in the legacy of the fighters until Israel will return to his land . . ." (3).

At first, this Irgun broadcast seems poorly designed to fulfill its purpose. The comparison of the Irgun martyrs to the martyrs of the fight against Rome might appear presumptuous to religious Jews. Moreover, the comparison does not seem to fit the Irgun's ideology. The martyrs of the fight against Rome sacrificed their lives for nothing. They would seem to be the very last group with whom the Irgun would identify.

However, the comparison drawn by the Irgun between the martyrs of the revolt against Rome and the martyrs of the revolt against Britain allows the message to function effectively. The Irgun broadcast functions at two levels. Despite the failure of the revolt against Rome, the martyrs of that revolt possess great ethos in Jewish culture. By linking the two sets of martyrs, the Irgun draws upon that ethos and answers those critics who said that the Irgun was sacrificing its men for nothing. At a second level, by pointing to the differences between the two generations of martyrs, the Irgun avoids offending religious Jews and establishes the inevitability of the Irgun's victory. The Irgun's victory is inevitable, in a situation similar to that in which the revolt against Rome was defeated, because its heroes are different from the heroes of the revolt against Rome. Irgun heroes are average men made great by their love of Israel. The heroes of the revolt against Rome were the great men of the age. But there were only a limited number of great men ready to die for the revolt against Rome. There are many average Jews who because of the "unbreakable link of love for the people, [and]

128

love of the homeland" (3) are willing to sacrifice
themselves for Israel. Irgun radio says, "But even
should the losses be tenfold--you know it, brothers-
in-arms we shall go on fighting" (4). Moreover, the
Irgun revolt will win because a mythic cycle is
brought to completion by the sacrifices of its martyrs. If there were ten martyrs at the beginning of
the exile then there must be ten martyrs to bring that
exile to a close. Thus, through their sacrifice, the
martyrs of the Irgun will bring to conclusion what
began in the revolt against Rome almost nineteen centuries before: "Our young brothers were born into the
last generation of enslavement and the first generation of freedom. . ." (2).

"The First Prerequisite of Freedom
Is Complete Victory."

Menachem Begin's May 15, 1948 speech, "The First
Prerequisite of Freedom," stands as a capstone, a
final statement of the goals and meaning of the
Irgun's fight for Hebrew independence. He begins the
speech by praising God for allowing the revolt to succeed. Later in the address, Begin reflects on the
meaning of the Irgun's struggle against the British
and announces that the Irgun will leave the underground in those areas of Palestine controlled by the
Israeli government. He also pledges the support of
the Irgun for the new government of Israel as long as
that government remains true to democratic principles
and fights for Jewish sovereignty over the entire land
of Israel. He argues for a strong army and a tough
military policy to reclaim the land of Israel. Begin
then discusses foreign policy and argues for estab-
lishing good relations with the United States, the
Soviet Union, France, and all other nations that treat
Israel fairly. On domestic issues, he calls for justice and fair treatment of the Arab population within
the Jewish state. On the surface, Begin's speech
appears to be nothing more than a policy address combined with a brief prayer of thanksgiving for the new
Hebrew state, but its import cannot be fully understood unless it is viewed from a mythic perspective.

"The First Prerequisite of Freedom" is really two
different speeches. Approximately the first nine-
tenths of the work is addressed to all of the Jewish
people living in Israel. In this section, Begin considers the meaning of the revolt and the problems

facing Israel. At the conclusion of his speech to the citizens of the newly established Israeli state, Begin addresses a few words to his comrades in the Irgun. Both sections of the speech follow the pattern of the myth of return.

The address to the people of Israel opens with two paragraphs explaining the significance of the birth of the Hebrew state. In the opening paragraph Begin calls for a "hymn of thanksgiving" over the birth of Israel. The modern citizens of Israel have returned to the ancient Jewish state: "We are giving thanks as our forefathers would be giving on the day of feast and celebration" (1). Begin then compares the Irgun's revolt against the British to the Maccabean revolt, "The Hebrew rebellion of the years 1944-1948 has been crowned with success: the first Hebrew rebellion that ended in victory since the uprising of the Maccabees" (1).

After comparing the Irgun's revolt to the Maccabean rebellion, Begin returns to the theme of thanksgiving with which he began the speech. It is now appropriate to give thanks to God that "70 generations of disperson, of defenselessness, of enslavement . . . [and] a period of total annihilation of the Jew" (1) have finally come to an end. It is the "Good Redeemer of Israel" who has wrought these miracles, "the same as He has done in days long past" (1). In paragraph two, Begin returns to the role which the Irgun played in bringing about the birth of the Israeli state. That state was created "Only Thus," that is through the fighting of the Irgun against British rule. In the two introductory paragraphs, Begin retells part of the Irgun myth. The Irgun fought against the defenselessness and dispersion which afflicted the Jews for seventy generations and which led to the holocaust. Through the aid of God, the Irgun regained their strength and fought to defeat the British. A nation is freed "Only Thus." Through the underground fight, the Irgun return the Jewish people to the greatness of ancient Israel. The Jewish people should now give thanks to God just as they had given thanks some twenty centuries before, for the strength of the Maccabees had returned to the people of the Maccabees. The Irgun triumphed over the British oppressor because it tapped the power of ancient Hebrew heroism and drew strength from God.

In the remainder of his independence evening speech, Begin considers the problems facing Israel in the coming weeks and months. He begins by explaining that while it is difficult to bring a state into being, it is still harder to protect that state once it has been established. The Jewish people are still threatened by holocaust. Hitler has been defeated, but the British have taken his place in threatening the Jewish people:

> Many peoples have surrounded us and they want to wipe us off God's earth. And that oppressor who is both Hitler's master and his disciple, that wily enslaver whom we smote in the battle is still trying to beat us by trickery; he is trying to beat us and subjugate us. . . . (4)

Israel needs weapons against this threat. Israelis need guns and tanks and bombs, but, more importantly, they need moral weapons to give them strength to fight against all those who oppose the Israeli state (4). Such moral strength comes only from the past history of the Jewish nation. Begin says: "If we shall stand in the next weeks armed with the strength of soul of an eternal nation resurrected to life again, we will in the meantime receive the arms we need to smash the enemy and we shall bring freedom and peace to our people and to our land" (4). This renewed strength will produce heroes unparalleled in human history. According to Begin, the Hebrew youth who fought the British are more courageous than the youth of any other nation or any other generation in Jewish history (5).

In the next three paragraphs, Begin describes his view of the proper foreign relations of the new Israeli state. The key word in his foreign policy is reciprocity: "There must be reciprocity in our relations with the peoples of the world. No submission, no surrender, and no flattery" (6). After discussing the future relations of Israel with the United States, the Soviet Union, and Europe, he turns his attention to domestic policy: "The cornerstone of this policy must be Return to Zion--homecoming" (9). Begin also calls for justice in dealing with all of the people of Israel and the Arabs. In dealings with the Arabs, "remember that you were a stranger in the land of

Egypt.⁵ This commandment will determine our relations with our neighbors" (10).

In paragraph eleven, Begin considers the role that the "fighting family" [the Irgun] will play in the new Israeli state. While the Irgun arose out of the underground and fought for the state, Begin implies that if Ben-Gurion strays from democracy or fails to claim all of the land of Israel, the Irgun will return to the underground. The Irgun will not allow the cause for which it fought with the "blood of heroes and martyrs" (12) to be sacrificed by "submission to tyrants and blackmailers" (12).

After defining the policies which he believes should guide Israel in the future, Begin considers the goals which Israel should aim for in its war of independence. While "Israel has arisen," the "homeland has not yet been freed" (13). The final disposition of that land will be determined with Hebrew arms. In this fight, the people of Israel must battle to regain all of Israel: "The Fatherland is an entity. Any attempt to dismember it is not only a criminal attempt, it is also a futile attempt" (13). To achieve "the vision of complete redemption, the vision of the homeland liberated" (13), all of the land of Israel on both sides of the Jordan must be captured. Begin says: "The soldiers of Israel will yet hoist our flag over the Tower of David. Our plows will yet plow the fields of Galad [a historical site in Jordan]" (13).

The portion of "The First Prerequisite of Freedom" addressed to the Israeli people concludes in paragraph fourteen where Begin describes the difficult struggle ahead: "Hard times are ahead. Blood the most precious of all treasures is being spilled and will be spilled. Strengthen your wills, steel your hearts, for this is the way of suffering and sacrifice and there is no other" (14). There is no alternative to struggle, because "we shall not buy peace from our enemies at the price of concessions. Yes, one kind of peace can be bought by submission. The peace of the graveyard, the peace of a new Treblinka. We must therefore strain ourselves to the utmost and be ready for the decisive test" (14). And that decisive test can be met because of the heroism of Hebrew mothers and the power of the Hebrew God:

132

> We shall stand our ground. The lord
> of Hosts will be with us and the hero-
> ism of the Hebrew youth and the hero-
> ism of the Hebrew mother, the mother
> who brings her son to the altar of
> God: this supreme heroism will save
> us from the hands of our enemies, and
> bring us out of slavery to freedom out
> of the peril of annihilation into the
> haven of safety. (14)

Even this policy-oriented central section of Begin's
address contains the essential elements of the myth of
holocaust and redemption through return. Begin
believes that the Jewish people are still threatened
by holocaust. At the beginning of this section, he
compares the British to the Nazis and actually suggests that they may be more evil than Hitler. At the
end, he refers to the threat of a future holocaust and
warns his audience that only one kind of peace can be
purchased, the "peace of a new Treblinka" (14).

Begin's answer to the continued threat of holocaust and to the British Nazis directing the Arab
invasion of Israel is return. Jews must return to the
ancient land of Israel, including the state of Trans-
Jordan (now Jordan). In the fight to reclaim all of
Israel, the Jews will be aided by the Hebrew God who
will again, as in the Old Testament period of Jewish
history, intervene to aid his people. Begin also
reemphasizes the tie to the heroic Hebrew past, a tie
he had made clear in the introduction. He refers to
the Jewish people as "an eternal nation resurrected to
life again . . ." (4). In his call for just treatment
of the Arab population of Israel, he relies upon
ancient Jewish law as the model for dealing with a
modern problem. In addition, he claims that now as in
the past the security of the Hebrew state depends upon
the willingness of her sons to defend it. Just as the
Maccabees and Bar Kochba refused to compromise, the
modern heroes of Israel, the "fighting family," must
not compromise.

Some of the policies Begin advocates are derived
from his mythic world view. Despite the precarious
military situation facing Israel, Begin calls for the
eventual liberation of all of the ancient Hebrew
state. This meant war with Trans-Jordan and Britain.
Begin advocates such a foolhardy policy because the
myth leaves him no option. He believes that strength

133

comes from the land of Israel; that land and strength
must be reclaimed. Begin's argument that the foreign
relations of Israel should be based on reciprocity can
also be traced to the myth of return. Israel must
demand equality in treatment because it was weakness
which produced the holocaust. It is strength and a
refusal to compromise that can prevent a future massacre. Therefore, the new state of Israel must demand
equal treatment and reject any slight, no matter what
the consequences.

The final section of Begin's radio speech was
addressed to the soldiers of the Irgun. At the beginning of paragraph fifteen, Begin's tone changes as he
shifts from the problems of the new state to address
"my brothers, children of the fighting family. . . ."
Begin tells them that in their fight the blood they
shed reaped a victory in "freedom" (15). He then pays
tribute to their bravery:

> You were alone and hunted, you were
> alone and martyred but you kept on
> fighting with invincible faith. You
> did not retreat. You were tortured
> but would not surrender. You were
> thrown into prisons but you would not
> give up. You were exiled from your
> homeland, but your spirit was not
> broken. You were walked to the gal-
> lows, but you sang a song. And so you
> wrote with your own hands a glorious
> page in the history of our people.
> And you will still write, not with
> ink, but with blood and sweat, not
> with pens, but with sword and the
> plow. (15)

While the underground fight of the Irgun has come to
an end, the war for the Israeli state is just beginning. It is that "battle . . . [which] will decide
our future" (16). In that battle, the Irgun will
again conquer because the spirit of the heroes of
Israel, both ancient and modern, goes with them:

> The spirit of our ancient heroes from
> the conquerors of Canaan to the rebels
> of Judea will go with us. Into this
> battle, the spirit of the revivers of
> our nation will go with us: Theodore
> Herzl, Max Nordau, Joseph Trumpeldor

and the father of reborn Hebrew heroism, Vladimir Jabotinsky. Into this
battle, will go with us the spirit of
David Raziel, the greatest of the war
leaders in our generation, and Dov
Gruner, the greatest of soldiers and
heroes. Into this battle will go with
us the spirit of the heroes of the
gallows, who overcame death. Into
this battle will go with us the spirit
of millions of our martyrs, of our
slain fathers, of our slaughtered
mothers, of our massacred brothers, of
our trampled children. In this battle
we shall smite the enemy and bring
freedom to a people surfeited with
persecution and thirsty for freedom.
(16)

Begin then prays to the ancient God of Israel to protect the soldiers of the Irgun: "God of Israel, keep
Your soldiers and bless their sword which gives a new
birth to the covenant that You sealed with Your
beloved people and Your chosen land" (17). Finally,
Begin exhorts his soldiers on to victory: "Forward to
the battle-grounds! Forward to victory!" (18).

The closing paragraphs of "The First Prerequisite
of Freedom" reflect the myth of holocaust and return.
The soldiers of the Irgun are treated as modern heroes
who learned the lesson of the holocaust--that compromise and weakness lead to death. They fought against
all odds and were aided in that fight by the spirit of
the ancient heroes of Israel and by God. In their
fight for the new state of Israel, they will again be
aided by those sources of strength and will give "a
new birth to the covenant" (17).

The four works of Irgun rhetoric which I have
considered are all dominated by the myth of holocaust
and redemption through return. Not all Irgun broadcasts contain the entire pattern of the myth of
return. Some works contain no references to the
strength flowing to the Irgun from the land of Israel.
Other works, such as "The Ten Martyrs," are built
around only one aspect of the myth (e.g., the return
to ancient Hebrew heroism). And there are works which
focus entirely on problems not directly tied to the
myth of holocaust and redemption. For example, the
Irgun complained bitterly about the treatment of Irgun

135

soldiers captured by the British. However, as a whole, the rhetoric and world view of the Irgun are shaped by the myth of holocaust and redemption through return.

Conclusion

The myth of return is built around three components. The first component is the holocaust. The Jewish people lived for nineteen centuries in weakness and dispersion. Their passivity led to persecution, to pogroms, and finally to the death camps.[6] The Germans massacred six million Jews because no one in the world cared enough to do anything.[7] According to the Irgun, the British were particularly guilty. They encouraged the Nazis, and when Germany was defeated, they became the major oppressors of the Jewish people.[8] In Begin's view, the British and the Germans are almost indistinguishable. But while the holocaust could have been stopped if the world had cared about the Jewish people, the fundamental cause of the holocaust was not lack of public concern for the Jews; it was Jewish weakness.[9] The Jews had not learned the lesson, known to all other peoples, that the world respects only those who are strong. Nineteen centuries of exile sapped the strength of the Jewish people, and they were led like sheep to the slaughter. Jewish passivity threatened both the physical existence of the Jewish people and their psychological well-being, because passivity leads to the mentality of the slave.[10] In sum, the Jews still lived in the holocaust world and would continue to be threatened until they put aside all passivity.[11]

The second component of the Irgun's myth is redemption. Begin's vision of redemption is quite different from traditional Judaism or labor Zionism. He describes neither a Messianic age to come nor a perfect society to be achieved on earth. Begin's vision of redemption is much simpler. When they have been redeemed, the Jewish people will be allowed to live in freedom and peace in their own homeland. In The Revolt, this final redemption is symbolized by Begin's description of the future Jewish state in which "Jewish children once more would laugh" (p. 377). In the essay on the memory of David Raziel, the Irgun makes the same point in somewhat different terms: "We make our own history, with our own hands . . ." (7). Redemption for the Irgun means that the Jewish people

will be allowed to live their lives in freedom and
safety in all of the ancient land of Israel.[12] Redemption will also cleanse the Jewish people of their
guilt. They will put aside the passivity of life in
the ghetto for the strength and honor of the ancient
Hebrew people.[13] Thus, the redemption promised in the
Irgun's myth will save the Jews both physically and
psychologically from another holocaust.

The third component of the Irgun's myth is
return. It is through return that the Jewish people
can regain the strength needed for redemption. Through
a return to the ancient land of Palestine[14] and to the
heroism of the Maccabees,[15] the Jews will regain their
strength. This return will be aided by the Hebrew God
who will again act in history to save his people.[16]
The return to the land and the heroism of ancient
Israel will save the Jewish people by turning "a
slaughtered herd into a fighting nation."[17] The
modern heroes of the Irgun who regained their strength
will lead the Jewish people to redemption.

In all essential characteristics, the myth of
return found in Irgun rhetoric in the 1940s and the
myth found in The Revolt are the same. In both cases,
the myths are built around the movement from the holocaust to redemption through return. If anything, the
myth found in the Irgun rhetoric in the 1940s is
stated in somewhat stronger terms than in The Revolt.
In The Revolt, Begin bitterly attacks the British, but
his comments are almost mild compared to the Irgun's
claims in the 1940s that the British were worse than
the Nazis. A close analysis of Irgun rhetoric in the
1940s also indicates that it was not just Begin who
saw the world through the myth of return. The jury
speeches of Irgun soldiers reflect this same perspective (see notes 14-16). In fact, the Irgun soldiers
went somewhat further than Begin. The Irgun soldiers
claimed that God aided the Irgun by blinding the British so that they might be utterly destroyed (see note
16).

There is one term common to the three Jewish
mythologies which I have described--return. For traditional Jews, return was the counterpart of exile.
Through the rituals and festivals of the Jewish faith,
the Jews symbolically returned to their homeland. The
traditional Jewish myth of exile and return also promised an ultimate physical return to Zion at the beginning of the Messianic age. Labor Zionists called for

137

return to Zion in order to build the perfect society on earth. They hoped that the perfect society would serve as "a light unto the nations of the world." The return promised in the labor mythology was an inverted version of the return in traditional Judaism. Where some traditional Jews opposed attempts to return to Zion physically and shaped their lives around rituals of return, the Zionists called for a mass movement to return to Palestine. Where traditional Jews spoke of a real Messianic age to come, labor Zionists referred to the Messianic age as a metaphor describing the perfect society which they hoped to build on earth. For the largely secular labor Zionists, the presence of return in their mythology reflected more the strength of the tie to Zion in Jewish culture than any logical link between a return to Zion and their goal of building the perfect society. The perfect society could have been built in Uganda or Argentina or even Poland. Palestine was the preferred homeland only because of the power of the image of Zion in Jewish tradition.

In Begin's myth, the meaning of "return" has been redefined. The evil to be confronted is no longer just exile or the threat of assimilation; it is the threat of physical and psychological annihilation. Because no other people in the world can be trusted, the Jews must be strong enough to defend themselves against all attacks. Redemption for the Jewish people means normal life, free from danger of attack, free from the psychology of the ghetto. The means to that redemption is return. Return is no longer the ultimate end, as in the messianism of traditional Judaism. Nor is return a rhetorical strategy to appeal to a wide variety of Jews, as in the labor mythology. For Begin and the Irgun, return is a means to an end, the end of protecting the Jewish people. Through a physical return to all of the ancient land of Palestine and the heroism of the ancient Hebrew people, the Jews could regain the strength they needed to confront the holocaust.

Begin's mythic vision of an Israel redeemed through return held great power for many Israelis. During the revolt, many Jews idolized Begin as a great hero: "Menachem Begin had already become a legendary figure. In growing circles his name was uttered with awe."[18] This awe translated into a political movement following the conclusion of the revolt. Despite Ben-Gurion's manipulation of the facts of the Altalena

138

incident to make it appear that the Irgun had attempted a coup,[19] Begin's party, Herut, received 11.5 percent of the vote in the first election to the Knesset. Begin's popularity was also evidenced by the large crowds which were drawn to the speeches he gave after leaving the underground drew.[20]

While much of Begin's popularity can be explained by the romance associated with the Irgun's underground fight, the myth of return explains some of his success. Part of the power of the Irgun's myth may have come from the elements of the other two Jewish mythologies which were incorporated into it, namely, the love of traditional Jews for Zion and the Zionist desire for a state. However, the main reason for the power of the Irgun's myth was that it served as a response to the holocaust. The holocaust was the force which motivated the Irgun to launch the revolt.[21] The power of the myth is evident in the large numbers of holocaust survivors who were drawn to the Irgun.[22] In addition, the testimony of Irgun soldiers indicates that the revolt filled a desperate psychological need to do something to fight the holocaust. Meir Feinstein explains to a British court that the holocaust left no option but revolt:

> Us--who have been repeatedly asking ourselves, why did fate treat us differently than the millions of our brothers? How come that we did not share their days of fear and moments of agony?
> To this we had only one reply: we have remained alive not in order to live in thraldom and repression for a new Treblinka. We have remained alive in order to make certain that life, freedom and honor will be our lot and the lot of our nation and the lot of our generations unborn.[23]

In another statement to a British court, Isaac Ganzweick speaks of the severe psychological pressure to fight against the holocaust:

> I asked myself: why did I deserve to remain alive? How am I better than my brothers that I was not destroyed like them? And my conscience gave one reply: If the Great God brought me

here it is a sign that he wills me to
be the messenger of all those who
remained on the other side of the
wall, that I should fight for them,
for their redemption and future.[24]

The enormous guilt created by the holocaust is also
evident by David Kripitchnkoff's statement:

Every morning, the newspaper brings
him [the Jew living in Palestine]
terrible tidings of his brethren in
Europe. And if he is a thinking man,
he despises himself and curses his
cowardice. There is no escape from
the shameful feelings that he enjoys a
quiet life, while his brethren and
sisters are exterminated in Europe.[25]

The Irgun's revolt provided an answer to the feelings
of powerlessness and guilt created by the holocaust.
David Kripitchnknoff speaks of the immense psychological relief provided by the revolt:

Among fighting men, one is suddenly
relieved of mental distress, one gains
an ideal and a faith. In spite of
physical distress and incessant persecution, life acquires a meaning, he
knows what he is living for and what
he is willing to die for. He becomes
free and liberated. He doesn't envy
the heroes of the past any longer, and
he doesn't feel ashamed in the presence of their shadows . . . Heroic
deeds efface the images of Maidanek
and Treblinka. . . .[26]

The myth of the revolt provided the soldiers of the
Irgun with the "ideal," the "faith" they needed to
face the holocaust.

Some of the Irgun's success can be traced to the
myth of holocaust and redemption which dominates Irgun
rhetoric. That myth proposed an answer to all three
of the crucial problems raised by the holocaust. To
those who said that the holocaust proved that God had
never existed, the myth answered that God was again
acting in the history of the Jewish people to redeem
their homeland. To the threat of future holocausts,

the myth provided the image of reborn Jewish heroes. The Jews no longer need go as cattle to the slaughter. They could fight as the Maccabees had fought, and through that fight, any danger of a future holocaust could be eliminated. And to Jewish guilt created by passivity, the myth provided models for renewed Jewish heroism. Through the imitation of those models, "the images of Maidanek and Treblinka" could be effaced. The myth of the Irgun responded directly to the needs of the Jewish people in the aftermath of the holocaust. The degree to which the myth succeeded in answering the problems raised by the holocaust will be considered in a later chapter.

While the myth of the Irgun developed in response to the problems raised by the holocaust, its application was not limited to the holocaust. The Irgun's myth functioned as a complete world view which shaped all important aspects of the ideology of the Irgun. For example, the Irgun's demand that the Ben-Gurion government claim all of the land of ancient Israel can be traced to the myth of return. In practical political and military terms this demand made no sense. The Israeli state was hard pressed to defend itself against the onslaught of Arab armies. There was obviously no chance that they could conquer the state of Trans-Jordan. And if they had tried, the British undoubtedly would have intervened. Moreover, a war of conquest against an Arab state could only have harmed Israel's precarious position in the world. Why, then, did the Irgun stick to its position that Palestine on both sides of the Jordan River belonged to Israel? When viewed from a mythic perspective this claim made perfect sense. Begin believed that the very strength of the Jewish people was derived from the land of Israel. To give up the land would mean giving up the sources of their strength.

The myth of the Irgun also explains the uncompromising perspective of that organization. While Ben-Gurion, Weizmann, and other Jewish leaders were willing to bargain with the British during the 1944-1948 period to get a good partition, the Irgun rejected any compromise. The heroic models provided by the ancient Hebrew heroes who fought at Modi'in, Bethar, and Masada made compromise unthinkable. Those heroes fought to their deaths rather than surrender to an oppressor. The Jews had compromised for centuries, and the result had been death and destruction. According to the myth of the Irgun, only through a rejection of all compromise could the Jewish people be saved. This attitude was reflected in all aspects of the Irgun's revolt. For example, the Irgun praised the passengers on the Exodus for their refusal to make practical calculations.[27]

The Irgun's myth also elucidates the retaliatory policy of the Irgun. The Irgun made every attempt to avoid killing civilians, but they retaliated against Arab attacks even when they knew that civilians inevitably would be killed. They retaliated in those situations despite a very real concern for protecting the lives of innocent people, because their ultimate aim was to prevent another holocaust. And the only way to fight the holocaust was through strength and instant retaliation. It was weakness that had created the situation which made the death camps possible. Such a situation must never be allowed to recur, even if innocent people must die to prevent it. Similarly, the Irgun's demand for reciprocity in foreign relations can be traced to the rejection of Jewish weakness. Only by demanding that they be treated as equals could the Jewish people gain the respect of the world.

Finally, the Irgun's unwillingness to strike against the Haganah and the Jewish Agency, even under the most severe provocation, also can be traced to the myth of return. In 1945, the Jewish Agency tried to destroy the Irgun in an operation called the "season." Irgun members were handed over to the British. Some members of the Irgun were kidnapped and even tortured by members of the Haganah. For reasons directly related to their mythic world view, the Irgun did not strike back. Begin recalled that in the revolt against Rome, which ended in the destruction of the temple, the Romans were aided by internal Jewish squabbles. The Irgun refused to strike back at the Haganah because it saw the modern history of Israel through the lens of Isarel's ancient past.

The myth of the Irgun did more than generate an ideology; it shaped the Irgun's understanding of the world. For example, according to the Irgun, the British occupation force in Palestine was continuing the work of the Nazis. In Irgun rhetoric the British are often referred to as Nazi-British or Nazo-British. In addition, the leaders of the Jewish Agency and Haganah are treated as people who have sold out to the British. According to the Irgun, the actions of the

142

Jewish leadership reflected the "psychology of the Warsaw ghetto"[28] and the "mentality of the slave: 'I love my lord.'"[29]

The Irgun's characterization of the British as Nazis and the leaders of the Jewish Agency as victims of ghetto mentality was far-fetched. The British took harsh action against the Irgun and failed to bomb the death camps during the war, but they built no death camps and enforced no ghetto regulations. The British were doing their best to balance the competing interest of the Jewish population of Palestine, the Arabs, and the British Empire. It is arguable that they did a very poor job of handling the Palestine mandate, but in no way did they act as Nazis. Nor was it fair to treat Ben-Gurion and the other representatives of the Jewish establishment as shaped by the attitude of the "Warsaw ghetto." Ben-Gurion walked a tightrope between moderation and violence. He wanted to put pressure on the British, but not so much pressure that they would respond with crushing military force. Begin may have been a better tactician than Ben-Gurion, but Ben-Gurion was no "willing slave."

Yet Begin was not a paranoid unable to respond realistically to facts. Rather, myth shaped his view of the world. In many ways, his interpretation of the conflict with the British was quite accurate. Of the important Jewish leaders, only Begin understood that the promise of the British Labour party to the Jewish community could not be trusted.[30] However, Begin's world view also predisposed him to see all threats to the Jewish people in terms of the holocaust and to view any compromise as a sellout. Thus, he saw the British as Nazis who threatened the existence of the Jewish people. The myth of holocaust and redemption through return functioned as a lens through which Begin and the Irgun understood the world.

Notes

1 All of these works were published in The Answer. See "A Message From the Commander-in-Chief of the Irgun to the Diaspora," The Answer, September 1946, pp. 11-12; "From Kishenev to Acre: On the Sixth Anniversary of the Death of David Raziel," The Answer, 30 May 1947, p. 6; "The Ten Martyrs Under Cursed Britain Compared to 10 Martyrs Under Rome," The Answer, 15 August 1947, p. 6; Menachem Beigin [sic], "The First Prerequisite of Freedom Is Complete Victory," The Answer, 28 May 1948, pp. 4-5. In the 1940s there was no single agreed upon spelling of Begin's name. It was often listed as Beigin. Further references to these works will be made in the text, by noting the paragraph number of the reference in parens. These works are reproduced in the appendix.

2 See Frank Gervasi, The Life and Times of Menachem Begin: Rebel to Statesman (New York: Putnam, 1979), p. 242; Gertrude Hirschler and Lester S. Echman, Menahem Begin: From Freedom Fighter to Statesman (New York: Shengold, 1979), pp. 154-155.

3 See Walter Laqueur, A History of Zionism (New York: Schocken, 1976), p. 123.

4 Bialik is quoted in Laqueur, p. 123.

5 Here Begin is citing Leviticus 19:33-34 or Exodus 22:21. See note 22 in chapter four.

6 Irgun rhetoric is filled with references to the holocaust. In Irgun Zvai Leumi, Memorandum to the United Nations Special Committee on Palestine, 1947, hereafter cited as Memorandum, there are seventeen references to the holocaust in the first twenty-three pages. References to the holocaust were often combined with attacks on the British. In Irgun Zvai Leumi, "Jewish Rule over the Homeland Immediately," Fighting Judea, April 1946, p. 4, the Irgun argues: "The British oppressors, with premeditation and malignity, closed the gates of our country, driving back in the very days of the blood-bath and with their own hand, millions of our unfortunate brothers into the crematoria. . . ." Their rhetoric makes it quite clear that the Irgun fight was motivated by the holocaust. In "Beigin [sic] in Stirring Address at Waldorf-Astoria Dinner," The Answer, 10 December 1948, p. 4, Begin notes:

It was not accidental that we raised the banner of revolutions in the days when the blood of our brethren was crying to us from all corners of

the earth. In the days when our children were
being slain and our parents were being annihilated. In the days when our people were being
trampled like dust. In those days we came to see
and rather instinctively to feel that we had
nothing more to lose, nothing but gas chambers
that were—and gas chambers that were to come.
The annihilation of six million of our people was
in itself a disaster beyond words, but we knew
that unless we raise and take our fate in our own
hand, the remnants of our people inescapably
would meet the same end.

The same point is made in Irgun Zvai Leumi, "The Night of Blood
at Acre," The Answer, 16 May 1947, p. 6: "For indeed it was for
them [holocaust victims] they [Irgun soldiers] had fought and for
them they had fallen, it was for them that they had sacrificed
their all, for them that they had taken the decision that was
stronger than death: to bring redemption to their people—or to
die."

7 According to the Irgun, the world responded with silence
to the death camps. In Irgun Zvai Leumi, "The Great Lesson of
the Exodus: Irgun Broadcast September 9, 1947," The Answer, 3
October 1947, p. 6, the Irgun says: "It was with this same
silence that our brethren marched to their death in the gas-
chambers; and it was with this same silence that the entire world
followed them on their long journey." The world refused to take
actions which could have saved thousands of Jews. In Memorandum
(p. 22), the Irgun argues:

And when later it was proposed that bombers
should attack the death factories at Treblinka
and Auschwitz, etc., attacks, which if properly
directed, could have saved thousands of the can-
didates from the gas-chambers and the ovens, the
British refused, on the typically hypocritical
pretext that the poor Jewish inmates of the camp
might be hit.

Of course, the United States refused to make the raids as well.
The Irgun's analysis in Memorandum of the failure of the world to
it against the death camps has been proved largely correct. See
Memorandum, pp. 20-23.

8 The Irgun made any number of bitter anti-British statements. In "Jewish Rule over the Homeland Immediately," pp. 3-4,
the Irgun writes:

Throughout those years when it would still have been possible, but for the British betrayal, to rescue millions of our brethren from extermination by Hitler, the representatives of the Jewish people have been appealing to the conscience, the justice and the humanitarianism of the British rulers. In vain. Their appeals and warnings were cruelly trodden underfoot; their outcries and pleadings interpreted as weakness and cowardice. As a result of that, most of European Jewry—our fathers, our mothers, our sisters, our brothers, our children, our relatives, our friends, our teachers, our scholars, our rabbis, and sages were massacred by the Germany murderers with the accomplicity of the British traitors.

Irgun statements often compared the British to the Nazis. In Irgun Zvai Leumi, "Irgun Offers Plan of Action," The Answer, 29 October 1947, p. 6, the Irgun claims that, "The Nazi-British enemy is interested in sapping our strength in a prolonged and sterile battle of defense." The same perspective is clear in Irgun Zvai Leumi, "Attack Is Best Defense Against Rioting Arabs," The Answer, 26 December 1947, p. 6:

> Moreover, the Nazo-British enslaver must be attacked. His forces must be driven away from the area of operations. They are not there to establish peace. They are there to make the troubles greater, to murder Jews and to arrest defenders.

Average Irgun soldiers also referred to the British as Nazis. See Yoser Simchon's statement in Itzhak Gurion, Triumph on the Gallows (New York: Futoro Press, 1950), pp. 73-74. The Irgun placed much of the responsibility of the holocaust on the British. In Memorandum, p. 20, the Irgun writes, "Britain has encouraged and participated in the greatest of all crimes in human history: the extermination of the Jewish people in Europe."

9 In Irgun Zvai Leumi, "The Attack on Acre Fortress," The Answer, 13 June 1947, p. 6, the Irgun makes it clear that passivity equals death:

> Sacrifices made in battle are never useless. Only victims of massacres and victims of surrender are useless and such victims we have produced by the millions in the course of the centuries, because we feared to die for life and liberty; because we went to ghettos, because we dared not

rise up while we still had time; because we had
never accustomed ourselves to fighting for liberation.

The same position is clear in Irgun Zvai Leumi, "The First
Soldier of Rebellious Judea: On the Fifth Anniversary of His
Death," The Answer, September 1946, p. 10, "The curse of the
exile, the shame of the subjugation, the baseness of the massacres were caused by the amputation of this branch the branch of
militarism from Israel."

   10 Guilt is obvious in the many references to the passivity
with which the Jewish people responded to the holocaust.   In
Memorandum, pp. 3-4, the Irgun refers to "masses of Jews degraded
and persecuted, and even led--almost without resistance--to the
slaughter."   The refernce to "the curse of the exile, the shame
of the subjugation, the baseness of the massacres . . ." in "The
First Soldier of Rebellious Judea," p. 10, also suggests the
presence of great guilt.   Even after the end of the war, the
Irgun believed that passivity still threatened the Jewish people.
The statement in Irgun Zvai Leumi, "The Flogging Incident," The
Answer, 21 February 1947, p. 6, is revealing:

> For thousands of years our people has been the
> victim of the lash.   In the diversity of our
> exiles the whip--figuratively and actually--has
> come down upon our bent, beaten and bleeding
> backs.   Our ancestors became accustomed to it.
> One gets used to anything--even humiliation,
> debasement, beatings and scorn.   Some were even
> able to stroke the rod that beat them or pay
> homage to the hand that wielded the lash.   Some
> survivors of this school of thought, unfortunate-
> ly, are still with us even in the land of Israel.

The Irgun even attacked Ben-Gurion personally as a representative
of the passive perspective which had led to disaster.   In Irgun
Zvai Leumi, "Irgun Exposes British Tricks and Offers a Plan of
Action," The Answer, 31 October 1947, p. 6, they write:

> There are indications right now that these Brit-
> ish tactics are not as stupid as they would
> appear at first.   Many among the defeatist lead-
> ership who first greeted the impending British
> withdrawal with joy have already begun to express
> disappointment at the British refusal to partici-
> pate in the implementation of the United Nations
> recommendation.   Here we see the old mentality of
> the slave: "I love my lord."   Radical talk is
> one thing.   Slavish souls another.   One shouldn't

therefore dismiss lightly the weight of the British "threat" from the minds of the miserable "leadership." We have it on reliable authority that should the United Nations adopt a plan similar to the Morrison plan, Ben-Gurion would accept it.

The reference to the "mentality of the slave" clearly indicates that the Irgun felt disgust for the passivity of Jewish life in the Diaspora and feared that this passivity might take root in Israel. This perspective is also clear in Irgun Zvai Leumi, "Irgun Proclaims Iron Fund for Liberation," The Answer, 19 March 1948, p. 6, where the Irgun again attacks the official leadership of the Jewish community, "It is those leaders who grovelled like willing-slaves before every Nazo-British official."

11 Even after the end of the war, the Irgun believed that it was involved in a struggle for the survival of the Jewish people. In Irgun Zvai Leumi, "Irgun Offers Plan of Action," The Answer, 29 October 1947, p. 6, they write:

> Britain's scheme is visible to all. The enemy's plan has been and continues to be the perpetuation of our nation's dispersion and enslavement; the plunder of our homeland; our imprisonment inside a ghetto and, finally, our total extermination.

This position is also clear in Irgun Zvai Leumi, "To the People," The Answer, 21 May 1947, p. 6: "We are engaged in a life and death struggle. In a fight for the existence of our nation, and that such a fight demands human sacrifices and untold human suffering." (This article was originally printed entirely in caps.) In Memorandum, p. 5, the Irgun writes: "But it remains a fact; there is not an iota of exaggeration in our words: in fighting for the liberation of our Homeland, we are fighting for the very existence of our people" [emphasis in original]. According to the Irgun, the British aimed at placing the Jewish people in a new ghetto. In Irgun Zvai Leumi, ". . . Till the Enemy Has Gone," [ellipsis in original] The Answer, 15 November 1946, p. 6, they write:

> We are headed for a national catastrophe. We are heading toward a ghetto. We are going toward the abandonment of the nation in the diaspora. We are going toward the erection of a fortified wall which will separate us from the greater part of our territory, and which will separate the homeland from most of its children in exile.

148

¹² The Irgun claimed that all of the land of ancient Israel belonged to the Jewish people. In **Memorandum**, p. 1, the Irgun writes:

> Palestine (Eretz Israel) in its indivisible extent East and West of the Jordan river is the national territory of our people. It is its Homeland. In this country our forefathers set up their independent state and their original culture which, together with the culture of other ancient peoples, became part of the foundation of all human civilization.

The boundaries of the homeland had been established by God. In "The Irgun Appeals Against Partition: Let the People Have Their Say," The Answer, 27 June 1947, p. 6, they write: "Have we not a homeland? Have not its boundaries been set by God and history and the sacred blood that has been shed upon and for it from time immemorial?" In "Menachem Beigin [sic] Talks to the City of Jerusalem," The Answer, 20 August 1948, p. 5, Begin says "The Hebrew soldier will go forward and in the next months or in the next years, he will reach this goal, he will reach the Jordan and will go beyond it."

¹³ In Irgun rhetoric, the soldiers of the Irgun are described as great heroes. In "New Year's Greetings," The Answer, 15 October 1948, p. 6, Begin writes of some of their heroic actions:

> We conquered Jaffa and saved the Hebrew city of Tel Aviv from destruction and the Hebrew front from collapse. Were it not for our pioneering onslaught on the main base of the Arab rioters, the port of Jaffa would have been at the disposal of the Egyptian invaders and on the day of the Arab invasion hundreds of Hebrew soldiers would have been pinned down in the Tel Aviv line of defense.

Begin goes on to argue that the Irgun revolt succeeded against overwhelming odds:

> Within this tiny country and over this small nation there loomed a mighty enemy, an enemy enforced by one hundred thousand soldiers and policemen armed to their teeth; an enemy with centuries of experience and a great far-flung secret-service, an enemy which benefited by the collaboration of the "official" Jewish leadership. Nevertheless, the enemy was beaten and

149

repulsed. And it is our fighting family which brought this about.

In their revolt, the soldiers of the Irgun showed incredible courage. Irgun radio, "The Voice of Fighting Zion," spoke of the courage showed by the Irgun, even when they were ordered by the united command to retreat from Jerusalem. In "Jerusalem," The Answer, 6 August 1948, p. 6, Irgun radio says:

> But the soldiers of the Irgun Zvai Leumi, who with their blood had paved the way for the liberation of the Temple-site, were called upon to retreat. They did a great deed an historic deed. Once again they proved the strength of their attack, the power of their thought and ability of execution. Once again they displayed unlimited devotion and unprecedented spirit of sacrifice.

The soldiers of the Irgun also showed great courage when they were sentenced to death. In "The Night of Blood at Acre," The Answer, 16 May 1947, p. 6, the Irgun writes: "They [the martyrs of the Irgun] faced their torturers and murderers like bars of steel; and like men of iron believed to the last in the victory of their people and the liberation of their Homeland." The status of the Irgun as mythic heroes is most obvious in the example of Dov Gruner. In "The Legend of Dov Gruner," The Answer, 16 May 1947, p. 6, the Irgun writes of Gruner's unparalleled courage:

> Where in history was ever more clearly depicted the victory of the spirit over the barbarism of brute force? From that long struggle Dov Gruner emerged victorious, and his hangmen, the enemies of his people, they, with hands bloody and spirits cowering, it is they who were defeated.

Gruner's heroic status is also obvious in "The Night of Blood at Acre," The Answer, 16 April 1947, p. 17, where the Irgun writes: "Dov our great brother, the man of steel preserved his dignity, the honor of a captive soldier, to the last moment." According to the Irgun, Dov Gruner has taken his place among the great heroes of Hebrew tradition. In "The Legend of Dov Gruner," the Irgun writes:

> And the legend of Dov Gruner will fire his comrades and those who come after him. They will ensure that he shall not have died in vain. And children at their mothers' knees will imbibe the story of Dov Gruner, not only in this generation,

not only while the struggle for his people's liberation still lasts, but when peace returns to his people, in all generations to come, in the free Hebrew State for which he freely gave his life.

14 In many statements the Irgun emphasizes the tie between the Jewish people and the land of Israel. In "Partition Will Never Be Recognized Says Irgun," The Answer, 12 December 1947, p. 6, the Irgun writes: "Jerusalem was ever, and ever will be, its capital. Eretz Israel will be restored to the People of Israel. The whole of it. Forever." The Memorandum to the United Nations Special Committee on Palestine makes the link to the land quite clear:

> We remind you of these facts not out of abstract "romanticism." We recall them because in our consciousness it is they that constitute the decisive factor in the bond between us and this country. These facts, though they are enveloped in the mists of history, are not dead. They are alive. It is they that demonstrate that it is a lie to say that ours is a people without a Homeland. Our people has a Homeland, only was exiled from it by force of arms; and it is by force of arms that new invaders and occupiers are preventing its return. [emphasis in original] p. 3.

On the same page in Memorandum, the Irgun says, "To us here every stone and every rock speaks, and they all convey one message: this is our land, our country and our Homeland from the dim beginnings of time and for all future to come." Dov Gruner's jury speech, cited in Gurion, Triumph on the Gallows, p. 98, speaks of the tie to the land of Israel:

> For this you must know; there is no force in the world that can break the link between the people of Israel and its one and only country. He who attempts it shall have his hand severed and the curse of God shall be upon him forever.

According to the Irgun, the strength of the Hebrew people came directly from the land of Israel itself. In Memorandum, pp. 3-4, the Irgun writes of the direct link between the return to Zion and the rebirth of Hebrew heroism:

> You who have seen, whether closely or at a distance, masses of Jews degraded and persecuted, and even led--almost without resistance--to the slaughter, will see here a people risen to life

151

again, with its language and its culture; a new
generation, who have revived the soil of the
Homeland, as the soil of the Homeland has revived
them and restored to them the image of free men,
free from fear, freed from the complexes resulting from two thousand years of persecution; a
generation healthy in body and mind, whose sons
know how to plough and how to shoot, how to
labour and how to fight. [emphasis in original]

The life-supporting properties of the land of Israel are emphasized in Chaim Luster's jury speech, which is included in Irgun
Zvai Leumi, The Hebrew Struggle for National Liberation, submitted to the United Nations Special Committee on Palestine, 1947
(hereafter cited as Hebrew Struggle), p. 53:

You will never succeed in bringing the inhabitants of this country to extermination camps
without resistance, without an emormous price
that you will have to pay with your own blood.
This was possible only there, in the damned countries of the diaspora, truly damned, on that soil
of the Exile that robbed our brethren of the
physical and spiritual will of resistance, which
had led them to be completely defenceless. . . .

In "Menachem Beigin [sic] Talks to the City of Jerusalem," The
Answer, 20 August 1948, p. 4, Begin speaks to the city of Jerusalem as if it were a sort of goddess who could use her power to
protect the Jewish people:

Jerusalem our capital, I greet thee. I greet
thee, city of suffering, eternal city, Jerusalem.
When we began our resistance, when, from the
depths of the underground we brandished the flame
of insurrection, our hearts were full of thee,
Jerusalem. When we struck the enemy, your
oppressor, you were in our blood. when the best
of your sons were thrown into concentration camps
and torture chambers, you were in their sufferings. And when the greatest of your heroes went
to the gallows, you were in their last songs.
. . . For it was not only your own defense you
assured, but that of all of Israel, of its existence, its independence and its future. Like a
mother protecting the life of her children with
her body, you have defended the towns of Israel
and its settlements.

152

In many works, the Irgun compared its soldiers to the ancient Hebrew heroes of the biblical era. In "The New Miracle of Chanukah," The Answer, 17 December 1948, p. 7, Begin says:

> The analogy between the great liberation fight of the Maccabees and the fight of our own days is almost complete. In those days, too, before the fight began, we were a minority in our own country, under the yoke of a once-great empire whose strength began to wane. In those days, too, we faced surrender or complete annihilation. In those days, too, a minority within the minority raised the banner of rebellion against the enemy; in those days, too, there were collaborators and assimilationists who besmirched the noble patriots, betrayed them to the enemy and called them the same names we were called in our time. . . .

In "New Year's Greetings," The Answer, 15 October 1948, p. 6, Begin draws the same comparison: "The British enslaver who had plotted to perpetuate his rule over the sons of the Maccabees was drawn out of the land of the Maccabees by their heirs." The link between the Irgun and the Maccabees is also clear in "Partition Will Never Be Recognized Says Irgun," p. 6: "The people of the Maccabeans, whose valour has been renewed in the sight of the world, will liberate the land of the Maccabeans." The Irgun even claimed that the method of their revolt had been borrowed from the Maccabees. In ". . . Till the Enemy Has Gone," p. 6, the Irgun writes:

> We did not create the method of unrelenting warfare, the policy of a general revolt. They were created by our fathers from Modin [sic]. They fought on the hills and in the valleys, they fought for years, tirelessly. They never renounced one inch of the homeland. They never accepted the authority of the Hellenist "leadership"; and thus they reached Jerusalem through bloody battles and bloody sacrifices.
> Therefore we now resolve to follow the example of positiveness, the example of the victorious war of the Hasmoneans: Modin! [sic] That is the road which we will follow.

In some works, the Irgun goes beyond the claim that their revolt is modeled after the Maccabean revolt to claim that strength flows directly from the ancient Hebrew heroes to the heroes of the Irgun. In "To the People," p. 6, the Irgun writes: "Enormous forces, which have arisen out of the past of our nation and by instinct of self preservation. They are leading us and they will take us out of slavery into freedom, out of darkness into light" [Original all in caps]. In Memorandum, p. 4, the Irgun writes: "An ancient people has come to life again independent of mind, free in spirit, no better than other peoples, but no worse." In his address to the city of Jerusalem, p. 4, Begin says that Jerusalem drew strength from the ancient heroes of the Jewish people:

> You resisted, you did not surrender nor fall. The spirit of your ancient heroes supported you in the moment of siege, in the hour of war and distress. The heroism of those who went to the gallows sustained you into our State, they make a distinction in your days of war for the independence of Israel.

In other works, the Irgun puts the return to Hebrew heroism in a subordinate role compared to the return to the land of Israel. In these works, the Irgun claims that the return to Zion has revived the heroism of the ancient Jewish people. In a jury speech quoted in Hebrew Struggle, p. 77, Avshalom Haviv says:

> You wonder, do you not? Yet the thing is simpler than you imagine. The spiritual character of our generation has been determined by two factors. By the soil of our Homeland which has revitalized us and has given power to our muscles, courage to our hearts, belief in our future, which has restored to us in practice the tradition which our people carried in its heart for many generations: the tradition of heroism of the Maccabeans and of Bar-Kochba [emphasis in original].

In Hebrew Struggle, pp. 53-54, Chaim Luster makes the same point:

> Here, however, this [weakness] is not possible at all, here we stand in our country. Our country has given us the youthful vigour of the people of the Hasmoneans. Our country commanded us to take up arms against and to redeem it with our blood, as our forefathers once redeemed it with their blood, its ancient conquerors and liberators.

On page 54 Luster says: "Our country has revived in us the heroes of Masada and Jodefeth. It has given us strength, it calls us from the depths: 'Arise and fight for me and for the People that has been led away from me into exile.'"

16 The Irgun claimed that their revolt was aided by God. In "Jerusalem," p. 6, the Irgun says: "Who was there that could

154

stand in the way of their will which flows from the Almighty himself and from the command of tens of generations past to conquer at all costs?" Through God's aid and their heroism, the Irgun could give new meaning to the festivals of Jewish tradition. According to the Irgun, those festivals would be re-energized via the revolt. In "To all Soldiers: A Passover Message From the Irgun," The Answer, 8 April 1947, p. 6, the Irgun writes:

> THEREFORE, as we stated in our Chanukah message—the resplendent festivals of Israel which symbolize the ideas of unconquerable freedom, have ceased to be in our eyes abstract holidays which recall an ancient past which can return only—as it was for two thousand years—through imagination prayer, and soulful longing mingled with impotent sighs. No. The festival of freedom, the most glorious among the nation's holidays, is for us today a symbol of the future, a concrete festival of concrete freedom brought to the people by its sons, who are taking it out of Egypt with a believing heart, with supreme sacrifice, with clear supreme sacrifice, with clear thought, quiet courage, a strong hand and an outstretched arm.

"The New Miracle of Chanukah," p. 7, The Answer, summarizes a portion of a speech by Begin dealing with the revitalization of the festivals of the Jewish tradition:

> Mr. Beigin [sic], the principal speaker of the evening, recalled that for centuries Jews the world over used to celebrate the feast of Chanukah by lighting candles and reminiscing over the miracle of the Maccabean fight which once freed the Hebrew country from the yoke of the great Greek Empire. They recounted the story of the heroes of bygone days without understanding whether it was a miracle or a heroic achievement of man. This year, again candles will be lit the world over, but this time, the story that will be told will not be of a period long past, but a story of our own generation. A story that passed before our own eyes and in which almost every one of us played a direct part. The same story will be repeated: the story of how we regained our strength and courage and through it regained our land.

The Irgun's view of revitalized rituals and festivals is obviously at variance with the traditional Jewish myth of exile and return. The link between the Irgun's revolt and the Hebrew God is also emphasized by Irgun soldiers, who argue that the only credible explanation for British policy in the Middle East is that God has been blinding the British to the truth just as he once blinded the Pharaoh. Meir Feinstein's jury speech in Gurion, Triumph on the Gallows, p. 119, states this position:

> And, if you [the British] fail to see this vision of a nation that has nothing to lose but the irons of slavery, but the "hope" for a new Majdanek—then you are indeed stricken by blindness and doomed by Providence to share the fate of all those who have lifted arms against the Eternal People. Assyria, Babylon, Athens, Rome, Spain and Germany have tried before you, and you will share their graves.

Also see Yosef Simchon's statement in Gurion, Triumph on the Gallows, p. 74. In Hebrew Struggle, p. 73, Mordechai Alkoshi says that the British have been blinded by the Hebrew God:

> And if you have not yet understood this phenomenon of a people that has nothing to lose but the shackles of slavery and the "prospect" of a new Maidanek—it is a sign that you have been smitten with blindness, in order that you whould [sic] leave the stage of history, from which the Almighty removes all those who rise up against the eternal people to destroy it. Assyria and Babylon, Greece and Rome, Spain and German came before you—and you will follow in their footsteps. It is an everlasting law.

17 Through their fight, the Irgun claimed to cleanse the Jewish people of passivity. In "The Flogging Incident," p. 6, the Irgun claims that the revolt has revived a sense of honor in the Jewish people:

> But—and here is the rub—a new generation has arisen in the meantime. They do not look upon questions of honor as the special province of gentiles, of squires and drunken lords whom the "clever" Jew despised from the depth of his oppressed soul. To them honor is as natural as the air they breathe. This new youth will no longer strive to devise ingenious excuses for its lack of healthy human reactions when the need arises. The era of humiliation and degradation has ended. Jews are not to be whipped any more—

this is the moral which our people will draw from our reaction.

In a jury speech cited in Gurion, _Triumph on the Gallows_, p. 109, Dov Rosenbaum explains that the Irgun's whipping British soldiers was aimed at proving that the Jewish people had regained their sense of honor. Rosenbaum says:

> We set out that night [on an Irgun operation to flog British officers] to protect the honor of our comrade soiled by your rule; we came to prove how mistaken was your assumption that only Englishmen are capable of a sense of honor, whilst we--the sons of the Jewish people--have no such feelings; we came to demonstrate that a new Jewish generation has arisen in this country which will not forbear humiliation, which will not acquiesce in enslavement, which will fight for its honor at any cost.

18 Harry Hurwitz, _Menachem Begin_ (Johannesburg, South Africa: Jewish Herald, 1977), p. 24.

19 For a clear description of the Altalena incident, see J. Bowyer Bell, _Terror out of Zion: Irgun Zvai Leumi, LEHI, and the Palestine Underground 1929-1949_ (New York: Discus, 1977), pp. 400-413.

20 See Doris Katz, _The Lady Was a Terrorist: During Israel's War of Liberation_ (New York: Shiloh, 1953), pp. 177-178; Gervasi, p. 242.

21 See _Hebrew Struggle_, p. 55, and an interview with Begin in Robert St. John, _Shalom Means Peace_ (Garden City, NY: Doubleday, 1950), p. 175.

22 See Edward Morgan, "Terror in Tel-Aviv," _Colliers_, 24 May 1947, p. 103; Jan Gitlin, _The Conquest of Acre Fortress_ (Tel-Aviv: Hadar, 1977), p.82.

23 Meir Feinstein's statement is quoted in Gurion, _Triumph on the Gallows_, p. 119.

24 Isaac Ganzweick's statement is quoted in _Hebrew Struggle_, p. 18.

25 David Kripitchnkoff's statement is quoted in _Hebrew Struggle_, p. 40. Also see Avshalom Haviv in _Hebrew Struggle_, p. 78; Avshalom Haviv in Gurion, p. 163.

[26] Kripitchnkoff, p. 41.

[27] See Irgun Zvai Leumi, "The Great Lesson of the Exodus," The Answer, 30 October 1947, p. 6.

[28] Irgun Zvai Leumi, "Irgun Offers Plan of Action," p. 6.

[29] Irgun Zvai Leumi, "Irgun Offers Plan of Action," p. 6.

[30] See Bell, pp. 171-178.

CHAPTER VI

MENACHEM BEGIN'S MODERN RHETORIC

The situation facing the new Israeli state in
1948 and the situation facing Israel today are quite
different. In 1948, Israel was beset by enemies on
every side. The chances of survival for the first
Jewish state in 1900 years seemed dim. Today, Israel
is the dominant military factor in the Middle East and
is capable of defeating any single Arab country or all
of them in combination. Despite these changes in the
international situation, Menachem Begin's view of the
world has changed little since the conclusion of the
revolt. He has been called, not without reason, the
most consistent politician in the world.[1]

One sign of the consistency in Begin's thought
can be found in rituals celebrating the Irgun. When a
group of people ritually celebrate a story, the ritual
itself attests to the mythic character of the story
celebrated in the ritual. Begin and the soldiers of
the Irgun continue to treat the story of the revolt as
absolutely true and celebrate rituals recalling it.
In 1958, former members of the Irgun held a ceremony
honoring those killed in the Altalena incident. In
1962, services were held at the grave of David Raziel
and at the Dov Gruner monument honoring the soldiers
of the Irgun who died in battle. In 1964, medals were
presented to former Irgun men who suffered in British
prisons. In 1968, a monument was erected honoring the
soldiers of the underground who were executed by the
British, and Begin and other former members of the
Irgun marched in a pilgrimage to the grave of Jabotinsky. In 1969, Begin spoke at a ceremony commemorating
the Irgun's attack on the New Gate in Jerusalem.[2]

Begin and the soldiers of the Irgun continue to
celebrate such rituals because the revolt continues to
serve important psychological functions for them. An
indication of these functions can be found in Begin's
actions shortly after being admitted to the Government
of National Unity in 1967. He instructed his driver
to take him to Jabotinsky's grave, where he spoke to
his teacher, "Sir, head of Betar, we have come to
inform you that one of our followers is now serving as
a minister of the government of Israel."[3] Haber also

reports that Begin continues to visit the memorial to Irgun soldier, Dov Gruner, who was executed by the British.[4] As these acts indicate, for Begin the Irgun's fight against the British is not an incident from the now distant past; it remains one of the crucial events of our times.

Begin's continuing concern for the Irgun and its revolt against the British is also obvious in the political issues which have dominated his career since the 1940s. One might expect Begin to downplay his role as commander of the Irgun. After all, the Irgun represent a small minority in the Jewish community, and Ben-Gurion quite successfully blackened Begin's name for some Irgun actions. But despite political pressures to moderate his image, Begin has emphasized his ties to the Irgun. In a 1958 Anniversary of the Revolt Rally, he asked "'My Soldiers, My Sons' to help change the government."[5] In effect, the election campaign ten yers after the Irgun disbanded was an extension of the Irgun's revolt. For example, Begin attacked Ben-Gurion for turning over soldiers of the Irgun to the British some ten years earlier.[6] For Begin, the "season," the King David Hotel bombing, and the Altalena incident[7] are not ancient history but events which continue to shape Israeli politics.

The fight of the Irgun remains crucial to an understanding of Begin. In an essay on Herut, Segal argues that it is energized by the spirit of the Irgun.[8] Most of the leaders of Herut are former Irgun members,[9] some of whom Begin continues to address by their underground code names.[10] Begin's continuing commitment to the Irgun is also obvious in his request, at a program honoring Jabotinsky, to be introduced first as former commander of the Irgun and only second as prime minister of Israel.[11] Begin has explicitly stated several times that leadership of the Irgun was more important than his service as prime minister of Israel.[12] Meir Merhav puts this continuing emphasis on the Irgun into perspective:

> What many people do not realize is that Mr. Begin is still fighting the battle of 1944-1948, and that for him there is no other. Details may have changed. Essentials have remained. What they do not recognize is that Mr. Begin will not waver and will not go back on his word, for his stead-

fastness is the mainspring of his
leadership.[13]

Based on such data, Segal concludes that Herut is an
extension of the Irgun and serves similar psychological functions for its members:

> The gathering at the Kfar Maccabia
> Hotel [Herut 8th National Convention
> in 1966)] indicated in any case that
> for some people membership in Herut
> serves some profound psychological
> needs: and not just as an instrument
> for political action. Time and again
> the assembly took on the appearance of
> a mass revival rally where the faith-
> ful renew their loyalty by unquestion-
> ing reaffirmation of faith.[14]

Herut reflects the continued commitment of Begin and
his followers to the myth of return.

Begin's life also continues to be shaped by the
event which caused the Irgun to attack the British--
the holocaust. In his speeches on German war reparations in the 1950s and the recognition of Germany in
the 1960s, Begin showed his concern for the holocaust.
This concern is obvious today in his bitter speech
attacking Chancellor Helmut Schmidt for endorsing a
Palestinian state: "It seems the Holocaust has con-
veniently slipped his mind. The German debt to the
Jewish people can never end--not in this generation
and not in any other."[15] Begin believes that the Jewish people are still threatened by the holocaust. He
believes that the world does not care about Israel and
that a new holocaust could threaten the Israeli state,
unless the government of Israel places Israeli security above all other goals. Begin's all-consuming hate
for the Palestine Liberation Organization (PLO) and
his opposition to a Palestinian state are drawn from
his fear of a new holocaust. Begin sees the PLO as
the modern-day equivalent of the Nazi death squads:
The PLO is "the blackest organization other than the
Nazi murder organization--ever to arise in the annals
of humanity."[16] Like the Nazis, the PLO "murdered
Jews--just for being Jews."[17] Because they are
modern-day Nazis, the PLO must be shown no mercy. The
Nazis took advantage of Jewish weakness and humiliated
the Jewish people:

161

> This we shall remember until the last
> day of our lives, and this we shall
> bequeath to our children thereafter:
> He who, in this generation rose up to
> liquidate us, did not carry out his
> evil design until he had humiliated
> our people to the dust, until he had
> robbed them of their human dignity.[18]

However, if the People of Israel are strong, they can
avoid another holocaust:

> I believe: We the Jews, the Zionists,
> the people of Eretz Israel, the build-
> ers of Israel, free of all complexes,
> who are returning the people to their
> land and the homeland to its people
> and owners, will continue to follow
> our path and to overcome all the Nazi
> Arafats and their lackeys. . . [empha-
> sis added].[19]

For Begin, the holocaust is a living reality which the
PLO threatens to bring to completion. The Jewish
people must learn the lesson of the revolt and resist
all threats.

Other essential elements of the myth of return
are also present in Begin's contemporary rhetoric.
Prime Minister Begin viewed the history of the Jewish
people as moving from the hell of the holocaust to the
redemption of the rebirth of the Hebrew state. In the
1972 "Introduction" to The Revolt, he refers to the
period from the holocaust to the birth of the Israeli
state with the phrase, "From the holocaust to redemption."[20] One of his biographers, Harry Hurwitz,
explains the link which Begin sees between the holocaust and the birth of Israel:

> He is the product of, and has been
> moulded by the two main events affect-
> ing Jews in this century--the Holo-
> caust in which 6,000,000 Jews were
> massacred and the Jewish War of Inde-
> pendence or Liberation that paved the
> way for the renewal of Jewish State-
> hood and Peoplehood.
> He sees a direct link between the
> two events and at the 13th Herut
> National Convention in the first days

of 1977 we heard him reveal his ardent
desire to write a major work entitled:
"The Generation of Destruction and
Resurrection."[21]

For Begin, the two crucial events of our time are the
events described at the beginning and end of the myth
of return.

Other elements of the myth of return are also
present in Begin's modern rhetoric. For example, in
an address to the Egyptian people in 1977, he compared
the people of Israel to the Maccabees: "Ours is not,
as you know, a weak hand. If attacked we shall always
defend ourselves as our forefathers, the Maccabees,
did--and won the day."[22] In a 1981 ceremony honoring
Jabotinsky, Begin quotes a poem by Jabotinsky which
explicitly identifies the Israelis as reborn Maccabees:

> Do not say it be not there,
> The blood of our Maccabi fathers,
> In me are three of its drops,
> Mixed with my own heart's blood.
>
> When the enemy mounts ambush,
> Then we shall rise and fight,
> Alive is the youth, alive is the sword,
> Alive is the blood of the Maccabees.[23]

This poem also illustrates the continuing power of
blood as a symbol. In addition, Begin still treats
Jabotinsky as a prophet whom the Jewish people tragically ignored. In the 1981 address honoring Jabotinsky, Begin states:

> In dark days we saw you in your suf-
> fering, in your torment. We heard you
> cry out to the people who did not want
> to listen: Save yourselves, put an
> end to the exile before the exile puts
> an end to you. In those terrible days
> on the very brink of disaster, you
> said to us, your disciples, your sons:
> A time shall come and the people shall
> call upon you to administer their
> affairs, to dedicate yourselves to
> their future. This day has come.[24]

163

Here, Jabotinsky is the prophet who foresaw the holocaust and Begin the disciple whose time has come to lead the state of Israel. For Begin, Jabotinsky remains the guide who orients his life: "Happy are the disciples, Rosh Betar, [Commander World Betar, Jabotinsky] for whom a teacher as you arose and who lives on in their hearts."[25]

In addition to a return to ancient heroism, Begin calls for a return to the religious faith of the ancient Hebrews. It is not that the Jews of the Diaspora lost track of God, but that through the return to Israel, the Jewish people have regained contact with the living center of Judaism. As in the 1940s, Begin today claims that the rituals of Judaism no longer celebrate ancient history but modern realities. In his first speech after returning from the signing ceremony for the Egyptian-Israeli peace treaty, Begin explains:

> In another thirteen days we shall be holding the Passover "seder." For thousands of years now, our children have been asking us Four Questions, and we, the parents, and the parents' parents have been replying: "We were slaves in Egypt, and the Lord God took us out of there with a mighty arm . . ." [ellipsis in original] Four questions. If I may, I should like to ask that it be permitted for them, on this forthcoming Passover night, to put to us a fifth question: "That on all the other nights we were in a state of war with Egypt-[sic] but on this night we have peace with Egypt."[26]

Here, Begin uses the Passover ceremony in order to explain the meaning of the Eyptian-Israeli peace treaty.

Finally, Begin still believes that the strength of the Israeli people returned because of contact with the land of Israel. Consequently, there must be no compromise over the land which was once part of the ancient Hebrew state. In one speech, Begin addresses Jabotinsky to inform him that Jerusalem belongs to Israel. "We bring you tidings, Rosh Betar, that Jerusalem is the city bound inextricably together, the eternal capital of Israel and Eretz Israel, indivisi-

164

ble--this city is our liberated capital, reunited, and thus shall it be for ever and ever."[27] In the same speech, Begin claims all of the West Bank as part of Israel: "Western Eretz Israel is wholly ours; it shall not be partitioned again."[28] He even states his hope that there will someday be a covenant between Western Eretz Israel (Israel and the West Bank) and Eastern Eretz Israel (Jordan) to reunite the land[29] a hope with which the state of Jordan is unlikely to agree.

Begin not only continues to see the world through the myth of return, but his followers treat him as a mythic hero who guides their lives. A number of press critics have noted the similiarity between Begin and an Old Testament hero. Linowitz's comment is typical: "There is almost the fervor of an Old Testament prophet about him as he talks about the dangers confronting his small country."[30] Philip Gilion, cited earlier, argues that the Likud agrees about only one important point of policy, "the near divinity of Menachem Begin."[31] This is particularly apparent in the partisan biography of Begin by Harry Hurwitz:

> In the cause of peace and security for
> his nation he has devoted and is now
> devoting--his rare qualities of lead-
> ership and his many talents--his bril-
> liant oratory, that is capable of
> moving masses and persuading even the
> most pragmatic of statesmen; his
> inspiring prolific writings that have
> educated a generation in Israel and
> outside the country; his incisive
> political mind that brilliantly analy-
> zes and interprets events and develop-
> ments, cutting through all the haze of
> confusion, doubt and misunderstanding;
> his encyclopaedic knowledge and phe-
> nomenal memory; his optimism, confi-
> dence, and above all his selfless
> dedication.[32]

Begin is more than an extraordinarily brave and smart man. He is a man of destiny, a modern Bar Kochba[33] or Judas Maccabeus:

> That is how it must have been in
> Bar Kochba's time or in the days of
> Judas Maccabeus, when the enemy was

becoming ever more powerful and arrogant, and some Jews more timid.

Only a man of the greatest personal courage could withstand the decadence around him: only an exceptionally inspired being would find the will to continue, to carry on in spite of all. Menachem Begin combined all three qualities and more.[34]

The heroic role Begin plays for members of his party and former Irgun soldiers is reflected in Hurwitz's discussion of the relationship between Jabotinsky and Begin. Hurwitz retells several stories indicating that Begin was the chosen successor of Jabotinsky. If Hurowitz is correct, then Jabotinsky foresaw Begin's coming greatness.[35] According to Hurwitz, Jabotinsky said of Begin:

Yes, of course, there is another--and why didn't you choose him [to command World Betar]? He is young, the youngest amongst you. He was nurtured and grew up in this land (Poland) and he will continue to grow up in stature for the future is his. He is worthy of the command and the command is worthy of him--I mean Begin.[36]

For those who view Begin as a hero, the stories about the relationship of Begin and Jabotinsky identify Begin as the chosen successor to the greatest leader of Revisionism; they confer mythic power on Begin. The greatness of a hero is often foretold by a prophet. Jabotinsky is the prophet of the myth of return who saw Begin's coming greatness. The stories also establish Begin's bloodline. Symbolically, Begin is Jabotinsky's son, just as the men of the Irgun are Begin's sons.

The myth of return which dominated Begin's rhetoric in the 1940s continues to dominate his contemporary rhetoric. He views the problems facing the Jewish people today as similar to the problems which faced the Irgun. He continues to call for renewed strength through a return to all of the ancient land of Israel, the ancient heroism of the Hebrew warriors, and revitalized festivals of Judaism. Through this return, the Jewish people have regained their strength: "Gone forever are the days when Jewish blood could be shed with impunity. Let it be known: the shedders of innocent blood shall not go unpunished."37

Four Contemporary Speeches

The claim that Begin's contemporary rhetoric reflects the myth of return and influences his ideology can be tested through an analysis of key rhetorical acts. I consider four such acts: Begin's prayer at the Wailing Wall after the Israeli army recaptured Jerusalem in 1967, his speech in the Knesset during Sadat's visit to Jerusalem, his speech at the Egyptian-Israeli Peace Treaty signing ceremony, and his response to U.S. criticism of Israeli annexation of the Golan.

Following the capture of the Western Wall in the Old City of Jerusalem in 1967, Begin recited the following prayer:

> O God of our fathers Abraham, Isaac and Jacob, Lord of Hosts, be Thou our help. Our enemies encompassed us about, yea they encompassed us about and arose to destroy us as a people. Yet has their counsel been destroyed and their schemes will not be accomplished. For there has arisen in our Homeland a new generation, the generation of liberty, a generation of warriors and heroes. And when they went forth to engage the enemy there burst forth from their hearts the call which echoes throughout the generations, the call from the father of the Prophets, the redeemer of Israel from the bondage of Egypt: "Arise, O Lord, and let Thine enemies be scattered and let them that hate Thee be put to flight." And we scattered and defeated them and flee they did.
>   The defeated enemy has not yet laid down his arms. The Army of Israel continues to pursue and smite them. Lord, God of Israel, guard Thou our forces who with their arms are forging the convenant which Thou didst make with Thy chosen people. May they

return in peace, children to their parents, fathers to their children and husbands to their wives. For we are but the surviving remnant of a people harried and persecuted, whose blood has been shed like water throughout the generations.

Today we stand before the Western Wall, the relic of the House of our Glory, in Jerusalem, the Redeemed, the City that is now all compact together, and from the depths of our hearts there arises the prayer that the Temple may be rebuilt speedily in our days.

We shall yet come to Hebron, the city of the Four Couples, and there we shall prostrate ourselves at the graves of the Patriarchs of our people. We shall yet be on the way to Ephrath as thou comest to Bethlehem of Judah. We shall pray at the Tomb of Rachel and we shall bring to mind the prayer of the prophet: "A voice is heard in Raman, wailing and bitter lamentation, Rachel weeping for her children, she refuseth to be comforted for her children, for they are not. Refrain thy voice from weeping and thine eyes from tears for there is a reward for thy labour, saith the Lord, and they shall return from the land of the enemy. And there is hope for thy latter end and thy children shall return to their borders."[38]

Begin's wartime prayer at the Wailing Wall functions as overheard rhetoric. It is addressed to God, but it is designed to be overheard by the Israeli public. Public prayers generally possess a formal style and deal with the religious dimensions of a problem. They do not deal with specific issues. Public prayers in wartime are constrained by the need for unity in fighting the common enemy. During a war one does not stir up controversy which could divide the nation. Given these constraints one would expect Begin to thank God for the victory of the Israeli army in the Six Day War and pray for the continued safety of the army. Begin also might have been expected to speak of the tie between the Jewish people and Jerusalem.

At the level of content, Begin clearly violates the conventions associated with wartime prayer. In paragraphs one and two, Begin refers not only to the victory in the Six Day War, but also to the holocaust. His references to the massacre of the Jewish people in the death camps seem inappropriate in a prayer celebrating a great victory. In addition, in paragraphs three and four Begin calls for the annexation of the West Bank. He speaks of his hope that Israel will return to the borders of the ancient state of Israel, which included the West Bank, and mentions several places on the West Bank where he hopes Jews will again live. Not cnly does Begin bring a specific issue (the future of the occupied territories) into his prayer, but he advocates a position rejected by the majority of the Israeli government, who favored trading territory for peace. Finally, Begin challenges one aspect of traditional Judaism. He speaks of the soldiers of Israel "forging the covenant which Thou didst make with Thy chosen people." This statement reflects Begin's view that the Jewish people lost their strength and their tie to God during centuries of passivity. The covenant was not destroyed in the exile, but it lost its power. It can be forged again through battle and sacrifice by the army of Israel. Begin believes that the strength of the covenant lies in a fighting Hebrew army. This statement clearly contradicts Jewish tradition, which places a premium on avoiding conflict. Moreover, most traditional Jews do not believe that the Jewish people lost contact with God or the covenant during the exile.

The content of Begin's prayer at the Wailing Wall is shaped by the myth of holocaust and redemption through return. In the opening of the prayer, Begin addresses himself to the God of Abraham, Isaac, and Jacob and then refers to the holocaust: "Our enemies encompassed us about, yea they encompassed us about and arose to destroy us as a people." But the holocaust was not completed because "there has arisen in our Homeland a new generation, the generation of liberty, a generation of warriors and heroes." Unlike the weak and passive Jews of the Diaspora, this new generation of heroes was inspired by the ancient history of Israel. They had returned to "the call which echoed throughout the generations, the call from the father of the Prophets, the redeemer of Israel. . . ."

169

Inspired by this message, the heroes of Israel "scattered and defeated" their enemies. The first section of the prayer retells in short form the myth of return from holocaust to redemption.

The second section of the prayer applies the same pattern to the problem of Israel in 1967. Israel was again surrounded by enemies: "The defeated enemy has not yet laid down his arms." It is strength which protects Israel: "The Army of Israel continues to pursue and smite them." Begin asks God to protect that army: "Lord, God of Israel, guard Thou our forces. . . ." Yet, even with God's aid, the holocaust still dominates Israel: "For we are but the surviving remnant of a people harried and persecuted, whose blood has been shed like water throughout the generations." The second section of the prayer repeats the pattern found in the first section. A threat faces Israel which can be confronted only with strength. The army of Israel aided by the ancient strength of the God of Israel overcomes the threat. Yet, even with this strength, holocaust threatens Israel.

The final section of the prayer states the attachment of the Jewish people to all of the land of Israel. Begin speaks of Jerusalem "redeemed," evidently by the arms of the Israeli Defense Force, and calls for rebuilding the temple. He then speaks of the tie between the Jewish people and Hebron, Bethlehem, the Tomb of Rachel, and the other sites on the West Bank. Here, Begin refers to the holy places of the ancient Israeli state in order to legitimize claims of the modern state to that territory. He closes the prayer by promising that there shall be a reward for the labors of the army. They shall "return" from the "land of the enemy" to the borders of ancient Israel including Judea and Samaria. The references to the holocaust, reborn Hebrew heroism, and the West Bank in a prayer of thanksgiving indicate the influence of the myth of return on Begin's view of the world.

While the content of Begin's prayer at the Wailing Wall is shaped by the myth of return and violates the conventions associated with wartime prayers, at another level the prayer illustrates the capacity of the myth of return to cloak controversial claims in conventional forms and draw upon the love of Zion in traditional Judaism. Paragraph one takes the form of an Old testament prayer of thanksgiving to God for

170

saving the Jewish people. The opening sentence affirms the bond to the "God of our fathers. . . ." The remainder of the prayer stays close to the formal conventions of the Old Testament. In paragraph two, Begin prays for the return of the soldiers of Israel from battle. This is similar to Old Testament prayers for success in battle (see, for instance, Judas Maccabeus's prayer in First Maccabees 4:31-34). Paragraphs three and four speak of the return to the holiest sites in all Judaism. Jews throughout the ages prayed for a return to Hebron, Bethlehem, and most of all to Jerusalem and the Western Wall. While Begin's message is controversial, his form is purely conventional, and he uses the conventions of form to obscure the radical character of his message. He knows better than to demand explicitly that the government annex the West Bank, but instead prays for a return to the holy sites of Judaism on the West Bank. The prayer illustrates the capacity of the myth of holocaust and redemption to draw upon the formal conventions and the love of Zion found in traditional Judaism, while proposing actions which radically contradict the traditional myth.

Begin's prayer at the Western Wall reflects the influence of the myth of return on his rhetoric and world view in 1967 when he first served in the government of Israel. However, his experience in the government might have moderated his views and led him away from the myth of holocaust and return. In order to test whether the myth of return is still the dominant perspective through which Begin sees the world, I have examined three important rhetorical acts during Begin's contemporary tenure as prime minister of Israel. The speech to the Knesset during Sadat's visit to Jerusalem and the speech at the signing of the Egyptian-Israeli peace treaty are Begin's two most important rhetorical acts flowing from the peace negotiations with Egypt. His letter to President Reagan, answering U.S. criticism following the Israeli annexation of the Golan Heights, raised serious questions about the future of relations between the United States and Israel. If Begin's perspective is still dominated by the myth of holocaust and redemption through return, that myth should be apparent in these works.

Shortly after becoming prime minister, Menachem Begin initiated a series of foreign policy efforts which eventually resulted in the Sadat visit to Jeru-

salem.[39] Begin sent information gathered by Israeli
intelligence, about a Libyan plot against Sadat,
directly to the Egyptians. Begin also established
contact with Egypt through the king of Morocco and the
president of Rumania. These peace initiatives bore
fruit when President Sadat offered to go anywhere in
the search for peace, even Jerusalem. Following
Sadat's statement, Begin invited him to Jerusalem.[40]
After arriving in Jerusalem, Sadat toured the Vad
Vashem (the holocaust memorial), conducted a number of
private meetings with Israeli leaders, and gave a
speech to the Knesset. While Sadat's visit to Jerusalem showed great courage and opened the way for peace
in the Middle East, his speech at the Knesset was
hardly conciliatory. At one point Sadat said: "We
insist on complete withdrawal from these [West Bank]
territories, including Arab-Jerusalem."[41] Since all
major Israeli political parties rejected concessions
on Jerusalem, and Begin had explicitly rejected any
compromise on Israeli claims of sovereignty over the
West Bank, Begin could hardly have been pleased by the
content of Sadat's address. Sadat's message was so
tough that, during his speech, Defense Minister Ezer
Weizman reportedly leaned over and told Begin that
Israel had better begin planning for war.[42]

It is in this context that Begin responded to
Sadat. In many ways, Begin's address might best be
characterized as a traditional speech of welcome. He
clearly tries to adapt to the situation by praising
Sadat and appealing to the Arab world. Begin praises
Sadat's courage: "The duration of the flight from
Cairo to Jerusalem is short, but until last night, the
distance between them was infinite. President Sadat
showed courage in crossing this distance."[43] Begin
also appeals to the Arab peoples by sending greetings
to "all adherents of the Islamic faith . . . on the
occasion of the Feast of Sacrifice, Id el Adha" (1,
2). He also links the Jewish and Arab peoples together
by recalling the story of Isaac and arguing that it
was "our two peoples" (1, 3) who taught the world to
give up human sacrifice. Later in the address, he
offers a prayer to the "God of our common ancestors"
(8, 34). Begin also appeals to the Arab audience by
twice stating that past history should not prevent
peace. He says: "Let us not be daunted by memories
of the past, even if they are bitter to us all" (3,
11). In addition, Begin appears to make an enormous
concession by stating that all claims are negotiable:

I propose, in the name of the overwhelming majority of this Parliament,
that everything will be negotiable.
Anybody who says that, in the relationship between the Arab people--or
the Arab Nations in the area--and the
State of Israel there are subjects
that should be excluded from negotiations, is assuming an awesome responsibility. Everything is negotiable.
No side shall say the contrary. We
will conduct the negotiations with
respect. (6-7, 28)

Finally, Begin expresses the aspirations of all Israelis "to bring peace: peace to our nation which has
not known it for even one day since the beginning of
the Return to Zion . . ." (2, 9). Begin appears to be
anything but intransigent. His statement that all
issues are negotiable and that the past should not be
allowed to prevent peace seems surprisingly flexible
and very unlike the rhetoric described previously.

However, a closer look at Begin's address reveals
the same mythic outlook which dominates his other rhetoric. First, while Begin calls on both the Arab and
the Israeli peoples to forget the past, he emphatical-
ly does not mean that the holocaust should be forgotten. At one point Begin compares the situation facing
the Jewish people in the 1930s with the current day:

Then, too, we were told to pay no heed
to such words. The whole world heard.
No one came to our rescue; not during
the nine critical, fateful months following this announcement--the likes of
which had never been heard since God
created man and man created Satan--and
not during those six years when millions of our people, among them a million and a half small Jewish children
were slaughtered in every possible
way. (6, 25)

As a result of this hideous crime and the failure of
any civilized nation to come to the aid of the Jews,
the people of Israel have sworn never to forget the
holocaust:

And therefore, we, this entire generation, the generation of Holocaust and
Resurrection, swore an oath of allegiance: never again shall we endanger
our People; never again will our wives
and our children--whom it is our duty
to defend, if need be even at the cost
of our lives--be put in the devastating range of enemy fire. (6, 26)

While the wars between the Arab states and Israel may
be forgotten, the holocaust must never be forgotten.
And in response to that horrible crime, the Jewish
people must "never again" be weak. He will take no
risks with the security of the Jewish people. Another
indication of his mythic world view is the reference
to the "generation of Holocaust and Resurrection," a
phrase reflecting a view of recent Jewish history as a
journey from the ultimate evil of the holocaust to
redemption or resurrection in the Israeli state.

In addition to his comments about the holocaust,
Begin refers to the battle of the Hebrew underground
organizations against the British. He tells Sadat
that Israel cannot be bullied, because "in this democratic chamber sit commanders of all the Hebrew underground fighting organizations. They were compelled to
conduct a battle of few against many, against a mighty
world power" (2, 9). Begin's motives for focusing
upon the Irgun seem inexplicable. By referring to the
Irgun, Begin risks dredging up memories of the Dir
Yassin massacre. To Begin, however, the revolt seems
relevant because it revealed that only strength brings
peace. Begin refers to the Irgun because he sees the
problems which Israel faces in the 1980s as similar to
the problems Jews faced in Palestine in the 1940s.

And most pointedly, Begin speaks of the eternal
bond between Israel and the land of Palestine:

No, sir, we took no foreign land. We
returned to our Homeland. The bond
between our People and this Land is
eternal. It was created at the dawn
of human history. It was never severed. In this land we established our
civilization; here our prophets spoke
those holy words you cited this very
day; there the Kings of Judah and
Israel prostrated themselves; here we

174

became a nation; here we established
our Kingdom and, when we were exiled
from our country by the force that was
exercised against us, even when we
were far away we did not forget this
Land, not even for a single day. We
prayed for it; we longed for it; we
have believed in our return to it.
. . . (5,23)

The return to Zion of which Begin speaks was aided by
God: "This, too, is true: with the help of God we
overcame the forces of aggression and assured the survival of our nation, not only for this generation, but
for all those to come" (2, 7). He also claims that
Israel emerged victorious in battle because her forces
"defended right" (2, 8-9). Thus, the Arabs have no
right to Palestine. The land was given to the Jews by
God and the Jews have retained the land because of the
righteousness of their cause. This view leaves little
room for territorial compromise.

Begin also implicitly compares the conflict
between the Israelis and the Arabs with the attempt by
the Nazis to annihilate the Jews. He claims that the
attack by several Arab states upon the infant state of
Israel in 1948 was another stage in the holocaust:

But it is my duty--my duty, Mr. Speaker, and not only my privilege--to
assert today in truth that our hand,
extended in peace [to the Arabs], was
rejected. And, one day after our
independence was renewed, in accordance with our eternal and indisputable right, we were attacked on three
fronts, and we stood virtually without
arms--few against many, weak against
strong. One day after the declaration
of our independence, an attempt was
made to strangle it with enmity, and
to extinguish the last home of the
Jewish People in the generation of the
Holocaust and Resurrection. (2, 5)

Despite his statement that past history should not
stand in the way of peace between the Arab and Jewish
people, Begin pointedly assigns the blame for thirty-
five years of war to the Arabs. While Begin says that
the past should not prevent peace between the Arabs

175

and the Jews, his own world view is drawn from that past. In Begin's address during Sadat's visit to Jerusalem, all of the major portions of the myth of return are present, save a direct reference to the modern Israelis as reborn Maccabees.

It might be argued that while Begin's myth remains the same, the ideology underlying his remarks in the Knesset during Sadat's visit to Jerusalem is quite different from the ideology of Herut or the Irgun. Actually, Begin's comments about peace negotiations are consonant with the ideology I have described. For example, Begin explicitly calls for reciprocity in the peace negotiations: "We shall conduct the negotiations as equals. There are no vanquished and there are no victors. All the Peoples of the region are equal, and all will relate to each other with this respect" (7,30). The ultimate goal of these negotiations is a peace treaty (7,30). Moreover, while Begin says that all issues are negotiable, he does not say that any of his basic positions have changed. The development of the peace process since Sadat's visit to Jerusalem proves that while the Begin government was willing to listen to Arab claims on issues such as Jerusalem, they were not willing to compromise.[44]

In their speeches in the Knesset, Sadat and Begin were pulled in conflicting directions.[45] Sadat, who desperately wanted peace, was constrained by the reaction of the Arab world to his visit to Jerusalem. He hoped to maintain his credibility with other Arab nations and the Palestinians by making tough demands on the Israelis. On the other hand, he hoped to appeal to the Israelis through the visit itself. The visit to Jerusalem would serve as a symbol that peace could be reached. Begin was also pushed in conflicting directions. Many of his followers feared that the Sadat trip was a trick.[46] At the same time, Sadat's visit was clearly an opportunity for peace. Begin responded to that opportunity by speaking graciously to Sadat personally and the Arab peoples in general. However, his mythic world view allowed no symbolic concession comparable to the Sadat trip itself.

In March 1979, the peace negotiations between Egypt and Israel, which began in earnest with Sadat's journey to Jerusalem, came to fruition. Egypt and Israel signed a peace treaty. The negotiations for this treaty went through a number of difficult stages.

After the Sadat trip to Jerusalem, Begin visited Sadat at Ismailiya, Egypt, in December 1977 and proposed limited autonomy for the Palestinians under Israeli rule. Following that visit, military and foreign affairs committees were established to facilitate the negotiations between the two countries. These two sets of committees accomplished very little. In September of 1978, President Sadat, Prime Minister Begin, and their respective staffs met with President Jimmy Carter at Camp David. Carter hoped that by bringing Begin and Sadat together for intensive negotiations some compromise could be worked out. After very difficult negotiations, the Camp David accords were signed by all parties. The accords sketched the outlines of a peace treaty between Egypt and Israel, called for the return of the Sinai to Egypt, and proposed limited autonomy for West Bank Palestinians. Following the signing of the Camp David accords, a number of difficult problems developed and additional negotiations were needed until, in March of 1979, both the Egyptians and the Israelis were ready to sign a treaty of peace. Although Egypt and Israel had finally reached agreement on a peace treaty, there were still problems to be worked out, notably the question of how much autonomy the Palestinians should be given. However, the ceremony was not the time to deal with such issues. Rather, it was time for Carter, Begin, and Sadat to celebrate peace. The situation called for speeches paying tribute to the other leaders involved and praying for a generation of peace.

President Sadat responded to the exigencies of the situation and produced a hymn of peace. He praised Prime Minister Begin and especially President Carter for his work for peace. More important, President Sadat removed two paragraphs from his speech in which he called on Israel to grant full rights to the Palestinians.[47] Sadat evidently realized that the call for Palestinian rights could only offend Begin and the Israel people on a day on which it was more appropriate to praise the achievement of peace between the two nations.

To some extent, Begin also responded to the exigencies created by the treaty-signing ceremony. In his speech, Begin praised both Sadat and Carter and spoke with much emotion of the value of peace:

> Peace is the beauty of life. It is
> sunshine. It is the smile of a child,

177

the love of a mother, the joy of a
father, the togetherness of a family.
It is the advancement of man, the
victory of a just cause, the triumph
of trust. Peace is all of these and
more, and more.[48]

While some aspects of Begin's speech were adapted to
the situation, some commentators argue that in other
sections he makes statements which could only offend
the Arab world. Lippman's comment is typical of his
view:

Egyptians who watched the ceremonies
tonight winced as Begin went through
what they saw as an excessive and ill-
timed reminiscence about the Holocaust. They also criticized his
remarks about Jerusalem and his failure to offer anything new on the
Palestinian question.[49]

Begin's failure to adapt to the exigencies of the
treaty-signing ceremony can be traced to the myth of
return through which he continues to view the world.

The myth of return is obvious in much of Begin's
Peace Treaty speech. Initially, he focuses a great
deal of attention upon the holocaust. After the
introduction, in which he thanks all of those present,
Begin identifies himself as a member of the generation
of the holocaust: "I have come from the land of
Israel, the land of Zion and Jerusalem, and here I am
in humility and with pride, as a son of the Jewish
people, as one of the generation of Holocaust and
Redemption" (2). At the conclusion of his address, he
introduces the 126th Psalm by speaking of the holocaust:

Therefore, it is the proper place and
the appropriate time to bring back to
memory the song and prayer of thanksgiving I learned as a child in the
home of father and mother, that
doesn't exist anymore--because they
were among the six million people,
men, women, and children, who sanctified the Lord's name with their sacred
blood, which reddened the rivers of
Europe from the Rhine to the Danube,

178

from the Bug to the Volga, because--
only because--they were born Jews.
And because they didn't have a country
of their own, and neither a valiant
Jewish army to defend them. And
because nobody, nobody, came to their
rescue, although they cried out, "Save
us! Save us!" De Profundis, from the
depths of the pit and agony." (9)

In this statement, Begin spells out part of the position he encapsulates in the phrase "generation of
Holocaust and Redemption." The Jewish people were
murdered because they had no country of their own,
because they were weak, and because the West did not
care.

According to Begin, the day of peace finally
arrived because of the heroism of the Jewish youth:
"Let us turn our hearts to our heroes, and pay tribute
to their eternal memory. It is thanks to them, to our
fallen heroes, that we could have reached this day"
(3). He also uses the ancient history of Israel and
Egypt as a paradigm for understanding the modern day
history of the two nations: "However, let us not
forget that in ancient times, our two nations went
also in alliance. Now we make peace" (4). In addition, Begin links the ancient Hebrew people to the
modern Israelis. He speaks of the great vision of the
Hebrew prophets, Isaiah and Micah (2). Begin sees
modern Israelis as Hebrew heroes who can follow the
urgings of Isaiah and Micah in order to beat their
swords into plowshares.

Not only does Begin speak of the modern Israelis
as the spiritual sons of ancient Israel, but he says
that it was God who gave him the strength to reach
this day:

God gave me the strength to persevere,
to survive the horrors of Nazism and
of a Stalinite concentration camp--and
some other dangers. To endure--not to
waver in or flinch from my duty. To
accept the abuse from foreigners and,
what is more painful, from my own people and even from my close friends.
This effort, too, bore some fruit.
(8)

179

In this passage, Begin recalls his years as commander of the Irgun. The "other dangers" include the "season" and other attempts by the official Jewish organizations to crush the Irgun.

The most telling evidence of Begin's commitment to the myth of return comes when he explains that this day of signing a peace treaty with Egypt is the third greatest day of his life:

> And it is, ladies and gentlemen, the third greatest day in my life. The first was May the fourteenth, 1948, when our flag was hoisted. Our independence in our ancestors' land was proclaimed after 1,878 years of dispersion, persecution, humiliation and ultimately physical destruction. We fought for our liberation alone, and, with God's help, we won the day. That was spring. Such a spring we can never have again. The second day was when Jerusalem became one city, and our brave, perhaps most hardened soldiers--the parachutists--embraced with tears and kissed the ancient stones of the remnants of the wall destined to protect the chosen place of God's glory. Our hearts wept with them in remembrance: Now we stand within your gates, O Jerusalem, that is built to be a city where people come together in unity. (7)

This statement could only offend President Sadat and the Arab world. Begin slights the treaty-signing ceremony by naming it as only the third greatest day of his life. Moreover, references to the founding of Israel and the capture of Jerusalem could only open wounds for the Arabs. For the Arabs, May 14, 1948, was not a great day; it was the day that they lost control of territory they believed to be their own. Begin's comments about Jerusalem would be still more offensive to Sadat, for whom the unification of Jerusalem was a crime. Moreover, Begin seems to imply that the Israelis will never compromise over Jerusalem. There was no reason for Begin to include these comments in his speech. They serve no persuasive function. On the contrary, they strike a discordant note.

Begin's description of the three greatest days of his life underscores his commitment to the myth of return. The greatest day of Begin's life was May 14, 1948, the day that the Hebrew people finally returned to Zion. The second greatest day of his life was the day Jerusalem was united. Jerusalem's importance comes from its place at the center of Jewish mythology. On the second greatest day of Begin's life, the Jewish people finally returned to their eternal capital.

The final rhetorical act to be considered is Begin's public reaction to U.S. criticism following the Israeli annexation of the Golan heights. On November 30, 1981, the United States and Israel signed a "Memorandum of Strategic Cooperation," committing both countries to consult with each other on strategic issues, primarily the threat posed by the Soviet Union in the Middle East. In mid-December, following the Israeli annexation of the Golan, the United States suspended the memorandum in protest. In addition, President Reagan and various administration representatives publicly criticized the Israeli annexation. In response, Prime Minister Begin called in U.S. Ambassador Samuel Lewis and complained harshly about U.S. actions. The public statement released by the Begin government was the summation of Begin's earlier statement to Ambassador Lewis.[50] Begin's statement is a strident attack on the Reagan administration for its criticism of Israel. While Begin's statement does not take the form of a myth, it, too, cannot be explained adequately without reference to the myth of return.

Begin's first argument is that the Israeli actions criticized by the United States were justified. Begin defends an Israeli raid on the PLO headquarters in Lebanon as a defensive act in response to the PLO murder of three Israelis and the injury of twenty-nine. He notes that one of the dead was an Auschwitz survivor (4). Begin also charges that the United States has no right to criticize Israel for military attacks which result in civilian casualties. He argues:

> You have no moral right to preach to
> us about civilian casualities. We
> have read the history of World War Two
> and we know what happened to civilians
> when you took action against an enemy.
> We have also read the history of the

181

Vietnam war and your phrase "body-
count." We always make efforts to
avoid hitting civilian populations,
but sometimes it is unavoidable--as
was the case of our bombing of the PLO
headquarters. (5)

Begin also defends the Israeli raid, which destroyed
an Iraqi nuclear reactor, by claiming that the Israeli
government had proof that the reactor was to be used
to produce nuclear weapons. He implies that the
information came from U.S. intelligence sources and
characterizes the raid as "an act of salvation."
According to Begin, the raid "saved the lives of hundreds of thousands of civilians, including tens of
thousands of children" (2).

Begin's second important claim is that the United
States has no right to criticize Israel. He points
out that Israel is not an insignificant state to be
pushed around by U.S. power: "What kind of expression
is this--'punishing Israel'? Are we a vassal-state of
yours? Are we a banana republic? Are we youths of
fourteen who, if they don't behave properly, are slapped across the fingers"? (9) According to Begin,
Israel does not need the agreement on strategic cooperation with the United States: "The people of Israel
has [sic] lived 3,700 years without a memorandum of
understanding with America--and it will continue to
live without one for another 3,700 years" (15).

Begin then bitterly attacks attempts to pressure
Israel into withdrawing from the Golan by comparing
U.S. policy to the actions of anti-Semites who,
throughout the ages, have tried to pressure the Jews
into giving up their rights. He even compares the
demand that the Golan law be rescinded with the inquisition: "To 'rescind' is a concept from the days of
the Inquisition. Our forefathers went to the stake
rather than 'rescind' their faith" (24). Begin also
compares the attempts of the United States to force
the Israelis to compromise on the Golan with the
actions of British General Barker who said, following
the Irgun operation which blew up the King David
Hotel, that "this race [the Jewish people] will only
be influenced by being hit in the pocket" (20). Begin
sees this same philosophy of hitting the Jewish people
in the pocket as part of the policy of the Reagan
administration (21). He also sees anti-Semitism at

the heart of the Senate campaign for the sale of AWACS planes to Saudi Arabia.

Finally, Begin says that the Israeli government cannot be threatened. He informs the United States that his government is made up of people who endured the underground:

> Let me tell you who this government is composed of. It is composed of people whose lives were spent in resistance, in fighting and in suffering. You will not frighten us with "punishment." He who threatens us will find us deaf to his threats. We are only prepared to listen to rational arguments. (10)

Therefore, since the government cannot be threatened, Begin informs the U.S. ambassador that "there is no force on earth that can bring about its [the Golan law's] rescision [sic]" (29). He also redefines U.S. suspension of the memorandum of cooperation:

> I regard your announcement suspending the consultations on the memorandum as the abrogation (by you) of the memorandum. No "sword of Damocles" is going to hang over my head. So we duly take note of the fact that you have abrogated the memorandum of understanding. (14)

This statement is not in mythic form. There are no references to the return to the ancient land of Israel, nor are the Maccabees mentioned. Rather, Begin's statement is a vituperative attack on U.S. policy. Begin's comparison of U.S. actions to the inquisition is particularly harsh, as is the statement about the Vietnam war. In addition, Begin calls the U.S. government anti-Semitic. He claims that the lobbyists working closely with the Reagan administration, who pushed for the Saudi arms deal, used anti-Semitic arguments. He also compares the actions of the Reagan administration to the anti-Semitic actions of the British in the 1940s.

Begin's statement makes little political sense. He makes no real attempt to justify the annexation of the Golan, nor does he adequately justify the other

183

actions which had been criticized. He simply says
that the raids on the PLO headquarters and the Iraqi
reactor were acts of salvation. Nor does Begin provide adequate justification for violating the strategic agreement with the United States. Israel had
wanted some sort of formal agreement with the United
States for years. It did not make sense to abrogate
that agreement because the U.S. delayed certain consultations with Israel. Most important, it was not in
Israeli interest to criticize the United States so
harshly. Israel needs the United States. The United
States sends Israel a great deal of economic and military aid and is one of the last supporters of Israel
in the world community. Given Israeli dependence upon
the United States, it hardly made sense for Begin to
attack the U.S. government so vociferously.

Begin is no political innocent. He has been a
major figure in Israeli politics for over thirty
years. During his years as a political outcast, he
learned to take calmly criticism far more strident
than that of the Reagan administration. The myth of
return, not anger, was the underlying cause of Begin's
statement. The spectre of the holocaust is obvious
throughout the statement. When Begin mentions a PLO
attack on Israel, he notes that one of those killed
was an Auschwitz survivor. The import of his comment
is not that the death of an Auschwitz survivor is more
terrible than the death of any other human being.
Rather, the fact that an Auschwitz survivor living in
Israel could be killed by terrorists meant for Begin
that Israel still lives in the world of the holocaust. The Auschwitz survivor had been killed by the
modern Nazis, the PLO. This also explains why Begin
mentions the inquisition and the pressures which had
been put on the Jewish community through the centuries
to rescind decisions. Begin sees in the modern world
the same sorts of threats which have been made against
the Jewish people throughout the ages. Begin's concern with the holocaust also explains his reference to
the bombing of the Iraqi reactor as an act of "salvation." That bombing raid prevented a possible future
holocaust.

Begin's statement also reflects his experience as
commander of the Irgun. He reminds the Reagan administration that the Israeli government is made up of
former underground leaders who cannot be threatened.
Later, he compares the actions of the U.S. government
to the anti-Semitic actions of General Barker during

184

the revolt. Not only does Begin use the history of the Irgun as a way of conceptualizing the problems facing Israel in the 1980s, but he also adopts policies which are derived directly from the ideology of the Irgun. His response to U.S. criticism is to state that there will be no more compromise: "He who threatens us will find us deaf to his threats" (10).

Begin's comments about the agreement for strategic cooperation are also instructive. He declares it abrogated because the United States suspended it. Here, Begin demands that Israel be treated as an equal. In addition, Begin twice says that Israel does not need the United States. Begin demands reciprocal treatment and defends brute strength as the only Israeli defense.

The essential elements of the Irgun ideology are present in Begin's message to the United States. The Jewish people are threatened on all sides by destruction and can trust nothing but their own strength. They must be strong and demand equal treatment from all nations. An agreement with the United States is valuable only if it establishes reciprocal relations between the two nations.

Begin's statement to President Reagan makes no sense when considered as a practical message designed to achieve some end. However, when the situation is examined from the perspective of the myth of return and the ideology growing out of that myth, the statement becomes intelligible. Begin's vituperative outburst at the United States comes not from his spleen, but from the myth which shapes his view of the world.

Conclusion

Much of Begin's rhetoric from the 1940s through the 1980s follows the pattern of the myth of return identified in the rhetoric of the Irgun. Begin's life has been dominated by the holocaust and the fight to protect Israel. He still believes that the resurrection or redemption of the Jewish people, following the holocaust, can be assured only through a return to the glory of ancient Israel. So Begin speaks of the modern Israelis as reborn Maccabees and calls for a return to all of the ancient land of Israel. This explains his unwillingness to give up the West Bank. Finally, he still demands equality, strength for

Israel, and sees all major problems facing Israel as related to the holocaust.

Many of Begin's speeches since his election as prime minister possess the mythic pattern I have identified. The address to the Knesset during Sadat's visit and the address at the treaty ceremony possess most of the characteristics of the myth of return. These speeches are not in mythic form because they do not tell a story. Rather, they draw upon the pre-existing mythology of ancient Hebrew heroism and the myth of the Irgun. Other speeches and messages of Begin's are influenced by the myth. The Golan Heights annexation statement clearly fits into that category. The message in Begin's statement can be traced directly to the myth of the journey from holocaust to redemption through return.

Notes

¹ See Meir Merhav, "The Constancy of Menahem Begin," Jerusalem Post International Edition, 23 August 1977, pp. 7, 14; William Claiborne, "Begin Refuses to Compromise Principles," Washington Post, 25 March 1979, pp. A1, A18.

² See "Begin Presents Flag to I.Z.L.," Jerusalem Post, 5 August 1948; "10th Anniversary of Altalena Incident," Jerusalem Post, 8 June 1958; "Irgun Honours Dead," Jerusalem Post, 28 May 1962; Moshe Cohen, "I.Z.L. Awards Captivity Medal," Jerusalem Post, 11 February 1964; "Jabotinsky Memorial," Jerusalem Post, 26 July 1968; "Monument to Men Executed by Turks and Britain," Jerusalem Post, 25 April 1968; Abraham Rabinovich, "Memorial to IZL Dead in Attack on New Gate," Jerusalem Post, 17 July 1969. All of these articles are reprinted in the Inter-Documentation Company microfiche collection of articles on Begin printed originally in the Jerusalem Post. The microfiche do not list page numbers and some of the dates are indistinct.

³ See Eitan Haber, Menahem Begin: The Legend and the Man, trans. Louis Williams (New York: Delacorte, 1978), pp. 167-168.

⁴ Haber, pp. 180-181.

⁵ Mark Segal, "Herut 'Anniversary of the Revolt' Rally in Tel Aviv," Jerusalem Post, 9 April 1958, IDC microfiche.

⁶ "B-G [Ben-Gurion]: Dayan to Stop Speeches," Jerusalem Post, 26 June 1958, IDC microfiche.

⁷ See Haber, p. 240.

⁸ Mark Segal, "Herut Brings Down the Roof," Jerusalem Post, 8 July 1966, IDC microfiche.

⁹ Segal, "Herut Brings Down the Roof."

¹⁰ See Haber, pp. 231-232.

¹¹ See Harry Hurwitz, Menachem Begin (Johannesburg, South Africa: Jewish Herald, December 1977), p. 57.

¹² See for instance Menachem Begin, "Preface to the Revised Edition," The Revolt, rev. ed. (New York: Dell, 1977), p. 14.

¹³ Merhav, "The Constancy of Menahem Begin," p. 14.

187

14 See Segal, "Herut Brings Down the Roof."

15 Begin is quoted in "Sounding Off With a Vengeance," Time, 18 May 1981, p. 37.

16 Menachem Begin, "Statement Delivered in the Knesset by the Prime Minister, Mr. Menachem Begin, 13 March 1978," p. 3. This and other speeches of Prime Minister Begin are cited from texts of the speeches issued by the Israeli Embassy and the Israeli Information Service.

17 Begin, "Statement in the Knesset, 13 March 1978," p. 1.

18 Menachem Begin, "Address by Prime Minster Menachem Begin On the Occasion of the Centenary Year of the Birth of Zeev Jabotinsky, At a Memorial Meeting on Mt. Herzl Jerusalem," Embassy of Israel, 30 July 1981, p. 1.

19 Menachem Begin, "Statement By Prime Minister Begin in the Knesset, 7/9/79, Following the Visit By the Leader of the P.L.O. to Austria," Embassy of Israel, 20 July 1979, p. 3.

20 Menachem Begin, "From the Perspective of a Generation," The Revolt, rev. ed., p. 18. Also see Begin's statement quoted in David Ignatius, Frederick Kempe, and Seth Lipsky, "Begin on Begin: Soon I'll Retire to Write My Book," Wall Street Journal, 9 July 1982, p. 1.

21 See Hurwitz, pp. 10-11.

22 Menachem Begin, "Address by Prime Minister Menachem Begin to the Egyptian People," Embassy of Israel, 11 November 1977, p. 2.

23 Begin, "On the Occasion of the Centenary," p. 2.

24 Begin, "On the Occasion of the Centenary," p. 3.

25 Begin, "On the Occasion of the Centenary," p. 3.

26 Menachem Begin, "Address by Prime Minister Menachem Begin At Special Festive Ceremony, Held at Knesset Plaza, To Mark the Premier's Return Home Following the Signing of the Peace Treaty with Egypt," Embassy of Israel, 29 March 1979, p. 2.

27 Begin, "On the Occasion of the Centenary," p. 1.

28 Begin, "On the Occasion of the Centenary," p. 1.

29 Begin, "On the Occasion of the Centenary," p. 1.

[30] Sol Linowitz, "The Begin I Know," Newsweek, 14 September 1981, p. 42. Also see Dan V. Segre, A Crisis of Identity: Israel and Zionism (Oxford: Oxford University Press, 1980), p. 150; David Gross, "Israeli Premier: Menahem Begin Seen as Tough-minded Blend of Soldier-Prophet," Jewish Week Examiner, 24 September 1981, p. 31.

[31] Philip Gilion, "The Feud in Labour," The Jerusalem Post International Edition, 23-29 November 1980, p. 11.

[32] Hurwitz, p. 11.

[33] Hurwitz, pp. 38, 162-163.

[34] Hurwitz, p. 38.

[35] Hurwitz, pp. 59-60.

[36] Jabotinsky, is quoted in Hurwitz, p. 59.

[37] Begin, "Statement in the Knesset, 13 March 1978," p. 3.

[38] Begin's prayer is quoted in Hurwitz, pp. 89-91.

[39] For the story of peace negotiations between Egypt and Israel see Sidney Zion and Uri Dan, "Untold Story of the Mideast Talks," New York Times Magazine, 21 January 1979, pp. 20-22, 46-53, and 28 January 1979, pp. 32-43; Ezer Weizman, The Battle for Peace (Toronto: Bantam, 1981); Moshe Dayan, Breakthrough: A Personal Account of the Egypt-Israel Peace Negotiations (New York: Knopf, 1981); Eitan Haber, Zeev Schiff, and Ehud Yaari, The Year of the Dove (New York: Bantam, 1979).

[40] See Lally Weymouth, "Walter Cronkite Remembers," Washington Journalism Review, 3 (January-February 1981), p. 23.

[41] Anwar Sadat, "Text of Address by Mr. Muhammad Anwar Al-Sadat President of the Egyptian Arab Republic At a Special Session of the Knesset," 20 November 1977, Israel Information Centre, p. 8.

[42] Weizman, p. 33.

[43] Menachem Begin, "Text of Address by Mr. Menahem Begin, Prime Minister of the State of Israel, At a Special Session of the Knesset," 20 November 1977, Israel Information Centre, p. 1, paragraph 4. Future references to this address will be made in parens. in the text by citing first the page and then the paragraph of the reference. This speech is reproduced in the appendix.

44 See Richard H. Ullman, "The U.S. Should Press Israel to Pursue Peace," New York Times, 14 July 1981, p. A25.

45 For a discussion of the conflicting demands which the leader of a social movement may face, see Herbert W. Simon, "Requirements, Problems, and Strategies: A Theory of Persuasion for Social Movements," Quarterly Journal of Speech, 56 (1970), pp. 6-7.

46 See Haber, Schiff, and Yaari, pp. 29-30.

47 See Bernard Gwertzman, "Peace Treaty Signed by Egypt and Israel," New York Times, 27 March 1979, p. A10.

48 Menachem Begin, "Prime Minister Begin's Speech at the Signing of the Peace Treaty With Egypt," 26 March 1979, State of Israel Government Press Office, paragraph 3. Future references to this speech will be made in parens. in the text, with the paragraph number of the reference cited. This speech is reproduced in the appendix.

49 Thomas W. Lippman, "Egypt Greets Peace Treaty With Mix of Joy, Indifference," Washington Post, 27 March 1979, p. A12. Also see Suzanne Weaver, "Somber Gladness Pervades Carter's Party for Peace," Wall Street Journal, 30 March 1979, p. 14; David A. Frank, "In Celebration of Peace: A Rhetorical Analysis of the Three Speeches Delivered at the Middle East Ceremony of Peace 26 March 1979," paper presented at the Speech Communication Association Convention, Anaheim, California, 13 November 1981, p. 38.

50 Begin's statement is reprinted in "Israel Hits Back After U.S. Sanctions," The Jerusalem Post International Edition, 20-26 December 1981, pp. 1-2. Future references to this work will be cited in the text with the paragraph number of the citation in parens. Begin's statement is reproduced in the appendix.

CHAPTER VII

THE SOCIAL IMPLICATIONS OF MENACHEM BEGIN'S MYTHIC
RHETORIC

Menachem Begin's life and rhetoric, from the
1940s to the present, have been shaped by the myth of
holocaust and redemption through return. Begin continues to believe that the Jewish people are threatened with annihilation and that the only answer to
that threat lies in return to the heroism and land of
the ancient Hebrew people. In previous chapters, I
have focused on explaining the form and function of
Begin's myth itself. However, Begin's myth cannot be
fully understood without considering its relation to
Israeli politics and the Middle East. In this chapter, I describe the influence of the myth and evaluate
its worth as an answer to the holocaust.

The Myth of Return and Palestinian Rhetoric

One indication of the importance of the myth of
return is that some Palestinian groups have modeled
their activities after the Irgun and drawn upon its
mythology. The Jerusalem Post reported in 1969 that
fifty copies of the Arabic translation of The Revolt
were captured in the possession of a Palestinian terrorist group.[1] It can only be surmised that they were
using it for training purposes. In addition, the
slogan of the PLO, "Palestine fell in a storm of fire
and steel, and it will arise in a storm of fire and
steel," is a paraphrase of the Irgun slogan, "Judea
fell in blood and fire and in blood and fire it will
arise."[2] Further, Palestinian leaders often cite the
Irgun in support of their use of terrorism. Mroz
writes:

> Arabs frequently point to Mr. Begin's
> record as a terrorist during the fight
> to achieve an Israeli state. A remark
> by one of the West Bank mayors to the
> Western press in 1978 is typical: "As
> head of the Irgun in the 1940s, Begin
> organized bombings and attacks that
> killed hundreds, mostly innocent
> people, and now he is Prime Minister

of a Jewish state. How can a Palestinian look down on violence when we
have such a shining example of what
it can accomplish in Mr. Begin.[3]

Wolf quotes a solider and trainer for El Fatah,
William Naguib Nassar:

Menachem Begin, whom I consider to be
a great man, because, although he's my
enemy he knew what to do at the right
time in 1948. He massacred the Arabs,
so they ran away, and the Jews conquered the land. When the Arabs ran
away, they spread fear among other
Arabs. And I respect him for that,
because he taught us that civilian
massacres always lead to civilian mass
flight.[4]

Not only do some Palestinian groups treat the Irgun as
a model of a successful underground organization, but
their rhetoric contains mythic appeals quite similar
to those found in the rhetoric of the Irgun. For
example, the Palestinians express a strong desire to
return to their land. As Hirst notes: "There quickly
developed a whole mystique of The Return. The inmates
of the camps, particularly, thought and spoke of
little else. They made it an obsession."[5] Yodfat and
Arnon-Ohanna make the same point: "In hundreds of
interviews, addresses and statements, PLO personali-
ties repeat the same demand--to return to Jaffa,
Haifa, etc. . . ."[6] In addition, many Palestinians
view their struggle as a return to ancient Islamic
heroism. Yodfat and Arnon-Ohanna quote Professor
Bernard Lewis: "The imagery and the symbolism of the
Fatah is strikingly Islamic. Yasser Arafat's nom de
guerre, Abu Ammar, the father of Ammar, is an allusion
to the historic figure of Ammar ibn-Yasi, the son of
Yasir, a companion of the Prophet and a valiant
fighter in all his battles."[7] Hirst quotes a Fatah
leaflet which links the Palestinian resistance to the
heroic Islamic past:

To the heroes of the Arab people in the
occupied land. We call you in the name
of Arab heroes Omar and Saladin to rise
against the foregoing occupation and pro-
hibit the Zionist occupiers from treading
on our sacred Arab land. . . . The Zion-

192

ist occupation is nothng but the rise of a new Crusade. We shall continue to rebel until the final victory.[8]

In addition, like the Irgun, the Palestinians describe themselves as trapped in a ghetto which threatens their humanity. Fawaz Turki writes in "To Be a Palestinian":

> The world of the exile. The world of the occupied. The world of the stateless. All these are worlds with blackened walls surrounding them, all these have a special tension crystallizing their reality, all these have a mosaic of active mythology that is incomprehensible to others. Few can truly understand such encapsulated worlds, their truth, their devastation, their anguish and the desolate helplessness of their denizens.[9]

And, like the Irgun, Palestinians claim to be facing a holocaust. Terzi, the PLO representative to the United Nations, compares Israeli rule over the Palestinians to the holocaust:

> But the commission has witnessed a repeated holocaust, for how else can we describe the destruction of entire villages, rendering human beings homeless and displaced? Gas chambers are not used, but there is a slow death in the refugee camps, and lately it is not that slow because fragmentation and cluster bombs are being utilized to expedite the process of annihilation and of genocide—a process that the so-called civilized world does not even deplore or condemn.[10]

They claim that this holocaust can be prevented only through struggle. The terrorists who attacked the Israeli athletes at the Munich Olympics put this very clearly: "Our land will be liberated by blood and blood alone. The world only respects the strong. We shall not be strong through words alone, but only by acting on them. . . . We want Arab youth to know how to die for their people and their country."[11] This

position is strikingly similar to that of the Irgun.
Hirst puts the Palestinian view into perspective:
"How was The Return to be accomplished? It was no
good relying on others. Not on the world community
which, year after year, passed pious resolutions upon
which it did not act. The world's sympathy goes to
revolutionaries more than it does beggars."[12] The
Palestinians reject dependence on the West. I have
not sampled any sizable percentage of Palestinian rhetoric, but the works which I have considered bear a
striking similarity to the mythic rhetoric of the
Irgun.

A number of scholars have noted the use which the
PLO makes of Irgun slogans and the similar goals of
the two groups and treated them as essentially
alike.[13] And there are similarities between the Irgun
and the PLO, but there are also essential differences. The Irgun, unlike the PLO, never aimed its
attacks at innocent civilians. It carried out operations in which civilians were killed, but the goal of
its operations was always a military objective.[14] The
PLO is, by contrast, a terrorist organization which
has blown up airliners, attacked schools, and otherwise aimed its attacks at innocent civilians. In
addition, the Irgun never used personal terror. By
contrast, the PLO has relied upon assassination.
Begin is quite correct in objecting to the equation of
the tactics of the Irgun and the PLO.

Nor is the PLO's rhetoric similar to the rhetoric
of the Irgun. The PLO has shown a great ability to
produce slogans which are interpreted in one way in
the Arab world and in another way in the West.[15]
While the Covenant of the PLO and PLO statements to
non-Western audiences make it clear that their aim is
still the destruction of Israel,[16] PLO leaders have
adapted their rhetoric for Western audiences in order
to court support and obscure their aims. By contrast,
the Irgun stuck to its real position, even when that
position would not be palatable to the intended audience.

The most important similarity between the Irgun
and PLO comes at the level of myth. Both groups
describe themselves as oppressed peoples denied access
to a homeland that is rightfully theirs. However, the
similarities between the myth of the Irgun and Palestinian rhetoric do not reflect a Palestinian myth
mirroring the myth of the Irgun. The element which

energized the myth of the Irgun, the holocaust, does not afflict the Palestinians. Despite Mr. Terzi's comparison of Israel's West Bank policies to the death camps, the Palestinians have not been threatened with annihilation. Nor have the Palestinian people been forced to live for centuries in weakness and passivity in a forced exile. The factors which led the Irgun to develop the myth of holocaust and redemption through return do not apply to the Palestinian people. It seems likely that Palestinians compare Israeli occupation of the West Bank to the holocaust and call for liberation of their homeland through blood and iron because they recognize the power of those mythic symbols and hope to tap that power through the creation of a similar myth.

Myth and Israeli Politics

The identification of the myth of return underlying Menachem Begin's ideology and rhetoric is important, not only because it clarifies PLO rhetoric, but also because it may at least partially explain Begin's relatively rapid movement from the leader of a small party to prime minister of Israel. Between 1948 and 1967, Begin served as the party leader, first of Herut and later of the Gahal coalition. Although he was an important politician in Israel, he never came remotely near to winning the post of prime minister. Then from 1967-1970, he served as a Minister without Portfolio in the Government of National Unity. His new coalition, the Likud, gained seats in the 1973 election and then won the 1977 election.[17] A partial explanation for this increase in support is Begin's ability to confront the problems of the holocaust through the myth of return.[18]

Initially, the suggestion that Begin's mythic response to the holocaust has influenced recent Israeli elections may seem ridiculous. After all, the holocaust was over in 1945. And it would seem to have been played out as an electoral force by 1967. Actually, the opposite is true. For many years, the population of Israel failed to come to grips with the holocaust.[19] Given the enormity of the crime, it is understandable that they wished to avoid thinking about it. In his study of holocaust survivors, Brenner writes: "After the Holocaust, survivors found themselves charging through life, looking neither left nor right, least of all, aside."[20] The Six Day War

195

was the watershed which began the process of coming to grips with the holocaust. As I argued earlier, many Israelis believe that their astounding victory in the Six Day War was divinely inspired, God's answer to the death camps. Given this answer, the Israeli people could begin to come to grips with the holocaust. Brenner writes:

> The Six Day War opened the sluices in the dike of collective memory which had been restraining the backed up waters of Holocaust survivors' unshed tears. Then apparently the Yom Kippur war opened the floodgates wider still.[21]

Since the Six Day War, there has been a great increase in concern for the holocaust. Memorial days have been observed, books written, and so forth.[22] It is only natural that Begin would profit politically from that increase in concern. For Begin and the Likud, the holocaust is the seminal event of our time. For the Labor Party, by contrast, the holocaust is not a part of their basic mythology.[23] Thus, it is reasonable to believe that the increase in concern for the holocaust may have aided Begin politically.

One particular aspect of Begin's myth of holocaust and redemption, the return to the ancient Hebrew heroism and the use of biblical language which goes with it, may also help explain Begin's political resurgence. Begin's myth makes it easy for him to draw upon Jewish tradition and to use the language of the Bible in confronting contemporary problems. This symbolic advantage may partially explain his party's upswing beginning in 1967. For example, Segre argues that Israel's problems

> can best be articulated in the language of the Bible through definitions of Israel's destiny such as "to be a treasure of all peoples upon the face of the earth" (Deuteronomy 14.3). This language comes quite naturally to Begin, while no other Israeli secular leader (with the exception of the late premier David Ben-Gurion, who often spoke of Israel in biblical terms) could use such phraseology without sounding ridiculous.[24]

The myth of return allows Begin to draw upon the symbolic power of the Bible, while the labor Zionist myth
offers no such advantage.

It is important that the influence of the myth of
the Irgun on Israel as a whole not be overstated. The
myth is not the "root social paradigm" for Israel.[25]
The Likud coalition represents only a plurality of
Israelis,[26] and of the component parties which make it
up, only Herut is directly tied to Begin's myth.
Moreover, many Israelis explicitly reject the myth.
Polls in 1978 and 1979 showed that almost 70 percent
of all Israelis would be willing to give up the right
to settle on the West Bank and Gaza in exchange for
secure borders.[27]   Even some of the groups on the
right fail to accept the myth. For the "Land of
Israel Movement," the holocaust is not the overriding
concern it is for Begin. There is no mention of the
holocaust in their manifesto.[28] In addition, many on
the Israeli right opposed giving the Sinai back to
Egypt, even though the Sinai was never part of the
historical land of Israel.[29] Further, Israeli society
as a whole lacks the fervor of the Irgun, and there is
great resistance to calls for a return to the time of
the Maccabees and Bar Kochba.[30] Finally, the dominant
heroes in Israel are not the former soldiers of the
Irgun, but the soldiers of the Israeli army who have
fought bravely in four wars against the Arabs. It is
not Dov Gruner, but Moshe Dayan, Ezer Weizman, Arik
Sharon, and others who are heroes.

While the Irgun's myth is not the dominant paradigm of Israel, there is reason to believe that the
myth may have caused a small but important electoral
shift. Begin's political career took a sharp upturn
in 1967. It may be only coincidence that 1967 was
also the year in which many Israelis began to think
seriously about the holocaust, but it seems likely
that at least some of the success of the Likud coalition in the years since 1967 can be traced to their
mythic return which confronts the problems raised by
the holocaust.

The Influence of the Myth of Return
on the Policies of the Begin Government

In the United States, there is a general tendency
to treat Menachem Begin as an irrational ideologue. A
Washington Post editorial appearing immediately after

Begin became prime minister of Israel reflects this view:

> Mr. Begin is an ideologue--some would say a primitive--who has had the luxury of indulging old dreams and the lazy slogans of opposition. Whether he can be educated in the complexities of the issues, and even whether he can harness the disparate factions within the Likud is unclear.[35]

These criticisms did not disappear after Begin, along with Sadat, won the Nobel Peace Prize. If anything, the criticism became more strident. How, some commentators ask, could Begin be willing to give up the Sinai to Egypt and be unwilling to settle the Palestinian problem? They react with disbelief to Begin's claim that the Old Testament establishes Jewish sovereignty over the West Bank. It is, they argue, incomprehensible that the prime minister of a Western country could base a claim to sovereignty on biblical history. Some commentators dislike Begin so intensely that they refer to him in terms which they normally reserve for Third World dictators:

> Foreign leaders of all kinds are tired of Prime Minister Begin: Of his hectoring, his self-pity, his pedantry, his demagogy, his crude abuse of anyone who disagrees with him. Indeed, some of the warmest American friends of Israel are pained by the man and fearful that he will increase Israel's isolation.[32]

Others argue that Begin is insensitive to the rights of the Palestinians.[33] In this view, Begin might best be understood as the twentieth century version of the nineteenth century American Indian fighter. He is an Arab fighter who has built his political career calling for the Israel Defense Force to attack various Arab "threats." Brecher writes: "He has no sympathy for the plight and aspirations of the occupied Palestinians."[34] The former U.S. ambassador to Syria, Talcott W. Seelye, put it more bluntly: "It is impossible for Begin to divest Israel of the West Bank. . . he is totally blind to the Palestinian problem."[35] Begin's critics conclude that he is an obstacle to peace.[36]

198

There is some truth in each of these criticisms. Begin's view of the world is shaped by the holocaust. Safran writes of Begin, "Destruction or salvation lurks behind issues that may appear to others--Israelis included--as questions of prudence, convenience, advantage or what not."[37] It is also undeniable that Begin's government blocked proposals to grant full autonomy to West Bank Palestinians. The problem is that these criticisms are too simple. They treat the holocaust as just another event, albeit a tragic one, about which the Jewish people should no longer be especially concerned. And while Begin's proposal for the West Bank did not grant full autonomy to the Palestinians, it provided for considerably more political freedom than is found in many Arab countries. The anti-Begin view also ignores the political risks Begin has taken. He faced severe criticism from many in his own party over the decision to give Sinai back to Egypt. And Begin has a point when he argues that Sadat gave Israel nothing save the diplomatic recognition which the world, apart from the Arab bloc, had granted to Israel many years before, while Israel gave Egypt thousands and thousands of square miles of strategic depth in the Sinai. Israel has made sacrifices for peace.

Begin is far more complex than is recognized by many in the press. One key to explaining that complexity lies in the recognition that Begin is a nineteenth century liberal whose life has been dominated by the myth of the holocaust and redemption through return. Philosophically, Begin embraces liberalism; his greatest hero is Garibaldi. Dolav quotes Begin on Garibaldi:

> To me he [Garibaldi] represents the ultimate freedom fighter. A man who hated wars but fought for freedom, not only for the freedom of his own people but for that of other nations too. A republican by persuasion, who, for the sake of the unification of Italy agreed to a monarchy--for the single aim of achieving unification.[38]

Based on personal conversations with Begin, Sol Linowitz writes that Begin views himself as a sort of modern Garibaldi:

In Begin's view, Garibaldi was a hero
criticized and misunderstood in his
time but a true fighter for freedom
who history came to respect and admire
in the long run. I think this is very
much the way Menachem Begin sees himself: he believes that despite present criticism, history will come to
recognize him as a fighter for freedom
who preserved his nation's security
and led in the search for peace in the
Middle East.[39]

Begin's liberalism is obvious in his attitude toward
personal freedom. His political party's name, Herut,
means freedom, and the opening chapter of The Revolt
is entitled "The Gateway to Freedom." In addition,
Begin has fought for granting the Arab population in
Israel full freedom.[40]

    While Begin is a nineteenth century liberal whose
political philosophy commits him to human freedom,
freedom is not his ultimate value. Begin's commitment
to freedom and other values has been shaped by the
holocaust. His comments about Garibaldi are particularly instructive. Begin argues that Garibaldi was a
universal freedom fighter who supported a monarchy in
order to unify Italy. Garibaldi's overriding goal was
the unification of Italy and he was willing to compromise his republican principles to achieve it. In the
same way, the overriding value for Begin is Jewish
survival in the generation of Auschwitz. The redemption which occurred, for the saved remnant of the
Jewish people, with the founding of the Israeli state
is precarious. According to Begin, the PLO is a
modern-day Nazi organization which would destroy the
Jewish people if it could. Just as no one cared about
the plight of the Jews in the 1930s, no one cares
today. Europe is more concerned with oil supplies
than it is with the survival of the Jewish state.
Even the United States cannot be counted on in a
crisis. Thus, the Jewish people must remain strong.
The world respects only those who are strong. If the
Arabs come to the conclusion that Israel is defense-
less, then the Jewish state is doomed.

    Identification of the myth of return as the
driving element in Begin's life explains why he sees
the threat of the holocaust in even small attacks on
the state of Israel. Begin is not irrational. He

knows that Israel is strong, but he believes that it was many small compromises by the West and the Jewish people that led to the death camps. Thus, he fears that compromise with the anti-Semites of the world, on even small issues, could lead to new death camps. There are grounds for his fears. The recent outbreak of vicious anti-Jewish violence in France is but one sign of continuing anti-Semitism in the world. Moreover, there are former Nazis in high positions in the West German government. It is easy to understand why Begin sees meetings between West German officials and PLO leaders, who have sworn to destroy Israel, as threatening an alliance between former and modern Nazis. Begin believes that the Jewish people still live in the world of the holocaust. Western commentators should think carefully before they criticize this attitude. A generation ago, one-third of the Jewish people were killed by a madman, and the West watched and did nothing. Moreover, the most important theologians of the holocaust—Berkovits, Rubenstein, and Fackenheim—do not believe that the holocaust world has passed. If they can see signs of a future holocaust, perhaps Begin should not be so roundly criticized for his "paranoia."

The myth through which Begin views the world also helps explain why he rejects all slights to the honor of Israel. He believes that it was the willingness of the Jewish people to put up with such slights that led to the holocaust. It was the conviction that they had to be passive and put up with abuse which made European Jews targets for the Nazis. Therefore, Begin is resolved to demand absolute equality of treatment. If President Mubarik of Egypt is unwilling to come to Jerusalem during a trip to Israel, then that shows that he does not regard the Israelis as equals; Begin, after all, went to Cairo. Begin reacted bitterly to U.S. pressure following the Golan annexation because in his view the United States was not treating Israel as an equal. It pressured Israel for concessions just as Jewish leaders have been pressured for centuries.

The myth of return also motivated Begin to order retaliatory raids in response to PLO shelling and to order the Israeli Air Force to bomb an Iraqi nuclear reactor. He was not willing to take any chances with Israeli security. No weakness must be allowed to precipitate another holocaust. Moreover, since it is only strength which deters the enemies of Israel, no

201

force on earth could prevent Begin from acting, if he were convinced that Israel was endangered. The raid on the Iraqi reactor illustrates this point. The leaders of the Israeli Labor party opposed the raid and Begin undoubtedly knew that the United States and Western Europe would roundly criticize the action. He also knew that the Soviets and the Arab bloc would treat the raid as evidence of Israeli expansionist tendencies, and he knew that the raid might fail. Yet, none of these concerns prevented Begin from acting. The reactor was a potential threat to Israeli security. Therefore, Israel must destroy it. Were Begin still prime minister, he would not hesitate to order the use of military force in a preemptive invasion of an Arab country if he believed Israeli security were at stake. Where other leaders might temporize or call for United Nations action or superpower intervention, Begin would reject all dependence on outside forces and act. He trusts in nothing but the strength of the Israeli Defense Force to prevent aggression against Israel. Begin's model for the defense of Israel is the ancient Hebrew army which dealt out seven blows for every one it received. The modern state of Israel can remain safe only by following a similar policy.

In addition, the myth of return is the energizing force behind Begin's commitment to fight for all of Israel. Begin does not view the West Bank as territory available for settlements or even as land, some of which is needed to establish a defensible border. The West Bank is Judea and Samaria. It was given by God to the people of Israel. And it is from the land God gave the Jews that the strength of the Jewish people comes. Begin was able to compromise on Sinai because it was not part of ancient Israel. Once his fears about defense of the Negev were satisfied, Sinai could be exchanged for a peace treaty with Egypt: "For Begin, the equation is simple: Sinai is not part of the historical Land of Israel, so he could be generous about it: Hebron is part of the historical Eretz Israel, so it is 'inconceivable' to him that Jews should not be able to live there."[41]

The myth of return also explains Begin's "inability to understand the Arabs." Begin is not racist or anti-Arab. On the contrary, he is a liberal who undoubtedly wishes that the Arab people of Palestine could live in a democratic state. From the beginning of the revolt, the Irgun promised equal treatment for

202

the Arab minority in Palestine, and since the revolt, Herut has supported full freedom for the Arab population in Israel. Begin is a genuine republican who is concerned with freedom. Nor were Begin's West Bank policies, at least until the fall of 1981, particularly harsh. A November 1978 <u>Middle East</u> report described the West Bank occupation:

> It is certainly a subtle form of occupation. Overseas journalists are free to roam around the whole West Bank and meet prominent Palestinians openly.
> On a physical level, the Israeli occupation is equally discreet. The 2,200 or so Israeli soldiers stationed in the areas are rarely seen especially during the day. Their job is essentially manning check-points for identity control. . . ."[42]

In addition, the policies of the Begin government were not appreciably tougher than the policies of the Labor governments that preceded it. In fact, a scholar of Tel Aviv University's Shiloah Centre found that there had been significantly fewer homes destroyed, prisoners put in administrative detention, and Palestinians expelled in the first three years of the Begin government than under previous Labor governments.[43] And prior to the crackdown on the PLO in the spring of 1982, the Begin government tried to liberalize its policies on the West Bank. United Press International reported:

> New directives issued by the Defense Ministry forbid troops to enter school campuses or set up roadblocks, considered a harrassment by the local populace. The sources said the directives also require Israeli troops to refrain from invoking collective punishment measures.[44]

While Begin is genuinely concerned with the rights of all people, his driving concern is to protect the Jewish people from a future holocaust. The myth of return through which he fights the holocaust has no room for the Arabs. According to his view of the world, the rights of the Jews take precedence over Arab rights. Unlike the Jews, the Arabs were not threatened with the holocaust. In fact, a number of Arab leaders actually sided with the Germans. Nor have the Arabs suffered for 2,000 years without a state of their own. Today, the Arabs have a number of states. Most important, in Begin's view, the Arabs have no right to the land. The land of Israel was given to the Jewish people by God.

Begin's references to the Arabs in The Revolt support the claim that his mythic perspective prevents him from recognizing Palestinian rights. First, Begin describes the Arabs as dishonest and not particularly brave. He tells the story of an agreement between Jewish and Arab forces in Jerusalem not to use the Christian church as a base for fighting. The Arabs broke their word: "Several hours after our men had withdrawn, the Arabs came into the church and opened murderous fire on the Hebrew defenders."[45] Begin also describes the bloody Arab attacks on the Jews in 1920, 1921, 1929, 1936, and 1939 and concludes that the Arabs attacked not because of their own bravery, but because of Jewish weakness:

> The psychological consequence of these one-sided attacks were as disastrous as their political aftermath. The Arabs who, while they cannot be accused of undue cowardice, are not regarded as particularly courageous, began seriously to look upon the Jew as a walad-al-mawt--child of death-- and to look forward to the great festival of "bashel-yahud," of general slaughter. (48)

In addition, Begin undercuts the Arab claim to Palestine by noting that the "region is almost entirely empty. Here and there, in the wide expanse you see a Bedouin hovel or a camel" (p. 24). These statements reflect the Irgun's attitude that the Palestinian Arabs had no legitimate nationalist movement. Unlike the heroic soldiers of the Irgun, the Arabs fought because of the bloodlust and the ease of killing Jews. Begin's reference to Jewish passivity as the factor which led to Arab attacks is also revealing. Here, Begin argues that passivity in Palestine leads to disaster for the Jewish people, just as passivity led to the holocaust in Europe. Begin also denies the legitimacy of the Arab movement in Palestine by claim ing that it was instigated by the British (pp. 48, 334).

Also, Begin believed that the Arabs had very little to lose if a Jewish state were established:

> We [the Irgun] told the Arabs that we had no desire to fight or harm them; that we were anxious to see them as peaceful citizens of the Jewish State-to-be; we pointed to the undeniable fact that in our operations in Arab areas there had been not the slightest intrusion on Arab peace or security. (pp. 49-50)

The key point is that they could become free citizens in the "Jewish State." When various parties proposed arrangements in which the Jews were to be granted substantial local autonomy within an Arab state, the Irgun angrily rejected the proposals. The Irgun believed that the land was granted by God to the Jews. Why should they have to share it with anyone? By contrast, the Irgun's proposals did not even grant the Arabs cultural autonomy. They were to be Arab citizens in a Jewish state. Begin believes quite strongly that the Palestinian Arabs deserve freedom and political equality. He does not believe they deserve a state of their own. Again, it is Jewish claims which take precedence.

It also should be noted that Begin views Jewish security as much more important than the rights of the Arab population of Palestine. For example, Begin writes of Irgun reprisals against Arab "rioters":

> After two weeks of Arab attacks the soldiers of the Irgun launched the first counter-attack by Jewish forces. For three days, from 11th to 13th December, our units hammered at concentrations of rioters and their offensive bases. We attacked at Haifa and Jaffa; at Tireh and Yazur. We attacked again and again in Jerusalem. We went up to the aggressive village of Shaafat on the road to the Hebrew University. We penetrated Yeudiyeh and dealt preemptorily with an armed band that had established its base in

the village. Enemy casualities in killed and wounded were very high. (pp. 337-338)

What Begin does not mention is that the retaliatory raids inevitably killed innocent civilians. In some cases, the Irgun threw bombs into crowds of Arab civilians.[46] As commander of the Irgun, he felt it was essential that the Arab attacks be met with Jewish retaliation. And it was necessary to retaliate even if the Arabs responsible for the original attack could not be identified. It was unfortunate that innocent people were killed, but in the age of Auschwitz, Jews would no longer passively accept their casualties. They would and must strike back, because the world is impressed only by strength.

It is this same attitude which lead Prime Minister Begin to order Israeli bombing raids into Lebanon. Some observers saw the Israeli raids, in the five years before the full scale invasion of Lebanon in June 1982, as totally out of proportion to the damage which the PLO caused in Israel. Many more people were killed in the Israeli attacks than were killed in the PLO raids.[47] To Begin, the Israeli air attacks on PLO camps were a necessity. It was important that the PLO and the world understand that the Jews will never die passively again. Israel will strike and strike hard against any attacker. In fact, the raids, in Lebanon might best be understood as rituals through which Begin enacted his continuing commitment to the myth of holocaust and return. Through the raids Begin could fight against the holocaust and prove to the world that the Jews were not weak. This is not to deny that the raids were aimed at military objectives, but the underlying motive behind them was mythic not military. Occasional PLO shelling of northern Israel did not necessitate massive air raids on Beirut. Begin ordered those air raids because he interpreted the PLO shelling as a sign that the Jews were still threatened by the holocaust. Through the raids, Begin ritually reaffirmed his commitment to the myth of return.

For Begin, the security of the Jewish population comes before the rights of the Arab population, even if many innocent Arabs must die or lose their homes. Begin believes that 2,000 years of suffering, the holocaust, and God's eternal grant of the land of Palestine to the Jews gave them rights which are more important than the rights of the Arab population. His comments about the Arabs in The Revolt appear paradoxical. On the one hand, he is committed to granting the Arab population of Palestine full rights within a Jewish state and encouraging economic and political cooperation between Arabs and Jews. On the other hand, he attacks the Arabs as liars and cowards, claims that there was no legitimate Arab nationalist movement, and justifies retaliatory attacks in which innocent Arabs were killed. These apparently contradictory positions can be explained as growing out of the interaction between the myth of return and Begin's nineteenth century liberal perspective. Begin supports democratic principles and believes that all humans possess certain basic rights. However, viewed through his mythic perspective, the rights of Arabs are less important than the rights of Jews.

Begin is not anti-Arab as such, but his mythic perspective makes it impossible for him to see the Arab point of view. In this light, his position on autonomy for the West Bank is understandable. The autonomy regulations which Begin offered to Sadat at Ismailiya provided considerably more freedom than is found in many Arab countries, but they did not offer real autonomy.[48] Moreover, the Begin government ruled the West Bank under the Emergency Defense Regulations promulgated by the British in September 1945,[49] regulations promulgated to fight Begin and the Irgun. This is not the only irony. The autonomy plan which Begin proposed at Ismailiya bears a striking resemblance to the autonomy proposal for all of Palestine which the British made in 1947.[50] In the British proposal, Arab and Jewish residents of Palestine were to be granted some local autonomy for five years, at the end of which time the situation was to be reviewed. Begin's original autonomy plan granted local autonomy to Arab residents within the confines of Israeli military rule. The Camp David accords incorporated the five-year review period. It is a mistake to interpret Begin as an "Arab fighter" or Arab-hater.[51] He undoubtedly regrets the necessity of using force on the West Bank and he is committed, in general, to freedom of speech and press and free elections. But in the generation of holocaust and redemption, he sees no other choice than to strike hard at the PLO and limit Arab rights in Judea and Samaria. Begin will never willingly cede Israeli claims of sovereignty over the West Bank or allow a truly autonomous Palestinian state to be established. Such a state would inevitably deny Jews the right to settle on land given to their heroic forefathers by God, and it could threaten the existence of Israel.

The influence of the myth of return on Begin's ideology and policy decisions is also made clear in the most controversial act of his government, the June 1982 Israeli invasion of Lebanon. To many, the Israeli decision seemed totally irrational.[52] The attempted assassination of the Israeli ambassador in London was a horrible act, but, in this view, it hardly justified a full-scale invasion of Lebanon. Nor, according to Begin's critics, did PLO shelling of northern Israel. There had been relatively little shelling after the cease fire between the PLO and Israel negotiated by U.S. envoy Philip Habib in 1982. Some critics of Israel admitted that a limited Israel invasion to clear the PLO out of southern Lebanon and establish a buffer zone protecting northern Israel could be justified, but they drew the line at the Israel advance on Beirut. According to this view, the civilian casualties created by the Israeli assault were out of proportion to the defense needs of Israel. Even supporters of Israel opposed the war. Some argued that the political costs of the invasion were far too high. Others opposed the war on moral grounds. They argued that in its previous wars Israel had fought for its very survival, but in Lebanon it needlessly killed innocent civilians. In John Chancellor's words, the invasion of Lebanon represented the actions of a radically new Israel, an "Imperial Israel."[53] To many critics and supporters of Israel alike, the invasion of Lebanon seemed the height of folly and reinforced their view that Begin was irrational.

When viewed from the perspective of the myth of return, Begin's decision to invade Lebanon is not surprising. If anything, it is surprising that he waited so long to order the army of Israel to attack. The myth through which Begin sees the world requires that Israel strike against any threat, and the PLO gunners in southern Lebanon were a very real threat to the Israeli people. They killed relatively few Israelis but posed a constant danger to all of the citizens of northern Israel. Moreover, Begin believes that it is weakness which precipitates attacks on the Jewish people. If Israel allowed the PLO gunners to shell Israel occasionally, the result would eventually be disaster. In addition, the invasion of Lebanon was a chance to strike at the modern Nazis, the PLO. In an

208

interview in the <u>Wall Street Journal</u> published during the invasion of Lebanon, Begin compared Yassir Arafat to Hitler. He said that he would never trust Arafat regardless of the promises Arafat might make: "I wouldn't believe Hitler, or Goering or Goebbels and I will never believe Arafat. . . ."[54] From Begin's perspective, the invasion made perfect sense. It was necessary to defend the Israeli people, prove to the world that Israel was not weak, and strike at the new Nazis.

The Israeli decision to push on to Beirut after having cleared out a buffer zone in southern Lebanon is also comprehensible in light of Begin's mythic world view. When the first days of the war went very well, Begin saw the chance to destroy the new Nazis and took it. Israeli shelling of civilian areas can be explained in this light. The Israel Defense Force (IDF) made every effort to avoid killing civilians,[55] but overriding this aim was the commitment to destroy the PLO. There must be no weakness which the PLO could use. The PLO must not be allowed to hide behind women and children even if some women and children were killed as a consequence. And the PLO, in fact, attempted to hide behind innocent civilians.

Further, it was also the myth of return which lay behind Israel's hard-line negotiating stance during the invasion. For example, on August 3, 1982, Israel launched a major assault into Beirut despite word from U.S. envoy Habib that an agreement was all but worked out. Begin ordered the attack because he believed that the PLO would take advantage of any weakness.[56] He believed that only military pressure would force the PLO to negotiate in good faith. The Israeli rejection of a U.N. peace-keeping force is also explicable in light of the failure of the U.N. peace-keeping force in southern Lebanon to prevent PLO shelling of Israel. Moreover, Begin's mythic perspective predisposed him to trust only the Israel Defense Force.

Finally, Begin's response to criticism of the invasion also reflected the myth of return. At several points, Begin reacted quite sharply to Israel's critics. While on a trip to the United States, he angrily rejected criticism of the invasion by members of the U.S. Senate Foreign Relations Committee.[57] When he heard a rumor that the United States was considering sanctions against Israel, he sent a message to the Israeli cabinet to ignore all threats and base their decision only upon the security needs of Israel.[58] He responded angrily when Senator Charles Percy called for sanctions against Israel saying: "Nobody is going to bring Israel to her knees. You must have forgotten that Jews do not kneel but to God."[59] Politically, Begin's bitter responses to criticism seemed ill-advised. Israel needs the United States, and his harsh statements could only offend U.S. leaders. However, his absolute rejection of all criticism is understandable in light of his beliefs that the world respects only strength, and that it was weakness which led to Auschwitz. Begin saw the invasion of Lebanon in June 1982 as part of the continuing battle against the holocaust. In a statement to the Conference of Presidents of Major Jewish Organizations he said:

> Not one Katyusha [Soviet-made PLO rocket] will ever again fall on our people. Never again. We don't ask for more than other people, but we will never accept a situation in which the Jewish people have less [sic] rights than other nations. These attacks must be stopped under all circumstances.[60]

The phrase "Never again" links the invasion to the holocaust. "Never again" is a code phrase expressing the commitment of the Jewish people to reject weakness in order to guarantee that there are no new death camps.

At this point, it should be clear that the aspects of Begin's political ideology which are often criticized as irrational or inconsistent are neither. Begin's political views have been shaped by his liberal values and the myth of return. From the perspective of the myth, Begin's policies made perfect sense. Those commentators who treat Begin as a hopelessly irrational ideologue fundamentally misunderstand the man. In addition, their criticism of Begin's specific policies ignores the larger issue. If Begin is right about the continuing dangers of the holocaust and the need for return to all of the land of Israel in order to fight it, then the criticisms of his autonomy and retaliatory policies lose their force. Those policies may have unpleasant side effects, but if they are needed to fight the holocaust then they should be implemented. The validity of Begin's policies rests on the value of his myth as an answer to the holocaust. To evaluate Begin and his policies fairly, the critic must first critique the myth of holocaust and redemption through return as an answer to the holocaust.

The Social Worth of the Myth of Return

It is often difficult to evaluate fairly the quality of a rhetorical work. The effect of a given speech or essay may be difficult to measure. Moreover, effective rhetoric may succeed through unethical practices. Hitler's anti-Semitic rhetoric was quite effective, though highly unethical. It is no easier to utilize other critical standards. Aesthetic standards are notoriously difficult to apply objectively. It is also difficult to identify ethical standards which are both stringent and reasonable. Fortunately, in evaluating the quality of a rhetorical myth, there is an alternative method of analysis. Rather than applying a general standard drawn from a theory of the nature of good rhetoric to a particular work, the critic can evaluate the myth based on whether it serves its social function.

I argued earlier that the function of myth in modern societies is to resolve those social problems which cannot be answered through other means. Myths are used where discursive symbolism is inadequate. Based on its function, the critic can evaluate the symbolic quality of the myth, by asking whether it answers the question which led to its creation. The critic considers whether the world view encapsulated in the myth resolves the social problem facing the society. Here, the myth is evaluated much as the value of a theorem as an answer to a scientific problem would be evaluated by a scientist. The critic asks whether the myth symbolically answers the problem it confronts.

By evaluating myth as a symbolic answer to a problem, the critic avoids the problems associated with other methods of evaluation, e.g., the dangers associated with evaluating the effectiveness of a work and the problem of identifying universally applicable aesthetic standards. Finally, by evaluating myth as a problem-solving model the critic avoids the difficulty of developing objective and fair ethical standards. The critic is not concerned with applying universal ethical standards to the myth, but with whether a

211

specific myth fulfills its function. Of course, this
standard loses its value if there is any question
about the ethical value of solving the problem at
which the myth is aimed. For example, it might be
argued that the problem to which Hitler's Nazi myth
responded was the Jewish problem. If the goal of the
Nazi myth were defined in such a manner, then the myth
must be judged a horrible success. In that case, the
goal of the myth could not serve as a useful evalua-
tive standard, because the goal itself is unethical.
However, in the case of Begin's myth, this problem
does not arise. There is no ethical problem with
searching for a solution to the questions raised by
the holocaust.

At this point, some might object that the critic
has no means of evaluating whether the myth solved its
problem, save a consideration of audience response.
While there is no scientifically precise means of
making such an evaluation, the critic, as an unbiased
expert,[61] can ask whether the "logical model"[62] contained in the myth adequately resolves the social
problem which the myth confronts. In this case, the
question to be considered is whether the myth of holocaust and redemption through return resolves the three
fundamental problems raised by the holocaust: 1) Where
was God during the holocaust? 2) Why did the Jewish
people obey the Nazis and go willingly to their
graves? 3) How can the Jews survive in a world which
does not care?

The myth of return faces the same religious problems as do the traditional responses to the holocaust,
critiqued by Rubenstein. According to Begin, God acts
in history and intervened to aid the revolt. This
position leads quickly to the conclusion that God
could have intervened to prevent the death camps, but
chose not to act. A God who could intervene at Jaffa
could also intervene at Auschwitz. This raises the
question: Why would God give miraculous assistance to
the Irgun, but not the six million? While Begin does
not directly consider this question in either The
Revolt or Irgun rhetoric, there is one factor which
might explain God's inaction: Jewish passivity in the
face of death. The Jews at Auschwitz were weak; they
died on their knees. The soldiers of the Irgun were
active; they fought as heroes. Thus, the Irgun's myth
might be interpreted as a logical model explaining
that God acts in history to aid those who help themselves. God did not act at Auschwitz, because passive

212

Jews did not deserve his aid. The sin of passivity was punished with divine inaction.

While this interpretation resolves the logical difficulty of explaining the existence of a God and his failure to act during the holocaust, it is an unsatisfying answer. It suggests that the Nazis were the agent God used to punish the Jews for the passivity. Most Jews find this answer unacceptable. In his study of holocaust survivors, Brenner found that only nine percent see the holocaust as a manifestation of God's will.[63] Only two percent of survivors see the holocaust as punishment for the sins of the six million.[64] Brenner does not report any Jews who believe that the holocaust was punishment for Jewish weakness. They reject this answer, because it does not avoid Rubenstein's argument that no heavenly purpose could justify the slaughter of six million Jews. According to Rubenstein, a God who would sentence six million Jews to death for the crime of passivity (or any other reason) can only be characterized as a cosmic sadist.[65] Begin's myth may be interpreted to explain God's inaction at Auschwitz, but not to justify it. The myth of return fails to resolve the religious problems raised by the death camps.

The myth is more successful in resolving the psychological problems raised by the holocaust. It explains that the Jewish people did not fight back against the Nazis because they lost their strength during twenty centuries of dispersion and exile. It thus serves as a logical model explaining Jewish passivity in the death camps. At the same time, the myth provides the Jewish people with models of bravery. David Raziel, Dov Gruner, and others serve as the examples who prove that the Jews can fight heroically. The myth provides both the explanation for past passivity and a model of future heroism. Thus, by participating in the myth (through the underground fight itself, political action in support of the Irgun or later Herut, or through rituals supporting the myth) a Jew could wash away the guilt created by Jewish passivity during the holocaust. It is not only "heroic deed [that] efface the images of Maidanek and Treblinka . . ."[66] but also the retelling of those deeds and ritual participation in them through the myth of holocaust and redemption through return that serves the same cleansing function.

While the myth of return resolves the guilt associated with the holocaust, this resolution is not
achieved without a cost. The myth resolves the problems of the holocaust by placing responsibility for it
on Jewish passivity and, therefore, on the Jewish community itself. Although Begin bitterly attacks the
British and the Nazis for their actions against the
Jewish people, it is really the Jewish people themselves who are to blame. Jewish defenselessness is
the sin which precipitated the holocaust. He writes
in The Revolt that the "inexcusable" defenselessness
of the Jewish people was "a standing invitation to
massacre them" (p. xii). It was the Jews who caused
the holocaust through their own powerlessness. Thus,
while the myth of return resolves Jewish guilt created
in the holocaust, it does so by placing the blame for
the holocaust on the Jews themselves.

Begin's myth also calls upon the Jewish people to
throw away 2000 years of Jewish culture because that
culture was based on passivity and weakness. Hans
Kohn writes of this reaction in Israeli youth:

> Many of the young Israeli generation
> in Palestine not only look down on the
> native Arabs; they have turned also,
> with pride in their own valor and in
> bitter disgust, from the two thousand
> years of the diaspora, from the life
> of the fathers and grandfathers, which
> they reject. They have cut themselves
> off from the "ghetto" and they try to
> restore a link with a far-off primi-
> tive past. Over thousands of years
> they stretch out their hands to reach
> the zealots who died defending Bethar,
> Masada, and Jerusalem; the Maccabees
> who threw off the foreign yoke. . . .[67]

Begin may personally love the culture of the Diaspora
and pay tribute to the greatness which was once the
Jewish community in Poland and Germany, but his myth
leads Israelis, like the young Israelis of whom Kohn
writes, to reject it. This attitude led many Sabras
to refer to those who had survived the extermination
camp as "soap."[68] In Fackenheim's terms, the myth
grants Hitler a final victory, because it puts the
blame for the holocaust not on Hitler's evil, the
bureaucratic mentality of the Germans, or the amorali-
ty of the Allies, but upon the Jews themselves.

214

While Begin's myth of return resolves the guilt created by the holocaust, it does so only by placing the ultimate blame for the holocaust on the Jews themselves. Begin's answer to the holocaust is too simple. He does not recognize, as does Fackenheim with his 614th commandment and Commanding Voice, that no single answer to the holocaust can be both adequate and consistent. A myth is needed which recognizes the need for Jewish strength, vigilance, courage, and blood and which also recognizes that it was not the Jews, but the evil of the Nazis and others which caused the holocaust. The myth should recognize that the passivity with which Jewish leaders in the Diaspora responded to the Nazis was a strategy that had been used successfully to respond to persecution for over two thousand years.[69] Both Wiesel and Fackenheim have created complex myths which contain a number of competing answers to the holocaust. In Wiesel's mythology, the Jews who fought in the Irgun are heroic, but so are the Jews who died anonymously in the death camps.[70] Wiesel's myth presents in story form several answers to the holocaust. It is the nature of myths which confront a very difficult problem to respond through stories creating several competing answers to the problem. Similarly, with his Commanding Voice and 614th commandment Fackenheim creates several responses to the holocaust. He argues that the presence of inconsistent stories in a single mythology may reveal important truths.[71] Compared to the holocaust mythology of Fackenheim and Wiesel, Begin's myth of return is simplistic.

The final question to be considered is whether the myth of return so energizes Jews that a future holocaust is made impossible. Begin believes that by returning to the entire land of Israel and the heroism of the ancient Hebrew soldiers that Jewish people can be protected forever. At one level, the myth of return responds to the issue of Jewish survival. It guarantees that the Jews will be capable of defending themselves. If such a myth had energized Jewish life in the 1930s, the death camps could not have occurred. The Jewish people would have armed themselves and fought the Nazis. They might have been slaughtered by the S.S., but they would have died fighting.

While the myth of return fills the need for a model of Jewish resolve and heroism in the age of the holocaust, the myth also contains elements which make it likely that the Jewish people will be forced to

215

fight for their security. In other words, if the myth of return is accepted by the government of Israel, the chances for peace in the Middle East are reduced. There are two specific aspects of the myth which make it difficult for Begin and Israel to make peace with the Arab world. The myth requires that Israel respond instantly with overwhelming force to any threat and forbids compromise on the sovereignty over the West Bank.

If Israel is threatened, the myth of return requires that Israel act immediately. Therefore, Begin sent raids into Lebanon and bombed the Iraqi nuclear reactor. If there is any evidence of danger to the Israeli state, Israel must act instantly. They cannot wait to see if the threat is a bluff or if negotiations can eliminate the threat. In a region as explosive as the Middle East, it is inevitable that incidents will occur which will force the Israelis to attack. Any time an Arab country develops a weapon or a weapons capability which could someday threaten Israel, the myth requires that Israel attack preemptively. In their novel, The Fifth Horseman, Dominique Lapiere and Larry Collins, two journalists who have written about the 1948 Arab-Israeli war, create a fictional scenario to which Libya obtains nuclear weapons. After discovering that the Libyans have the bomb, Begin immediately orders a preemptive nuclear strike.[72] The work is fiction, but Lapiere and Collins accurately portray Begin's attitude. If Israel is threatened, he would order an immediate and overwhelming attack.

The myth also makes compromise on the sovereignty of the West Bank impossible. The West Bank is Judea and Samaria. It is part of God's original land grant to the Jewish people. The Arab inhabitants of the West Bank may be given some local autonomy. They may be given the right to vote for their own mayors. They may be given some modern Israeli services. But they will never be given title to the land.

The Palestinians view the situation from a very different perspective. They believe that the land is theirs by right of centuries of use. In his novel about the Irgun, Arthur Koestler states the Palestinian view through the mouth of an Arab character: "I care not for their hospitals and their schools. This is our country, you understand? We want no foreign benefactors. We want not to be patronised. We

216

want to be left alone, you understand! We want to live our own way. . . ."[73] As long as Israeli leaders view the West Bank as land which was given to the Jewish people by God, the chances of responding to the needs of the Palestinians and successfully resolving the West Bank dispute are quite slim.

Despite the annexation of the Golan Heights and the extremely bitter relations between Syria and Israel, there is a greater chance of an agreement between Syria and Israel on the Golan than of resolving the West Bank dispute. The Golan was never part of the land of Israel and part of the Golan could be returned to Syria without hurting Israeli security. Begin conceivably could compromise there. It is difficult to see how any such compromise could occur to resolve the West Bank dispute.

Without the resolution of the West Bank problem, the chances for war in the Middle East increase dramatically. As long as millions of Palestinians hate Israel and demand its destruction, there is always a risk of war. Moreover, with the high Palestinian birthrate, the Arab population in Israel and the occupied territories is increasing much faster than the Jewish population. If Israel annexes the West Bank with its massive Arab population, it is only a matter of time before there are more Arabs and Jews. In such a circumstance, the Arabs would undoubtedly demand self-determination, and Israel would either lose its Jewish character or be forced militarily to repress the Palestinian majority. In that case, it is hard to imagine Israel avoiding war.

A final indication that the myth of holocaust and redemption makes it difficult to achieve peace comes from comparing the myths of the Irgun and the PLO. I noted earlier that the PLO has imitated the myth of the Irgun. When two groups with mirror-image mythologies collide, the result can only be conflict. Both sides see the land as theirs by right. Both oppose any compromise and treat the other side as the devil incarnate. There is no room for peace.

When the myth of return is carried to its logical conclusion, the result can be only more war. The chance for peace in the Middle East depends upon compromise by both sides. It requires that both sides take small risks in order to reach a final settlement.[74] The myth of return precludes such action.

217

The myth provides the heroic models to energize the Jewish people in self-defense; however, it also makes it more difficult to achieve peace. Israel is surrounded by one hundred million Arabs. While Israel has defeated the Arabs four times in thirty-five years and is far and away the most powerful military force in the region, with each war the chances of defeat increase.[75] Three and one-half million Jews cannot defeat one hundred million Arabs forever. Several hundred years ago, crusaders tried to defend their state in the Holy Land with force of arms. They succeeded for a time, but eventually the sheer numbers of the Arab forces overwhelmed them. Israel faces a similar problem today.

This study is not intended to evaluate the military and political policies of Israel, but to note the implications of the myth of return for those policies. The myth of return makes it exeedingly difficult for Begin or any other Israeli prime minister who accepts the myth to resolve the Palestinian problem. It also makes it quite likely that the Israelis will strike preemptively against some future threat. Therefore, the myth makes it difficult to achieve a comprehensive peace.

Moreover, another myth might provide the heroic model for fighting the holocaust without including the dangerous elements found in Begin's myth. A myth which called for Jewish strength and courage, but which did not demand that every threat be crushed immediately and which did not demand Israeli sovereignty over the West Bank, would be more likely to protect the Jews from both a future holocaust and a future war than would Begin's myth. Such an alternative myth would energize the Jewish people in self-defense; at the same time it would increase the chances for peaceful resolution of disputes in the region.

At least one critic argues that a barrier to peace in the Middle East is that the Arab-Israeli problem has been raised to the level of myth. Yehiam Weitz writes: "But when the conflict is mythical there is no possibility of compromise--the solution must be total, radical and unambiguous--them or us. The conflict's end--black or white, but never anything in the middle."[76] I suggest that Weitz is wrong, not because he is mistaken about the danger inherent in myth, but because myth is inevitable. All societies

218

need myths to provide the ultimate answers. In the aftermath of the holocaust, the Jewish people needed a mythic response.

The real problem with the myth of return is that its answer is too limited. It tells religious Jews that they need not lose faith, God still acts in the world after the holocaust. But it does not explain why a just God would not act to save his people at Auschwitz. It resolves some Jewish guilt by creating a heroic model, but does so by placing the blame for the holocaust upon the Jewish people themselves. It creates a formidable model of heroism and self-defense, but only at the cost of making it very difficult to achieve peace.

A number of students of mythology have made a somewhat similar point in their analysis of the more general question: Which types of myth most successfully fulfill their social functions? Joseph Campbell argues that there is no longer room in the modern world for myths of a chosen people.[77] He claims that such myths inevitably divide a society into the chosen and the cabbage-growers and end by weakening the society. MacIver makes much the same point when he notes: "A multi-group society is a multi-myth society. Its appropriate form of government can be based only on some form of myth that accommodates conflicting myths, and as we shall see that condition is met by the myth of democracy."[78] Frye argues that myths define a culture both by inclusion and exclusion. In his view, a society with a single myth has a closed mythology. The closed mythology leads to the exclusion of some people from that society. The result is prejudice and discrimination.[79] The point which Frye, Campbell, and MacIver make is that in a society which possesses only a single myth, those who do not accept that myth are bound to be excluded. And when a society defines itself through a myth of the "chosen people," the rights of those who are chosen (the reborn Hebrew heroes) must take precedence over the rights of those who are not (the Palestinians).

In his analysis of the symbolic dimensions of language, Kenneth Burke develops the same point in a slightly different way. Burke argues that inherent in the nature of language is the desire to find the proper name for a particular object. In his view:

219

The principle of perfection is central to the nature of language as motive. The mere desire to name something by its "proper" name, or to speak a language in its most distinctive ways is intrinsically "perfectionist." What is more "perfectionist" in essence than the impulse, when one is in dire need of something, to so state this need that one in effect "defines" the situation? And even a poet who works out cunning ways of distorting language does so with perfectionist principles in mind. . . .[80]

This perfectionist tendency forces humans to carry out the implications of their symbolic systems:

A given terminology contains various implications, and there is a corresponding "perfectionist" tendency for men to attempt carrying out those implications. Thus, each of our scientific nomenclatures suggests its own special range of possible developments. . . . Insofar as any of these terminologies happen also to contain the risks of destroying the world, that's just too bad. . . . There is a kind of "terministic compulsion" to carry out the implications of one's terminology.[81]

Here, Burke explains why societies with a single myth often go haywire. The closed myth is the terminology which defines the society. Every terminology and, therefore, every myth contains the seeds of its own perfection. However, in the process of "perfecting it," those groups in the society who do not accept the myth may be discriminated against and ultimately destroyed. The Nazi myth defined Aryans as the chosen people and Jews as both subhuman and the cause of the world's evil. Given the human tendency to take a myth "to the end of the line," the Nazi myth led inevitably to the death camps. Begin's myth leads inevitably to more conflict in the Middle East.

Burke sees no way to eliminate the perfectionist tendency in humans. The seeds of destruction are inherent in any terminology. However, while the danger inherent in the perfectionist tendency to take myth to the end of the line cannot be avoided, it can be controlled. If a society possesses a number of myths, then those myths can compete against each other and control each other. Burke writes of the value of competing terminologies:

> Whereas there seems to be no principle of control intrinsic to the ideal of carrying out any such set of possibilities to its "perfect" conclusion, and whereas all sorts of people are variously goaded to track down their particular sets of terministically directed insights, there is at least the fact that the schemes get in one another's way, thus being to some extent checked by rivalry with one another.[82]

It is through such symbolic competition that the danger inherent in myth can be controlled.

Burke, Frye, Campbell, and MacIver all make the same point in slightly different ways. Every society needs myth, but the vast symbolic powers of myth pose dangers as well as fill needs for a society. Any single myth may be perfected and end up excluding some members of the society. The only hope is for a society with a plurality of myths or a single myth which contains multiple elements. The various myths can answer the needs of the various groups in the society and compete against each other to prevent the perfectionist disaster of which Burke writes.

Conclusion

The views of Campbell, Frye, MacIver, and Burke help explain the failings of Begin's myth of return. The myth is too simple. When taken to the end of the line, this myth places the blame for the holocaust on the Jews themselves, depicts God as a sadist, and makes it almost impossible to attain peace. The only answer lies in a group of competing myths. Israel needs myths which call for a return, not only to the warriors of ancient Israel, but also the prophets and peacemakers. It needs myths which glorify the culture developed in two thousand years of exile, as well as myths which attack passivity. It needs myths which

221

emphasize the traditional Jewish desire to aid the poor (in this case the Palestinians) as well as myths which tell the story of Jewish heroism against Arab attacks. Israel needs a group of myths which each contain a measure of the truth, a part of the answer.

Emil Fackenheim's response to the holocaust illustrates the needs for a plurality of myths to respond to a given problem. The four fragments of Fackenheim's Commanding Voice contradict each other.[83] How can the Jewish people place their own survival above other questions and not give up their concern for the rights of all people? What if the two positions conflict? I suggest that Fackenheim's answer to the holocaust is more satisfactory than that of Rubenstein, Berkovits, or Begin, because he recognizes that truth is not singular. There is a need for the Jewish people to protect themselves, but if such self-protection were the only value, then Jewish aggression might be condoned. There is also need for the Jewish people, after the holocaust, to fight for the rights of all people. But the Jews must beware of fighting for the freedom of all people while allowing their own security to be threatened. Fackenheim is saying that there is no one answer to the holocaust. His four fragments from the Commanding Voice function as four myths which compete with each other. The four fragments limit the others to protect the Jewish people from the danger inherent in any single terminology. Fackenheim's insight explains the flaw in Begin's myth of holocaust and redemption. Begin is quite right to be concerned with protecting the Jewish people, but by making this the only value his myth fails to accomplish its aim. What is needed, then, is a competing mythology against which the ultimate value of security can be balanced. A new mythology is needed which recognizes Israel's need for strength to survive, but which also recognizes that strength by itself is not the answer to the holocaust.

Notes

[1] "Begin, Mao in Arabic Found in Gaza Strip," _Jerusalem Post_, 8 April 1969, Inter-Documentation Company Microfiche. IDC collected articles from the _Jerusalem Post_ on Begin and reprinted them on microfiche. The IDC microfiche do not include page numbers.

[2] See Eitan Haber, Zeev Schiff, and Ehud Yaari, _The Year of the Dove_ (New York: Bantam, 1979), p. 242.

[3] John Edwin Mroz, _Beyond Security: Private Perceptions Among Arabs and Israelis_ (New York: Pergamon, 1981), pp. 125-126.

[4] Nassar is quoted in Leonard wolf, _The Passion of Israel: Interviews Taken and Edited in Collaboration with Deborah Wolf_ (Boston: Little-Brown, 1970), p. 154.

[5] David Hirst, _The Gun and the Olive Branch: The Roots of Violence in the Middle East_ (London: Faber, 1977), p. 267.

[6] Aryeh Y. Yodfat and Yuval Arnon-Ohanna, _PLO Strategy and Politics_ (New York: St. Martins Press, 1981), p. 70.

[7] Lewis is quoted by Yodfat and Arnon-Ohanna, p. 56.

[8] Hirst, p. 282; also see p. 274.

[9] Fawaz Turki, "To Be a Palestinian," in _Israel and the Palestinians_, ed. Uri Davis, Andrew Mack and Nira Yuval Davis (London: Ithaca Press, 1975), p. 188.

[10] Mr. Terzi, United Nations Security Council, Provisional Verbatim Record of the Two Thousand One Hundred and Fifty-Sixth Meeting, 18 July 1979, p. 76.

[11] This is quoted in Hirst, p. 314.

[12] Hirst, p. 272.

[13] See Thurston Clarke, _By Blood and Fire: The Attack on the King David Hotel_ (New York: Putnam, 1981), p. 259.

[14] See Eitan Haber, _Menahem Begin: The Legend and the Man_, trans. Louis Williams (New York: Delacorte, 1978), p. 288. Abba Eban, no friend of Begin, attacks the PLO for striking at innocent women and children. See Abba Eban, "U.N.'s Rhetorical

Pogrom," The Jerusalem Post International Edition, 3-9 August 1980, p. 11.

15 For examples of this adaptation, see Haten Hussain, ed., Toward Peace in Palestine (Washington: Arab Information Center, 1975). For the argument that PLO has adapted their rhetoric to different audiences see Y. Harkabi, The Palestinian Covenant and Its Meaning (Totowa, NJ: Valentine Mitchell, 1979), especially p. 52.

16 See Josef Bell, "Words Not Enough," Jerusalem Post International Edition, 14-20 January 1979, p. 11; Menahem Milson, "The PLO's Real Aims," Jerusalem Post International Edition, 7-13 December 1980, p. 11; "Fatah again Affirms 'Liberation by Force,'" The Jerusalem Post International Edition, 8-14 June 1980, p. 10; Harkabi, pp. 43, 52.

17 For a graph which shows the increase in support after 1965 for Begin and Likud, see Harry Hurwitz, Menachem Begin (Johannesburg, South Africa: Jewish Herald, December 1977), p. 108.

18 For a somewhat similar argument see Raël Jean Isaac, Party and Politics in Israel: Three Visions of a Jewish State (New York: Longmans, 1981), p. 125.

19 See A. B. Yehoshua, Between Right and Right, trans. by Arnold Schwartz (Garden City, NY: Doubleday, 1981), p. 3.

20 Reeve Robert Brenner, The Faith and Doubt of Holocaust Survivors (New York: The Free Press, 1980), p. 5.

21 Brenner, p. 9.

22 Yehoshua, p. 4. Also see Eliezer Berkovits, Faith After the Holocaust (New York: Ktav, 1973), p. 67.

23 See the discussion of the relation between the labor myth and the holocaust in chapter three.

24 Dan Segre, "The Symbolic Sources of Begin's Power," Washington Post, 28 August 1977, p. B5. Also see Nahum L. Gordon, "Since the Exile He's First Leader to Talk Judaism to World," Jewish Weekly American, 18 September 1977, p. 23; Hurwitz, p. 153.

25 Frank develops the argument that Begin's views represent the new root social paradigm of Israel. See David A. Frank, "'Shalom Achshav'--Rituals of the Israel Peace Movement," Communication Monographs, 48 (1981), p. 174.

224

26 For example, in 1977 the Likud coalition received 33.4 percent of the vote.

27 See Mroz, p. 156.

28 The "Manifesto of the Land of Israel Movement," is reprinted in Raël Jean Isaac, Israel Divided: Ideological Politics in the Jewish State (Baltimore: Johns Hopkins University Press, 1977), p. 165.

29 For the best development of this view see Shmuel Katz, The Hollow Peace (Jerusalem: Dvir and the Jerusalem Post, 1981).

30 For the argument that Israel is secular see Boas Evron, "The Demise of Zionism?" New Outlook, 23, no. 8 (November-December 1980), p. 30. For an attack on the view that Bar Kochba and the Maccabees are good models for Israeli society see Arthur Hertzberg, "It Is Not Because of the Masada Zealots that the People of Israel Lives," New Outlook, 22, no. 2 (March 1979), pp. 45-47.

31 "The Israeli Mess," The Washington Post, 19 May 1977, p. A16.

32 Anthony Lewis, "The Price of Mr. Begin," New York Times, 2 July 1981, p. A19.

33 Richard Cohen, "Holocaust Is Trivialized for Political Purposes," Washington Post, 29 June 1980, p. B2.

34 John Brecher, et al., "A Roadblock to Peace?" Newsweek, 14 September 1981, p. 40. Also see Raymond Carroll, et al., "Why Begin Is Tough," Newsweek, 30 January 1978, p. 42.

35 Seelye is quoted in Associated Press, "Retiring Envoy Doubts Peace under Begin," Lawrence Daily Journal World, 1 September 1981, p. 2.

36 See Arthur Hertzberg, "Begin and the Jews," New York Review of Books, 18 February 1982, p. 12.

37 Nadav Safran, "Makers and Witnesses of History," New York Times Book Review, 7 May 1978, p. 41.

38 Begin is cited in: Aharon Dolav, "White Nights and Tempestuous Days in the Life of Menahem Begin," Embassy of Israel Reprint, From Ma'ariv, 10 June 1977, p. 11 of reprint.

39 Sol Linowitz, "The Begin I Know," Newsweek, 14 September 1981, p. 42.

[40] See Isaac, Party and Politics in Israel, p. 141.

[41] Shlomo Avineri, "History versus Security," Jerusalem Post International Edition, 1-7 June 1980, p. 13; also see Angus Deming, "Egypt's New Friends," Newsweek, 10 May 1982, p. 62; Bernard Avishai, "The Road to Disaster," New York Review of Books, 10 January 1982, p. 25; David K. Shipler, "West Bank Is Israel's, Begin Asserts," New York Times, 4 May 1982, p. 43.

[42] "West Bankers Told: Bark, but Do Not Bite," The Middle East, no. 49 (November 1978), p. 20.

[43] Zvi Elpeleg, "PLO Calls the Tune," Jerusalem Post International Edition, 23-29 November 1980, p. 11.

[44] United Press International, "Israeli Defense Minister Relaxes Tough Policies on West Bank, Gaza," Washington Post, 13 August 1981, p. A22.

[45] Menachem Begin, The Revolt, trans. Samuel Katz (New York: Nash, 1972), p. 161. Future references to The Revolt will be cited in parens. in the text.

[46] See J. Bowyer Bell, Terror Out of Zion: Irgun Zvai Leumi, LEHI, and the Palestine Underground 1929-1949 (New York: Discus, 1977), pp. 335-337.

[47] See Anthony Lewis, "Might Makes Wrong," New York Times, 24 June 1983, p. A23; Anthony Lewis, "Operation Peace," New York Times, 7 June 1982, p. A19; James Reston, "The Podium and the Pit," New York Times, 20 June 1982, Sect. 4, p. 21; Nathan Glazer and Seymour Martin Lipset, "Israel Isn't Threatened. The War's Ill-Advised," New York Times, 30 June 1982, p. A23.

[48] See "Text of Prime Minister Menachem Begin's Autonomy Plan for Judea, Samaria and the Gaza District as Presented in the Knesset, December 28, 1977," Embassy of Israel, N.D., pp. 9-11. Also see Matityahu Peled, "Autonomy as a Gambit," New Outlook, 22, no. 1 (January-February 1979), p. 11; Hertzberg, "Begin and the Jews," p. 11.

[49] See "West Bankers Told: Bark, but Do Not Bite," p. 26.

[50] For the 1947 British proposal see "Text of the British Memorandum for Palestine Solution," New York Times, 11 February 1947, p. 12.

[51] The anti-Arab view is typical of much of Israeli society. According to Weizman, for most Israelis, "there was no such thing

as a good Arab. . . ." Ezer Weizman, The Battle for Peace (New York: Bantam, 1981), p. 31.

[52] For a sample of criticism of Israel following the invasion of Lebanon, see Roger Hurwitz and Gordon Fellman, "U.S. Jews and Lebanon," New York Times, 26 June 1982, p. 25; Lewis, "Might Makes Wrong"; Fouad Ajami, "The Oasis Goes Dry," New York Times, 21 June 1982, p. A19; Stanley Hoffman, "Israeli Self-Defense? No Self-Deceit," New York Times, 16 June 1982, p. A31; Edward W. Said, "Begin's Zionism Grinds On," New York Times, 11 June 1982, p. A31; Anthony Lewis, "Combing the Wreckage," New York Times, 10 June 1982, p. A31.

[53] Chancellor made his statement on August 2, 1982 on NBC's "Nightly News." For a similar view, see David K. Shipler, "A Crisis of Conscience over Lebanon," New York Times, 18 June 1982, p. A6.

[54] Begin is quoted in David Ignatius, Frederick Kempe, and Seth Lipsky, "Begin on Begin: Soon I'll Retire to Write My Book," Wall Street Journal, 9 July 1982, p. 1. In the August 16, 1982 Newsweek, John Brecher, et al., quote Begin as commenting in reference to Israeli attacks on Beirut: "I feel as a prime minister empowered to instruct a valiant army facing 'Berlin' where, amongst innocent civilians, Hitler and his henchmen hide in a bunker deep beneath the surface." See John Brecher, et al., "Beirut: A City in Agony," Newsweek, 16 August 1982, p. 10.

[55] See Martin Peretz, "Lebanon Eyewitness," New Republic, 2 August 1982, pp. 16-17, 19-20.

[56] The Israeli position is clearly described in William Safire, "PLO Won't Be Talked Out of Propaganda Haven," Kansas City Times, 6 August 1982, p. All.

[57] See John Lindsay, "A 'Lively' Discussion," Newsweek, 5 July 1982, p. 38.

[58] See David K. Shipler, "Begin Tells Cabinet to Ignore Reported U.S. Threat," New York Times, 17 June 1982, p. A22.

[59] Begin's response to Percy is quoted in Associated Press, "Tanks Close in; Vow Made to Step Up Pressure on PLO," Kansas City Times, 5 August 1982, p. A8.

[60] Begin is quoted in Paul Montgomery, "Begin Tells Leading U.S. Jews of Invasion Goals," New York Times, 18 June 1982, p. A6.

61 The view that the critic as an unbiased expert can fairly evaluate the quality of a work of rhetoric is clearly developed in Lawrence W. Rosenfield, "The Anatomy of Critical Discourse," Speech Monographs, 25 (1968), pp. 91-92. For a discussion of a similar idea found in Artistotle's Poetics, see S. H. Butcher, Aristotle's Theory of Poetry and Fine Art: With a Critical Text and Translation of the Poetics, 4th ed. (New York: Dover, 1951), pp. 204-207.

62 Claude Lévi-Strauss refers to myth as a logical model for solving problems. See Claude Lévi-Strauss, "The Structural Study of Myth," in The Structuralists from Marx to Lévi-Strauss, ed. Richard and Fernande De George (Garden City, NY: Doubleday, 1972), p. 193.

63 Brenner, p. 218.

64 Brenner, p. 229.

65 See Richard L. Rubenstein, "God as Cosmic Sadist: In Reply to Emil Fackenheim," Christian Century, 29 July 1970, pp. 921-923.

66 David Kripitchnkoff is quoted in Irgun Zvai Leumi, The Hebrew Struggle for National Liberation, submitted to the United Nations Special Committee on Palestine, 1947, p. 41.

67 Hans Kohn, "Zion and the Jewish National Idea," in Palestine: A Search for Truth, ed. Alan R. Taylor and Richard N. Tetlie (Washington, D.C.: Public Affairs Press, 1970), p. 50.

68 See Constance A. Katzenstein, "Israel--The Jewish Response to Feelings of Helplessness," New Outlook, 23, no. 1 (1980), p. 32.

69 This position is developed in Lucy S. Dawidowicz, The War Against the Jews 1933-1945 (New York: Bantam, 1975), pp. 463-466.

70 For works of Wiesel which show the courage of those who resisted and those who were unable to resist, see his first two novels. Elie Wiesel, Night, trans. Stella Rodway (New York: Avon, 1958); Elie Wiesel, Dawn, trans. Frances Frenoye (New York: Discus, 1960).

71 See Emil Fackenheim, God's Presence in History: Jewish Affirmations and Philosophical Reflections (New York: Harper, 1970), pp. 84-91.

72 See Larry Collins and Dominique Lapierre, The Fifth Horseman (New York: Avon, 1980), p. 123.

[73] Arthur Koestler, Thieves in the Night: Chronical of an Experiment (London: Hutchison, 1946), p. 203.

[74] See for instance Hertzberg, "It Is Not Because," p. 46.

[75] For a somewhat similar argument see Hertzberg, "Begin and the Jews," pp. 11-12; Uri Avnery, Israel Without Zionists: A Plea for Peace in the Middle East (New York: MacMillan, 1968); Lewis, "The Price of Mr. Begin," p. A19.

[76] Yehiam Weitz, "The Holocaust Analogy," New Outlook, 20, no. 7 (October-November 1977), pp. 45-46.

[77] Joseph Campbell: Myths to Live by Part 1, an interview by Bill Moyers of Joseph Campbell, "Bill Moyers Journal," 17 April 1981, Show 718, p. 9.

[78] R. M. MacIver, The Web of Government (New York: MacMillan, 1965), p. 39.

[79] Northrup Frye, The Critical Path: An Essay on the Social Context of Literary Criticism (Bloomington: Indiana University Press, 1971), pp. 106-107.

[80] Kenneth Burke, Language as Symbolic Action: Essays on Life, Literature and Method (Los Angeles: University of California Press, 1966), p. 16.

[81] Burke, p. 19.

[82] Burke, pp. 19-20.

[83] Fackenheim, pp. 84-92.

CHAPTER VIII

THE VALUE OF A MYTHIC APPROACH TO CRITICISM

The most important conclusion about the nature of myth which can be drawn from a study of Menachem Begin's myth of return is that there is no single theory of myth or method of mythic criticism which is appropriate for treating all mythic discourse. For the critic, this means that, rather than reasoning deductively from a theory to the explanation of a given myth, the critic should begin with the myth and, based upon its formal and functional characteristics, choose the most appropriate theoretical perspective for explaining and evaluating it.

Evidence that no single theory of myth is adequate to explain all myth comes from the analysis of the three Jewish mythologies I have considered. The traditional myth of exile and return responded to the problems created by the Diaspora. Through the promise of a physical return to Zion at the beginning of the Messianic age and through symbolic returns via the rituals and festivals of Judaism, the myth provided a portion of the Jewish people with an ultimate goal and a pattern to shape their daily lives. The form and function of the myth of exile and return reflect characteristics of myth treated in several theories. The cycles of exile and return in the myth seem to support Lévi-Strauss's claim that the myth possesses a repetitive formal structure. Lévi-Strauss argues that this repetitive structure functions to guarantee that the myth will transmit its message.[1] The myth of traditional Judaism also supports the view of theorists who emphasize the close tie between myth and ritual.[2] Moreover, characteristics of the myth of exile and return support several aspects of Mircea Eliade's work on myth. Eliade emphasizes the importance of the sacred in myth and the presence of cyclical returns to a moment of creation.[3] The myth of exile and return includes both sacred and cyclical elements.

The myth of labor Zionism developed in response to the problems of assimilation and anti-Semitism. Labor Zionists called for a return to Zion in order to escape oppression and to build the perfect earthly society. Their aim was to make the desert bloom and

231

to create a state which would be a "light unto the nations." In sharp contrast to the myth of exile and return, the labor myth seems to deny key elements in Eliade's work. First, the labor myth is largely secular. Although it draws upon the tie between the Jewish people and the land of Israel, the myth is not religious. Rather than promising other worldly salvation, the labor Zionist myth promises a perfect earthly society. God plays no role in this mythology, and many adherents to the labor myth were and are atheists.[4] Thus, the labor Zionist myth could be cited as evidence that some myths lack a sacred dimension. In addition, because the labor myth is oriented toward creating a perfect society on earth, it seems to violate Eliade's claim that all myths tell of a creation. Nor can the myth be interpreted as a return to Eden. The proponents of labor Zionism do not speak of a return to a perfect past when all men lived in harmony, but of creating a perfect future society based on socialist principles.

The labor myth has elements that fit a functionalist approach to myth. Malinowski argues that the primary function of myth is to provide a pragmatic charter for society.[5] Political scientists have adopted this perspective in their analyses of the relation between myth and social structure. The labor myth supports the functionalist theory. For example, Isaac argues that two of the essential institutions of the Israeli state--the Kibbutz and the Histadrut (an organization of labor unions)--draw support from the labor myth of a perfect earthly society.[6]

Begin's myth developed in response to the holocaust. Begin called on the Jewish people to take up arms to defend themselves, never to give in to weakness again. According to the myth, the strength needed to save the Jewish people could come only from a return to the land of Israel and to the heroism of the ancient Hebrews. The emphasis in the Irgun's myth upon return as a means to tap the power of ancient Israel clearly fits Eliade's conceptions. In addition, the use of blood as a symbol could be cited in support of an archetypal approach to myth.[7] Joseph Campbell's analysis of the structure of heroic myth is also supported by The Revolt.[8] In addition, Begin's use of return as a means to explain the rebirth of Israeli heroism can be interpreted as reflecting Lévi-Strauss's view that myth functions as a "logical model" for resolving contradictions.[9]

The myth of holocaust and redemption through return can also be used to question aspects of Lévi-Strauss's work on myth. Analysis of Begin's myth clearly demonstrates that the plot as well as the repetitive internal structure is an important aspect of the myth. However, this conclusion contradicts Lévi-Strauss's claim that the meaning of a myth lies beneath the surface in what might be called its deep structure.[10] The repetitive logical structure of myth can only be discovered, according to Lévi-Strauss, by going through a series of inversions and transformations through which the deep structure of the myth is discovered.[11] In this view the story told in the myth is unimportant. It is the logical structure, not the plot of the myth, which matters.[12] However, in the myth of holocaust and redemption through return, the plot is absolutely essential. The myth tells the story of the movement from the holocaust to redemption through return. The meaning of the myth is not hidden, but is obvious in the development of the story.

The characteristics of all three Jewish mythologies seem to deny other aspects of Lévi-Strauss's work with myth. For example, Lévi-Strauss's argument that myths do not serve a practical function[13] is clearly contradicted. The myth of exile and return responded to the problems of exile, the labor myth to assimilation and anti-Semitism, and Begin's myth to the holocaust. My conclusion is not that Lévi-Strauss's theory of myth is wrong or that his method is useless, although it is largely inapplicable here.[14] Rather, I conclude that no one theory or method of analysis fits all myth. The works of Eliade, Campbell, Jung, Malinowski, Lévi-Strauss, and others are useful, but only when applied in the proper circumstances. The critic should not adopt a single theory of myth, but move from a specific myth to the appropriate theory.[15]

In determining the proper method to be applied to a given work, the critic should use what might be called an inductive functionalist approach. In this approach, the critic begins with a general definition of the form and function of myth. This definition does not act as a critical method, but is used to distinguish those works which can be appropriately treated through mythic analysis. The proper method can be identified only after the critic has carefully analyzed the form and function of a given myth.

The starting point for the analysis should be the function fulfilled by the myth. The critic should identify the specific problem the myth confronts. Once the problem has been identified, it should be relatively easy for the critic to identify the formal structure of the myth responding to that problem. At that point, the critic can choose the theory or method capable of explaining the myth. If the myth is dominated by archetypal imagery, then a Jungian approach might be most appropriate. If it is built around a repetitive structure, in which the same message is stated at several points in slightly different form, then Levi-Strauss's structuralist approach might be useful. In this study of Begin's rhetoric, the form of Begin's myth led to the theoretical work of Mircea Eliade on the mythic significance of "return" and to the work of Joseph Campbell on the typical structure of heroic myth.

In most social scientific research, it is axiomatic that the scholar first picks a method and then applies it to the subject area. To adapt the method to the specific subject area would bias the study. However, in the study of myth (as in all rhetorical criticism),[16] this methodological axiom should be reversed. To analyze a myth adequately, the critic should begin with the myth and then move to the proper method. The position that the theory or method appropriate for explaining and evaluating a given myth can be discovered only after a close analysis of that myth is similar to that of anthropologists and linguists who argue that the researcher should approach a study with as few preconceptions as possible. Rather than imposing a perspective on a subject area, the researcher should develop a theory to fit the subject. For example, William writes of the danger of imposing a theoretical framework on an alien culture.

> An anthroplogist must avoid classification of observations in terms of his own cultural experiences. If a man is observed beating a woman and the population census reveals that the couple is married, it would seem proper to file the observation as an instance of "wife-beating." However, you may become aware later that in the local community men and women generally agree that some sickness is best driven away through public flogging,

or that women learn best when struck hard in public, or that married women must periodically show the strength of their husbands through suffering a public beating. If such meanings obtain for the form observed, classification under the heading of "wife-beating" is so misleading as to be a grave distortion of the local culture.[17]

Many linguists endorse a similar view. For instance, Pelto argues that progress in explaining the structure of American Indian and Eskimo languages occurred only after linguists put aside the view that all languages possess a formal structure similar to Latin and instead described the "languages in terms of their own 'natural' grammatical elements."[18]

The anthropological and linguistic view that method should be developed inductively out of the subject is generally characterized as an "emic" approach to research. The term "emic" was coined by Kenneth Pike who distinguished between etic methods of research, in which a theory is applied deductively to a culture, and emic approaches, in which the theory is generated in the process of studying the culture.[19] According to Pike: "The etic viewpoint studies behavior as from the outside of a particular system and as an essential initial approach to an alien system. The emic viewpoint results from studying behavior as from inside the system. . . . The etic organization of a world-wide cross-cultural scheme may be created by the analyst. The emic structure of a particular system must, I hold, be discovered."[20] Pike argues that the emic approach is valuable because it allows the anthropologist to put aside cultural preconceptions and describe a culture in its own terms.[21] He also notes that the emic approach is particularly useful for isolating the meaning or purpose behind a cultural artifact.[22] The emic approach described by Pike is quite similar to the inductive functionalist approach I have described.

Edwin Black has applied Pike's distinction between etic and emic to criticism. According to Black, the emic critic "approaches a rhetorical transaction in what is hoped to be its own terms, without conscious expectations drawn from any source other than the rhetorical transaction itself."[23] Black goes

on to argue that the emic critic seeks to explain a
rhetorical act in its own terms, while the etic critic
seeks to judge that act based upon external standards.[24] The emic critic acts as a psychoanalyst who
explains the act; the etic critic acts as a judge who
evaluates it.[25] Black concludes by arguing for a
combination of the two approaches.[26]

The work of Pike, Black, and various anthropologists supports the value of the inductive functionalist approach I have described. They all argue that
the imposition of a theory or method on a subject
produces "sterile" results.[27] It is their view that
the theory should be derived from the material being
studied. There is reason to believe that the emic
approach is particularly appropriate for mythic criticism. It would be inappropriate to approach a myth
serving one function with a critical theory focusing
on a different function. Moreover, myths are shaped
by cultural needs. A critic who imposed his or her
cultural preconceptions on a myth might totally misunderstand the myth. This explains why Black writes
that the "mode that subsumes emic criticism [is] the
mythic."[28]

The inductive functionalist method allows the
critic to combine etic and emic approaches to criticism as Black suggests. Theory should not be imposed
upon a myth, but discovered from an analysis of its
form and function. Only an emic approach can hope to
adequately explain a myth. My experience suggests
that critics should proceed from mythic function to
the formal characteristics developed to serve that
function and, from those characteristics, to a critical method. This approach is emic in that it allows
the critic to discover in the myth itself the appropriate theory for explaining the myth. It is etic in
that it uses standards based on mythic function for
evaluating the myth.

This study of Begin's rhetoric as myth is additional evidence for the distinction made earlier
between rhetorical acts in which myths are used strategically and rhetorical acts informed by myths which
function on the anagogic level as all-encompassing
world views. Begin is misunderstood primarily because
his use of myth is perceived as a strategic device
which he could cast aside. However, for Begin, the
myth of holocaust and redemption is no rhetorical
ploy. It is an all-encompassing world view shaping

236

his policies and rhetoric. It is obviously important that the critic be able to distinguish between these two uses of myth in rhetoric. While the strategic use of myth is important, rhetoric informed by a mythic world view is still more important because it has the power to shape a society.[29]

This study suggests that myths which function at the anagogic level can be distinguished from the merely strategic use of myth based on three characteristics: function, audience reaction, and form.

At the anagogic level, rhetorical acts create or rely on myths responding to crucial social problems. Humans do not create myths to deal with trivial difficulties. Consequently, if the rhetoric rests on a mythic world view, there should be evidence on the crucial nature of the problem which the rhetoric confronts. In the mythic rhetoric of the Irgun, the crucial problem was the holocaust. The Revolt, as well as Begin's other rhetoric, is replete with references to the physical and psychological threat to Jewish existence posed by the death camps. The holocaust is the paradigm of a problem for which there is no rational answer. The functions served by Begin's rhetoric are consistent with the conclusion that his discourse functions at the anagogic level as a mythic world view.

In addition to function, rhetorical acts which operate at the anagogic level are distinguishable from rhetorical acts using mythic elements strategically by the audience reactions produced in each case. If the rhetoric presents a total vision of reality, there should be evidence that, for those who accept its premises, the rhetoric shapes their view of the world. In other words, there should be evidence that the myth developed in and through the rhetoric is accepted as a living reality or total vision of the world. Such evidence might take the form of testimony about the meaning of the myth developed in the rhetoric from the members of the group that embraces it. Alternatively, the critic might point to rituals enacting the mythic message as proof that the rhetoric creates a reality lived. Societies do not create rituals about what they take to be pure fiction. Rather, rituals retell stories believed to contain fundamental truths. In the case of the Irgun's myth, both forms of support are available. Over the thirty-five years since the conclusion of the revolt, the former soldiers of the Irgun have continued to celebrate rituals recalling their fight for independence. In addition, the jury speeches of the Irgun soldiers who were tried by the British were dominated by the same myth found in Begin's rhetoric. Thus, there is good reason to believe that the myth of holocaust and redemption through return functioned as an encompassing world view for members of the Irgun.

In addition to the problem confronted and audience reaction elicited by rhetoric functioning at the anagogic level, mythic rhetoric is also formally distinguishable from the strategic use of myth. If a body of rhetoric is mythic, then the myth should form the core of the rhetoric under consideration. The myth is more than one appeal among others; it is the center from which all other aspects of the rhetoric draw meaning. The test for whether the rhetoric is mythic is to ask whether the essential meaning of the rhetoric would be altered if the mythic elements were removed. If the meaning would not be significantly changed by removal of the mythic elements, then the myth functions strategically. In Begin's case, the removal of the myth dramatically changes his rhetoric. All aspects of Begin's rhetoric and ideology flow from the myth. Without the mythic underpinnings, his rhetoric has little or no meaning.

An analysis of Menachem Begin's speeches and writings demonstrates the value of treating some rhetoric as mythic. Some modern rhetoric reflects the form and fulfills the function of myths found in primitive societies. The rhetoric responds to crucial problems. It tells the story of great heroes who operate outside historical time in a place of great symbolic power. In the story told in the rhetoric, these heroes symbolically resolve the problem facing the society. Such rhetoric cannot be explained adequately if it is not treated from a mythic perspective.

Mythic rhetoric needs to be explained and evaluated because of its social functions. Myths generate values, produce world views, and respond to crucial social problems. In Begin's case, the myth of holocaust and redemption through return encompasses the issues raised by the holocaust and shapes both Begin's world view and that of a portion of Israeli society. Begin is misunderstood primarily because the mythic underpinnings of his ideology have not been recog-

nized.   He is not irrational, nor an Arab hater;
instead, his view of the world is shaped by the myth
through which he continues to fight the holocaust.

Notes

1 Claude Lévi-Strauss, "The Structural Study of Myth," in The Structuralists from Marx to Lévi-Strauss, ed. Richard and Fernande De George (Garden City, NY: Anchor, 1972), p. 193. Future references to this work will be cited as "SSM."

2 The most cited work on the relation of myth and ritual is Clyde Kluckhohn, "Myths and Rituals: A General Theory," Harvard Theological Review, 35 (June 1942), pp. 45-79. Some theorists argue that myth is merely a ritual text. For a summary of this view, see Joseph Fontenrose, The Ritual Theory of Myth (Berkeley: University of California Press, 1966).

3 The best short work summarizing Eliade's view is Mircea Eliade, "Myth in the Nineteenth and Twentieth Centuries," Dictionary of the History of Ideal, vol. III, pp. 314-315.

4 See Raël Jean Isaac, Party and Politics in Israel: Three Visions of a Jewish State (New York: Longmans, 1981), p. 3.

5 Bronislaw Malinowski, Magic, Science and Religion (Garden City, NY: Doubleday-Anchor, 1954), p. 101.

6 See Isaac, pp. 92-95.

7 See C. G. Jung and C. Kerenyi, Essays on a Science of Mythology (New York: Pantheon, 1949). In addition, some argue that mythic archetypes can be explained based on the common experience of all humans. For this view, see Shirley Park Lowrey, Familiar Mysteries: The Truth in Myth (New York: Oxford University Press, 1982).

8 See Joseph Campbell, The Hero With a Thousand Faces (Princeton: Princeton University Press, 1948).

9 Lévi-Strauss, "SSM," p. 193.

10 Lévi-Strauss, "SSM," p. 174.

11 See Edith Kurzweil, The Age of Structuralism: Lévi-Strauss to Foucault (New York: Columbia University Press, 1980), pp. 17-19.

12 Lévi-Strauss, "SSM," 174.

13 Claude Lévi-Strauss, The Raw and the Cooked, trans. John and Doreen Weightman (New York: Harper and Row, 1969), p. 10.

[14] For treatments that emphasize the value of Lévi-Strauss's structuralism, see Robert Scholes, Structuralism in Literature: An Introduction (New Haven: Yale University Press, 1974), p. 73.

[15] For a similar argument, see G. S. Kirk, Myth: Its Meaning and Functions in Ancient and Other Cultures (London: Cambridge University Press, 1970), p. 7.

[16] See Edwin Black, Rhetorical Criticism: A Study in Method (New York: Macmillan, 1965); Lawrence W. Rosenfield, "The Anatomy of Critical Discourse," Speech Monographs 25 (1968), pp. 50-69.

[17] Thomas Rhys Williams, Field Methods in the Study of Culture (New York: Holt, Rinehart and Winston, 1967), p. 24. This was also the position of Boas and Sapir and is the position of the "New Ethnography" movement in anthropology. See Pertti J. Pelto, The Structure of Inquiry (New York: Harper and Row, 1970), pp. 68-70.

[18] Pertti J. Pelto, The Nature of Anthropology (Columbus, OH: Charles Merrill, 1966), p. 39. For a description of a psychological theory of perception which is somewhat similar to the emic view, see the summary of constructivism in David L. Swanson and Jesse G. Delia, The Nature of Human Communication (Chicago: S.R.A., 1976), p. 13.

[19] Pike develops this distinction in Kenneth L. Pike, "Etic and Emic Standards for the Description of Behavior," in Communication and Culture: Readings in the Codes of Human Interaction, ed. Alfred G. Smith (New York: Holt, Rinehart, and Winston, 1966), pp. 152-163. Pike coined the words etic and emic from phonetic and phonemic.

[20] Pike, pp. 152, 153.

[21] Pike, pp. 154-155.

[22] Pike, pp. 158-160.

[23] Edwin Black, "A Note on Theory and Practice in Rhetorical Criticism," Western Journal of Speech Communication 44 (1980), pp. 331-332.

[24] Black, "A Note," p. 334.

[25] Black, "A Note," p. 334-335.

[26] Black, "A Note," p. 335-336.

[27] Black, "A Note," p. 333.

28 Black, "A Note," p. 335.

29 For a brilliant essay illustrating the power which myth may exercise in a society, see Kenneth Burke, "The Rhetoric of Hitler's 'Battle,'" in The Philosophy of Literary Form, 3rd ed. (Berkeley: University of California Press, 1973), pp. 191-220.

APPENDIX

"A Message from the Commander-in-Chief of the Irgun
to the Diaspora."[1]

1   In the name of our tormented people and for the sake of its freedom-seeking sons we have unfurled the holy banner of revolt for our mother land. We have risen in order to restore to the Hebrew national his country, his sovereignty, his liberty; we have risen in order to liberate Palestine from British rule, the despotic government which bears the responsibility for the annihilation of millions of our brethren; from the rule of oppression which tramples with arrogant foot international obligations, which attacks the elementary rights of men and nations. We have risen in order to put an end to the curse of dispersion and to the stigma of servility. We have risen in order to introduce political freedom, social justice and cultural progress in the Hebrew Homeland. We have risen in order to reunite the sections of our land west and east of the Jordan which had been severed by the British tryants with the help of mercenary desert princes. We have risen and we have sworn that no sacrifice shall be too great and that we shall not put down our weapons nor cease our struggle so long as our nation's historic goal has not been attained: the whole of Palestine as a free and independent Hebrew state.

2   For years we stood alone in the field. The ruthless world war caused the severance of our land from the wide world and from our dispersed people. From the continent of Europe there came to us the moan of Hebrew blood, the blood of our parents and our brothers, the blood of the best of our people and our loved ones. We knew the identity of their murderers; we also knew who it was that helped hurl them into the abyss. We knew very well that had it not been for British perfidy; had it not been for the rule of foreign oppressors in our land; had it not been for the closing of the gates before the war and during the war, the German murderers would not have trapped our people, and millions of our brethren would still be alive today as free, proud and creative individuals. For this reason we did not yield to British intimidation; we did not mind our standing alone, and we did not delude ourselves with vain hope. We began to fight. We made dozens of attacks. We made precious sacrifices. Tens of our soldiers fell

---

[1]Irgun Zvai Leumi, "A Message from the Commander-in-Chief of the Irgun to the Diaspora," The Answer, September 1946, pp. 11-12.

in battle. Hundreds were wounded and taken prisoner. We were harassed mercilessly; we were tortured in cellars; we were exiled to distant points. But we remained unbroken. In the place of the absent there came others who continued the struggle. No one came to our aid. Like our brothers, the partisans in the forests of Poland, we too acquired all that we have with our strength and with our brains. We penetrated into the camps of the enemy. We took from him hundreds of rifles, light and heavy machine guns, countless bullets, and money, which also—according to our testament—is converted into steel. Thus was repeated the phenomenon of a struggle of the weak against the strong and the few against the many. Thus the entire world learned that a new generation has arisen in Israel, a generation which draws superhuman strength from the mother land, hallowed from ancient days with the blood of the brave and the holy; a generation which knows how to love liberty and to despise slavery, a generation who knows how to revolt and to fight with weapon in hand for justice and right.

3   The world war is now ended, but the war of Israel goes on. The nations of the world have celebrated the first anniversary of their triumph; we mourn the third of the people which has been erased from the book of life and the land which remains subjugated by foreigners and shut to our brethren who are rowing toward it with their last strength. And if they do not reach their destination; if they are not returning, like all of the peoples, to a life of peace and liberty, it is only because their way is blocked by the perfidious rulers of Britain, who have spread a network of espionage and anti-Hebrew concentration camps along the shore of the Mediterranean sea and its waters, along the highways of Europe and its boundaries, in order to sever for all time the people from the Homeland and in order to condemn its sons both in the Diaspora and in Zion to extinction, annihilation or eternal enslavement.

4   But precisely because of this, our struggle, the struggle of Hebrew liberation, is growing stronger. Here in this country the eyes of the masses and even the eyes of the leaders have been opened to see that there is only one alternative before us and none other: either to fight and be redeemed or to live in the status quo and be destroyed. For this reason there are no longer any internal strife against us—those degrading persecutions which would have brought on a civil war of the gravest consequences, had we not known, in the period of collective blindness, how to enforce the policy of self-restraint internally just as we knew how to conduct the struggle externally. That policy cost many victims as well; the best among our commanders were condemned to imprisonment and exile by the blind collaborators, but this policy was enforced unconditionally and today, after the

awakening, there have been laid the foundations for the erection of a united front of the Hebrew forces which are battling the tryannous rule of the British.

5   Outside Palestine the British oppressors are confronted by the united spirit of those saved from the sword, by the peculiar strength of a people which has been tried as no other on earth, which learned in the course of years filled with inhuman suffering that without a native land and without freedom there can be no life and that freedom is acquired only through struggle. Hardened by persecution, tested by suffering, taught by war, thousands of our brethren stand on the bloody Continent with but one determination: to reach the shores of the homeland at any price, in order to build it and to make fruitful its fields—if it is free, and—if it is enslaved—to fight for freedom, to die or to triumph.

6   We are convinced therefore that the British war against the Hebrew nation is a war without any chances of success for the aggressors. They, the cruel rulers, can of course prolong our suffering and extract an additional measure of blood from the open veins of the nation. But they will not attain their goal. The Hebrew nation will not forego its land, the Hebrew nation will not surrender nor will it continue to live the life of exile and degradation which terminates—as its history in every era indicates—in physical decimation. Despite everything, the Hebrew people will of itself cut a path to the land of its fathers, will redeem it and renew its days as of old.

7   And in order to shorten the period of suffering, all freedom-loving people, wherever they may be, must band together about their fighting allies in their regenerated homeland. The struggle of Israel against perfidious Britain must be universal, just as the war of Britain against our decimated people is universal. An organized boycott of British goods can be a useful weapon in our struggle; it must therefore be enacted on a world-wide scale. Also in other areas—political, public opinion and even military—the freedom-loving people can act against this evil government.

8   Obviously, embattled Zion, the main battlefield, is in need of help. This help—in manpower, financial means and arms—the Hebrew people can use in ever increasing amounts. If this is done the hands of the fighting Hebrews will be strengthened; the tempo of the struggle will be stepped up. Its scope will be widened. And we shall be ready, under proper military and international conditions, to stage an open revolt by the underground forces—to conquer.

9   This is therefore our call to you, the disciples of freedom, wherever they may be. The hour of fateful decision has come. The war for Hebrew liberation has begun. From the rivers of blood, from the depths of our people's endless history, there have come the rejuvenated forces which have undertaken the campaign, that will decide our fate for generations. Before our eyes there has taken place the miracle of the return of Zion; before our eyes there was born the Hebrew soldier, the fearless fighter, champion of freedom whose hands are trained for war and whose heart is filled with love for his people and for his land.

10   This soldier will fight; this soldier will fulfill his duty to the end. He will not retreat. And if his life will be demanded as a sacrifice he will give it with a willing heart, for he knows that from his blood there will grow the tree of life for his people. In the name of this unknown soldier--we are addressing you with a call of faith and with the message of resurgence:

11   The hour of redemption is near! Take on strength! Rise to the aid of fighting Zion! Rise to the struggle of the nation!

"From Kishenev to Acre: On the Sixth Anniversary
of the Death of David Raziel."[2]

1   He appeared in the history of our people, as do all makers
of revolutions—in anonymity. And he became immortal.

2   David Raziel made revolution in Israel. He laid the foundation of the Hebrew Army, a fighting army, an army of liberation.

3   The idea was not new. But it was David who gave it its
bayonets. And so started the revolution. The revolution of
Hebrew renewal. One of the great revolutions within the history
of humanity.

4   For tens of generations, we went among the peoples with a
mark on our foreheads: Hefker. We had become accustomed to it.
We thought that there simply was no alternative. And it was
still with this mark that we started to return to our Homeland,
as "protected" Jews (Shutzjuden), with pogroms as an inescapable
part of our daily existence, with books as "answers" to attacks,
with self-restraint as "reply" to the shedding of our blood. And
if here and there one of us stood up and defended himself—a
normal thing for every living being—this was considered a unique
act of heroism. There is no wonder in that. In the decayed
diaspora, even this did not happen.

5   Until David Raziel came and gave the signal. No longer
passive defense, but attack. No longer "self defense," but the
defense of the nation, in the broad sense, just as other nations
understand it.

6   Then arose the Hebrew Army, the Army of the revolution,
bearing the idea of freedom, which erases with burning steel the
mark of shame, Hefker, and writes on its flag the mark of glory:
"Conquest!"

7   The long era has ended during which our people disarmed
itself—the only people in the world to do so—and never used
arms otherwise than in the service of foreigners under the orders
of foreigners, or—very rarely—in self defense. A new epoch is
begun. We have taken up arms. We have wiped off the shame of
the butcheries. We have come out into the limelight of history.
We have become a factor. We have become a nation. No longer is
our history made by foreign hands, by those who arise to destroy
us. We make our own history, with our own hands, with the hands

---

[2]Irgun Zvai Leumi, "From Kishenev to Acre: On the Sixth
Anniversary of the Death of David Raziel," The Answer, 30 May
1947, p. 6.

of our sons, who have arisen to take us out of slavery and into freedom.

8   A miracle? So it is, a great miracle. For all this renewal took place during a small number of years, with continual mass extermination as its background, an extermination which has been going on for hundreds of years, and has reached its peak in this century of mechanized cruelty. This sudden transformation of a slaughtered herd into a fighting nation, of terrified persecuted beings into awe-inspiring fighters—let all those whose spirit is small, who laugh at the "shortcut," who preach surrender, who themselves retreat, who whimper and say: "What are we, and what is our force, that we should try, that we should measure ourselves?"—let all these defeatists understand that there are within the nation hidden forces which only appear in days of trial and tragedy, because the source of all our strength is the force of renewal, the force of rejuvenation that transforms an anonymous soldier into an immortal hero, a weak nation into a strong one, and enslaved people into a free one.

9   And our people has shown an unusual force of renewal. Look and see: It was only a few years ago that a Yugoslav partisan told a Hebrew parachutist: "The Jews are cowards. The Jews are afraid to die, and that is why they get killed. They are not a people. He who is afraid to die in battle has no right to exist." And today, tens of millions of people in the east and in the west, in the north and in the south, praise and respect the heroic acts of Hebrew men, acts of bravery the like of which are but few in the history of the world.

10   The basis of this renewal was laid by David Raziel. By his spirit; by his brain; by his acts; by his personal example. He gave to the people of Israel the type of the Hebrew Soldier. He taught, he fought and led into battle. He knew how to put a load of responsibility—even the most difficult ones—upon himself and upon others. He believed and inspired belief around himself. He blazed the trail for those who came after him: "Difficulties were created to be overcome; there is no 'impossible.'"

11   So it is, there is no "impossible." Within only two generations, a slaughtered people made the jump from Kishenev to Acre. Within a short number of years, we made the jump from that death cell in the Maidanek to this death cell in Jerusalem. This is the sign that the spirit of heroism has returned to Israel. And more than anyone in his generation David Raziel embodied that spirit.

"The Ten Martyrs Under Cursed Britain Compared to
10 Martyrs Under Rome."[3]

1   It has been consummated. Our generation, the same as our
forefathers in the days of Rome, has had its ten martyrs. Shlomo
Ben Yosef, Dov Gruner, Dov Rosenbaum, Eliezer Kashani, Mordecai
Alkoshi, Meir Feinstein, Moshe Barzani, Meir Nakan, Jacob Weiss
and Absalom Habib. These are the ten who in our generation were
marched to the gallows in our homeland by the foreign cruel
oppressor. There are, of course, some basic differences between
the ten martyrs in the days of Rome and the ten martyrs of the
days of cursed Britain.

2   The former were men of great renown in their lifetime, our
younger brothers were anonymous, completely unknown men who came
from the people and whose names became immortal in the fight and
the supreme sacrifice. The ancient martyrs lived in times which
saw the last generation of freedom and the first generation of
dispersion that was to last for 2,000 years. Our young brothers
were born into the last generation of enslavement, and the first
generation of freedom after the 2,000 years of dispersion.

3   But an unbreakable link of love for the people, love of the
homeland and a supreme heroism of the soul exists between these
two groups. Generations were brought up on the legacy left by
the martyrs and generations will live on the legacy of the fighters until Israel will return to his land, dwell in it in safety,
and until there will be no more martyrs in the Hebrew land until
it will be a Hebrew state.

4   Rest in Peace, heroes of Israel, you who broke down the
walls of the British Bastille, liberators of your brothers,
redeemers of your people. In the graveyard of Safet there are
seven of you. And who knows who will come after you, for the
enemy is ruthless and the fight is fierce. But even should the
losses be tenfold,--you know it, brothers-in-arms--we shall go on
fighting.

---

[3]Irvun Zvai Leumi, "The Ten Martyrs Under Cursed Britain
Compared to 10 Martyrs Under Rome," The Answer, 15 August 1947,
p. 6.

"The First Prerequisite of Freedom Is Complete Victory."[4]

1   Citizens of the Hebrew homeland, soldiers of Israel, Hebrew
youth, sisters and brothers in Zion!

After many years of underground fighting, of torture and persecution, of moral and physical sufferings, the rebels who rose
against the rule of evil stand before you today, with a hymn of
thanksgiving on their lips and a prayer to heaven in their
hearts. We are giving thanks as our forefathers would be giving
on the day of feast and celebration. We are giving thanks as
they would on seeing a new crop. And today is a holiday in our
tents, and a new tender sapling is shooting up before our eyes.
The Hebrew rebellion of the years 1922-1948 has been crowned with
success: the first Hebrew rebellion that ended in victory since
the uprising of the Maccabees. The British regime of enslavement
in our homeland was beaten, shattered and done away with. Out of
the war of bloodshed, the land of Israel came into being. A path
was cleared for the homecoming of our masses in exile. A foundation was laid--and this is only a foundation--for real Hebrew
independence. One phase came to an end--just one phase--of the
Hebrew war of liberation. The final aim of that war is to bring
back the people of Israel--all of them--into the land of their
own, and to bring back the land of Israel--all of it--to its
people, its rightful owners. And when we remember that this
overwhelming event came to pass after 70 generations--70 generations of dispersion, of defenselessness, of enslavement, of endless wanderings and endless persecution: when you remember that
this came to pass in the midst of a period of total annihilation
of the Jews because he was a Jew, when we remember that once
again the few vanquished the many who stood up to annihilate
Israel--then we are entitled and impelled to give thanks, though
the bitter cup of suffering of our mothers and children is not
yet empty. Then we have to give thanks to the Good Redeemer of
Israel for the miracles and wonders which He has wrought for our
people in our days, the same as He has done in days past. And
with all our hearts and with all our souls, we say today--on the
first day of our liberation from the yoke of British enslavement
--blessed be He who made us live. Who made us stand up and
brought up to see this day.

2   The state of Israel came to be. It came to be "Only Thus,"
by fire and blood, by mighty fist and upright arm, by sufferings

---

[4]Menachem Beigin [sic], "The First Prerequisite of Freedom
Is Complete Victory," The Answer, 28 May 1948, pp. 4-5. The
speech is printed in its entirety with editorial notes from The
Answer.

and sacrifice. It couldn't be otherwise. And even before the state can build its proper institutions, it is compelled to fight--or rather to continue to fight--against the aggression of the wicked enemy and his bloodthirsty hirelings, on land, on the sea and in the air.

3   Under these conditions of founding our national indepen-dence, there is profound meaning in the words with which the great statesman and philosopher, Thomas Masaryk, greeted his people, the people of Czechoslovakia, at the dawn of their lib-eration after 300 years of enslavement. In 1918, on his arrival in Prague, Masaryk said to the jubilant crowds: "It is awfully difficult to bring a state into being, but remember that it is much more difficult to keep a state alive." It was hard for us brethren in Zion, terribly hard indeed, to bring our state into being. It took scores of generations of wandering from massacre to massacre. It took exiles burning at the stake and suffering in the torture chambers. It took stunning blows to destroy blinding illusions. It took unheeded warnings of seers and prophets. It took the toll of generations of builders and pio-neers. And it took the uprising of rebels who smote the enemy, of heroes walking to the gallows and undaunted pilgrims wandering over seas and across deserts--to bring us to this day. To bring to their homeland 600 thousand Hebrews, to bring us to the liqui-dation of the regime of oppression; to bring us to the declara-tion of independence in part of that homeland which is all ours.

4   It was hard indeed to bring our state into being. But it certainly will be much harder to keep our state alive. Many people have surrounded us, and they want to wipe us off God's earth. And that oppressor who is both Hitler's master and his disciple, that wily enslaver whom we smote in the battle is still trying to beat us by trickery; he is trying to beat us and sub-jugate us through his mercenaries from the south, from the north and from the east. This is why our nation stands today in the flames of war, and that is why the prerequisite of our freedom is victory, full and complete victory in the war which is ravaging our country all through its width and length. For this victory, without which we shall have neither freedom nor even life, we need weapons--two-fold weapons; military arms, modern arms, heavy arms to beat the enemy, to expel the invader, to free our land, and also, and this goes for every one of us, another kind of weapon: weapons of moral strength; weapons that steel one's soul, weapons that make one stand without budging in the face of overwhelming odds, weapons that make one disregard bombings from the air, heavy losses of life, weapons that make one stand his ground without quivering in the face of local setbacks and pass-ing defeats, weapons that make one stand fast without retreating or whining. One does not go without the other. If we shall stand in the next days, if we shall stand in the next weeks,

251

armed with the strength of soul of an eternal nation resurrected to life again, we will in the meantime receive the arms we need to smash the enemy, and we shall bring freedom and peace to our people and to our land.

* * *

Victory Will Be Ours

5   But even after victory in this war—and victory will be ours—supreme effort will be needed to maintain our independence and to free our country. First and foremost, we shall have to increase, strengthen and develop the armed might of Israel, for without it, we shall not have homeland, freedom or even mere existence. The Hebrew army can be and must be among the best and most skilled of the armies of the world. In modern warfare, it is not numbers that decide, it is the spirit, it is the brains. And what the spirit of our fighters is, the Hebrew youth has shown, all of it: the youth of the Haganah, the youth of the Fighters for Freedom of Israel, the youth of the Irgun Zvai Leumi, the wonderful Hebrew youth, the like of which no other nation was privileged to have, the like of which no other generation in all the generations of Israel from Bar Kochba through the first pioneers has seen. And as for brains, the brains of Israel, the essence of 120 generations of thought, of 120 generations of thinkers, of seekers of God, has an unlimited scope of inventiveness. One might say that the development of these "natural resources" of ours is unlimited indeed. The military science based on Hebrew brains will be among the top-ranking of the world. We shall have strength, great strength, for we have brains, brains to think, brains that invent.

6   To maintain our freedom and protect our homeland, we shall also need a wise foreign policy. We must convert our declared independence into real independence, and this much must be clear to us; as long as a single British soldier, or any other foreign soldier tramps with his boots the soil of our country, our sovereignty is but as aspiration, an aspiration for the full attainment of which we shall have to fight not only on the battlefield, but also in the international-diplomatic arena. And this too we must realize: from the outset there must be reciprocity to our relations with the peoples of the world. No submission, no surrender and no flattery. Reciprocity must be the password: hate for hate, help for help, friendship for friendship.

7   We must cultivate relations based on understanding and friendship with the great American nation. The present American administration—the Forrestal administration—seems to have forgotten the teachings of Jefferson, Washington, Lee and Tom Paine,

but there are other forces in the American nation: they remember and will remember—they will remember both Cornwallis the Britisher and Lafayette the Frenchman. It is their forces that moved the Washington administration to recognize our provisional government. We must maintain and develop relations based on understanding and friendship with the peoples of the Soviet Union. Let us not evade the truth. There were—in the past—relations of hate between the land of the Revolution and the movement of Hebrew liberation. These relations have cost our people much blood and tears. But in the wake of the heroic fight of the Hebrew underground, these relations underwent revolutionary change. The Soviet Union has recognized our rights to sovereignty and independence in our homeland. And we shall never forget that the victorious Russian armies saved hundreds of thousands of Jews from the clutches of the Nazi beasts. We shall never forget that when our people stood at the crossroads of its history, the Soviet Union stretched out to it a helping hand and assisted it in gaining the road to independence.

* * *

Friendly Relations

8   We must develop relations of friendship and understanding with the peoples of Europe, who have a glorious tradition of fighting for liberation, and from whose midst will come, in the next months and years, the masses of those who will return to Zion. We must develop relations of friendship with the great nation of France, the lighthouse of nations and the carrier of the banner of freedom ever since the day of the Bastille. We must develop relations of friendship and understanding with every nation, big or small, strong or weak, near or far, which will recognize our independence, help our people and will be devoted, the same as we are devoted, to the reign of international justice and to peace among peoples.

9   No less important than our foreign policy is our domestic policy, and the cornerstone of this policy must be: Return to Zion—homecoming. Boats, for God's Sake, give us boatloads of repatriates! No stalling: no empty talk of absorptive capacity, of limitations for the sake of order, as it were. Quickly, quickly, our people is in a hurry! Bring in tens of thousands, bring in hundreds of thousands, and right now, right now! If there will not be houses for all of us, we shall find tents. If there will be no tents, what of it? There are skies above. The blue skies of our land. People don't die of living in hardship. Those who saw how the Russian people lived at the time they stood in the midst of a war for survival and freedom, know that there is no limit, simply no limit, to the sacrifice which a fighting nation is ready to undergo for the sake of its homeland, for the

sake of its future. And, as we stand in the midst of a war for survival, the speediest gathering in of the masses of our exiles will determine our fate and theirs.

10   Within our land, justice will reign supreme. Justice will rule even its rulers. There will be no domination. Those in high office will be the peoples' servants, and not its rulers. There will be no parasitism. There will be no exploitation. In our house, there will not be a man--citizen or alien--hungry for bread, without a roof over his head, without clothes or without an opportunity for education. "Remember that you were a stranger in the land of Egypt." This commandment will determine our relations with our neighbors. "And thou shalt seek justice." This commandment will determine the relations between men in our house. "And in this land will dwell in peace and happiness my son; the Moslem and the Christian native; for my flag is pure and just, and it will purify both shores of the River Jordan." (Vladimir Jabotinsky's song, "The Jordan"--ed.)

* * *

Out From Underground

11   For these principles, the Liberation Movement will fight within the framework of Hebrew law, within the framework of Hebrew democracy--that Liberation Movement which will arise from the depths of the Hebrew underground, that Liberation Movement which will comprise the great fighting family, the family that sprung from all walks of life, from all the dispersions, from all the trends, to rally around the banner of the Irgun Zvai Leumi. The Irgun Zvai Leumi now comes out from underground within the borders of the independent Hebrew State. We went down underground--one should rather say we went up underground--under a foreign regime of oppression, to beat it and liquidate it. And we beat it, we beat it good, and we destroyed it forever. And now, a Hebrew regime has emerged, for the time being only in part of our homeland.

12   In this part of our homeland, in the liberated part, in the part ruled by Hebrew law, and this is the only legal rule in this country, there is no need for a Hebrew underground. In the state of Israel, we shall be soldiers and builders. We shall abide by its laws, for they are our laws. We shall respect its government, for it is our government. But let the Hebrew government be warned, the provisional government and any other government that shall succeed it, not to give rise to a new underground through appeasement and concessions abroad, or through tryanny and domination at home. The Hebrew government must protect the independence which was bought at a cost of the blood of heroes and martyrs, and let it be warned not to squander that independence

254

by submission to tyrants and blackmailers. Let the government be the guardian of the rights of the men and citizens, without discrimination and without privileges. Let the government be the guardian of the principles of justice and freedom, and let our house bathe in the light of brotherly love and the brotherhood of Israel.

* * *

Not Freed Yet

13 The state of Israel has arisen, but let us remember that the homeland has not yet been freed. The war is going on, and you can see with your own eyes that your fighters did not err; Hebrew arms will determine the borders of the jurisdiction of the Hebrew sovereignty. So it is in this fight, and so it will be in the future. The Fatherland is an entity. Any attempt to dismember it is not only a criminal attempt, it is also a futile attempt. The Fatherland is a historic and geographic entity, and he who denies us the right to all of our government, denies us also the right to any part of its territory, and we shall never give up our inalienable birthright. We shall carry the vision of full liberation, we shall carry the vision of full redemption, and we shall make it true when the day comes. For this is an immutable law: there cannot be a dividing line between the national territory and the homeland, and if there is such an artificial line drawn, it is bound to disappear. Our national territory must be our homeland, and our homeland will be our state. Let us not be led astray by learned expressions. Let us not speak of irredenta, for it is not only a city that was robbed from us: five-sixths of our national territory is at stake. We must and can, reclaim it, for ourselves and for our generations to come, for our own security, for the security of our brethren and sons, and for the peace. And that is why we shall carry with pride the vision of complete redemption, the vision of the homeland liberated under the Hebrew flag, the flag of freedom, the flag of peace, the flag of progress. The soldiers of Israel will yet hoist our flag over the Tower of David. Our plows will yet plow the fields of Galad (historic Hebrew site in what is called Transjordan. Ed.)

14 Citizens of the Hebrew homeland, soldiers of Israel! We stand before an intensification of the battle. Hard times are ahead. Blood, the most precious of all treasures, is being spilled and will be spilled. Strengthen your will, steel your hearts, for this is the way, the way of suffering and sacrifice, and there is no other. We shall not buy peace from our enemies at the price of concessions. Yes, one kind of peace can be bought by submission. The peace of the graveyard, the peace of a new Treblinka. We must, therefore, strain ourselves in the utmost and be ready for the decisive test. We shall stand our

255

ground. The Lord of Hosts will be with us, and the heroism of the Hebrew youth, and the heroism of the Hebrew mother, the mother who brings her son to the altar of God; this supreme heroism will save us from the hands of our enemies, and bring us out of slavery to freedom, out of the peril of annihilation into the haven of safety.

* * *

How We Began

15   And now my brothers, children of the fighting family, do you remember how we began, and with what we began? Now you see with your own eyes those who sowed in blood reap in freedom. You were alone and hunted, you were alone and martyred, but you kept on fighting with invincible faith. You did not retreat. You were tortured but would not surrender. You were thrown into prisons, but you would not give up. You were exiled from your homeland, but your spirit was not broken. You were walked to the gallows, but you sang a song. And so you wrote with your own hands a glorious page in the history of our people. And you will still write, not with ink, but with blood and sweat, not with pens, but with the sword and the plow. You shall not remember wrongs and you shall not ask for reward. Our only reward is that we lived to see the day when our nation is being freed and fights—all of it—for its freedom. Our true reward will be when we shall be privileged—if we come back alive from the battlefront—to roam the cities and towns of our land, its hills and valleys, and to see Hebrew children playing peacefully; and when a soldier will walk in their midst, he will be a Hebrew soldier, and when from afar, a train will roar by, it will be a Hebrew train.

* * *

Forward to Victory

16   But right now, we must think of the battle, of nothing but the battle, for this will decide our fate, this will decide our future. Into this battle, the spirit of our ancient heroes, from the conquerors of Canaan to the rebels of Judea, will go with us. Into this battle, the spirit of the revivers of our nation will go with us: Theodore Herzl, Max Nordau, Joseph Trumpeldor and the father of reborn Hebrew heroism, Vladimir Jabotinsky. Into this battle will go with us the spirit of David Raziel, the greatest of the war leaders in our generation, and Dov Gruner, the greatest of the soldiers and heroes. Into this battle will go with us the spirit of the heroes of the gallows, who overcame death. Into this battle will go with us the spirit of millions of our martyrs, of our slain fathers, of our slaughtered mothers, of our massacred brothers, of our trampled children. In this

battle we shall smite the enemy and bring freedom to a people surfeited with persecution and thirsty for freedom.

17 God of Israel, keep Your soldiers and bless their sword which gives a new birth to the covenant that You sealed with Your beloved people and Your chosen land.

18 Forward to the battle-ground! Forward to victory!

"Text of Address by Mr. Menahem Begin, Prime Minister of the State of Israel, At a Special Session of the Knesset."[5]

1   Mr. Speaker, Honourable President of the State of Israel, Honourable President of the Arab Republic of Egypt, Worthy and Learned Knesset Members:

2   We send our greetings to the President and to all adherents of the Islamic faith, in our own country and wherever they may be, on the occasion of the Feast of Sacrifice, Id el-Adha.

3   This feast reminds us of the binding of Isaac on the altar, the test with which the Creator tried the faith of our forefather Abraham--our common father; the challenge which Abraham met. But, from the point of view of morality and the advancement of Mankind, this event heralded the principle of a ban on human sacrifice. Our two Peoples, in their ancient tradition, learned and taught that humanitarian prohibition, while the nations around us continued to offer human sacrifices to their idols. Thus we, the People of Israel and the Arab People, contribute to human civilization until this very day.

4   I greet the President of Egypt on the occasion of his visit to our country and his participation in this session of the Knesset. The duration of the flight from Cairo to Jerusalem is short but, until last night, the distance between them was infinite. President Sadat showed courage in crossing this distance. We Jews can appreciate courage, as exhibited by our guest, because it is with courage that we arose, and with it we shall continue to exist.

5   Mr. Speaker, this small People, the surviving remnant of the Jewish People which returned to our historic Homeland, always sought peace. And, when the dawn of our freedom rose on the 14th day of May, 1948, the 4th of Iyyar, 5708. David Ben-Gurion said, in the Declaration of Independence, the charter of our national independence:

> "We extend our hand to all neighbouring states and their peoples in an offer of peace and good neighbourliness, and appeal to them to establish bonds of cooperation and mutual help with the sovereign Jewish People settled in its own Land."

---

[5]Menachem Begin, "Text of Address by Mr. Menahem Begin, Prime Minister of the State of Israel, At a Special Session of the Knesset," 20 November 1977, Israel Information Centre.

258

A year earlier, in the midst of the fateful struggle for the liberation of the Land and the redemption of the Nation, while still in the underground, we issued the following call to our neighbours:

> "Let us live together in this Land and together advance towards a life of freedom and happiness. Our Arab neighbours--do not reject the hand which is outstretched to you in peace."

But it is my duty--my duty Mr. Speaker, and not only my privilege--to assert today in truth that our hand, extended in peace, was rejected. And, one day after our independence was renewed, in accordance with our eternal and indisputable right, we were attacked on three fronts, and we stood virtually without arms-- few against many, weak against strong. One day after the declaration of our independence, an attempt was made to strangle it with enmity, and to extinguish the last hope of the Jewish People in the generation of Holocaust and Resurrection.

6   No, we do not believe in might, and we have never based our relations with the Arab Nation on force. On the contrary, force was exercised against us. Throughout all the years of this generation we have never ceased to be attacked with brute force in order to destroy our Nation, to demolish our independence, or annul our right. And we defended ourselves.

7   True, we defended our right, our existence, our honour, our women and our children against recurrent attempts to crush us by brutal force, and not on one front alone. This, too, is true: with the help of God we overcame the forces of aggression and assured the survival of our nation, not only for this generation, but for all those to come.

8   We do not believe in might; we believe in right, only in right. And that is why our aspiration, from the depths of our hearts, from time immemorial until this very day, is peace.

9   Mr. President, in this democratic chamber sit commanders of all the Hebrew underground fighting organizations. They were compelled to conduct a battle of few against many, against a mighty world power. Here sit our top military commanders, who led the forces in a battle that was imposed on them, and to a victory that was inevitable, because they defended right. They belong to various parties, and have different outlooks. But I am sure, Mr. President, that I am expressing the views of them all, without exception, when I say that we have one aspiration at heart, one desire in our souls, and we are all united in this aspiration and this desire--to bring peace: peace to our nation which has not known it for even one day since the beginning of

259

the Return to Zion; and peace to our neighbours to whom we wish all the best. And we believe that if we achieve peace, true peace, we shall be able to assist one another in all realms of life, and a new era will be opened in this Middle East: an era of flourishing and growth, of development and progress and advancement, as in ancient times.

10   Therefore, allow me today to define the meaning of peace as we understand it. We seek a true, full peace, with absolute reconciliation between the Jewish People and the Arab Peoples. We must not permit memories of the past to stand in our way. There have been wars; blood has been shed; our wonderful sons have fallen in battle on both sides. We shall always cherish the memory of our heroes who gave their lives so that this day, yea even this day, might come. We respect the valour of an adversary, and we pay tribute to all members of the young generation of the Arab Nation who have fallen as well.

11   Let us not be daunted by memories of the past, even if they are bitter to us all. We must overcome them, and focus on what lies ahead; on our Peoples, on our children, on our common future. For, in this region, we shall all live together--the Great Arab Nation and its States and its countries, and the Jewish People in its Land, Eretz Israel--forever and ever. For this reason the meaning of peace must be defined.

12   As free men, Mr. President, let us conduct negotiations for a peace treaty and, with the help of God, so we believe with all our hearts, the day will come when we will sign it, with mutual respect. Then will we know that the era of wars has ended, that we have extended a hand to one another, that we have shaken each other's hand, and that the future will be glorious for all the Peoples of the region. Of prime significance, therefore, in the context of a peace treaty, is a termination of the state of war.

13   I agree, Mr. President, that you have not come here and we did not invite you to our country in order, as has been suggested in recent days, to drive a wedge between the Arab Peoples, or, expressed more cleverly in accord with the ancient saying, "divide et impera." Israel has no desire to rule and does not wish to divide. We want peace with all our neighbours--with Egypt and with Jordan, with Syria and with Lebanon.

14   There is no need to differentiate between a peace treaty and the termination of the state of war. We neither propose this, nor do we seek it. On the contrary, the first article of a peace treaty determines the end of the state of war, forever. We wish to establish normal relations between us, as exist among all nations after wars. We have learned from history, Mr. President, that war is avoidable. It is peace that is inevitable.

15   Many nations have waged war against one another, and sometimes they have made use of the foolish term "eternal enemy."
There are no eternal enemies. After all wars comes the inevit-
able--peace. Therefore, in the context of a peace treaty, we
seek to stipulate the establishment of diplomatic relations, as
is customary among civilized nations.

16   Today, Jerusalem is bedecked with two flags--the Egyptian
and the Israeli. Together, Mr. President, we have seen our
little children waving both flags. Let us sign a peace treaty
and establish such a situation forever, both in Jerusalem and in
Cairo. I hope the day will come when Egyptian children will wave
Israeli and Egyptian flags together, just as the Israeli children
are waving both of these flags together in Jerusalem; when you,
Mr. President, will be represented by a loyal Ambassador in Jerusalem, and we, by an Ambassador in Cairo and, should difference
of opinion arise between us, we will clarify them, like civilized
people, through our authorized emissaries.

17   We propose economic cooperation for the development of our
countries. God created marvelous lands in the Middle East--
virtual oases in the desert--but there are also deserts, and
these can be made fertile. Let us join hands in facing this
challenge, and cooperate in developing our countries, in abolishing poverty, hunger and homelessness. Let us raise our nations
to the status of developed countries, so that we may no longer be
called developing states.

18   With all due respect, I am prepared to endorse the words of
His Highness, the King of Morocco, who said, publicly, that, if
peace were to be established in the Middle East, the combination
of Arab and Jewish genius can together convert the region into a
paradise on earth.

19   Let us open our countries to free movement, so that you
shall come to us and we will visit you. I am prepared today to
announce, Mr. Speaker, that our country is open to the citizens
of Egypt, and I do not qualify this announcement with any condition on our part. I think it would only be proper and just that
there be a mutual announcement on this matter. And, just as
Egyptian flags are flying in our streets, there is also an hon-
oured Egyptian delegation in our capital and in our country
today. Let there be many visitors. Our border will be open to
you, just as will be all the other borders, for, as I noted, we
would like the same situations to prevail in the south, in the
north and in the east.

20   Threfore, I renew my invitation to the President of Syria to
follow in your footsteps, Mr. President, and to come to our country to begin negotations on the establishment of peace between

Israel and Syria and on the signing of a peace treaty between us. I am sorry to say, there is no justification for the mourning that has been decreed on the other side of our northern border. On the contrary, such visits, such contacts and discussions, can and should be a cause of happiness, a cause of elation for all peoples.

21   I invite King Hussein to come here and we shall discuss with him all the problems that exist between us. I also invite genuine spokesmen of the Palestinian Arabs to come and to hold talks with us on our common future, on guaranteeing human freedom, social justice, peace and mutual respect.

22   And, if they should invite us to come to their capitals, we shall respond to their invitations. Should they invite us to begin negotiations in Damascus, Amman or Beirut, we shall go to those capitals in order to negotiate there. We do not wish to divide. We seek true peace with all our neighbours, to be expressed in peace treaties, the context of which shall be as I have already clarified.

23   Mr. Speaker, it is my duty today to tell our guests and all the nations who are watching us and listening to our words about the bond between People and this Land. The President mentioned the Balfour Declaration. No, sir, we took no foreign land. We returned to our Homeland. The bond between our People and this Land is eternal. It was created at the dawn of human history. It was never severed. In this Land we established our civilization; here our prophets spoke those holy words you cited this very day; here the Kings of Judah and Israel prostrated themselves; here we became a nation; here we established our Kingdom and, when we were exiled from our country by the force that was exercised against us, even when we were far away, we did not forget this Land, not even for a single day. We prayed for it; we longed for it; we have believed in our return to it ever since the day these words were spoken:

"When the Lord brought back the captivity of Zion we were like those who dream. Then our mouth was filled with laughter and our tongue with joyful shouting."

That song applies to all our exiles, to all our sufferings, and to the consolation that the Return to Zion would surely come.

24   This, our right, has been recognized. The Balfour Declaration was included in the Mandate which was recognized by the nations of the world, including the United States of America. And the preamble to that authoritative document states:

262

"Whereas recognition has thereby been given to the historical connection of the Jewish People with Palestine (or, in Hebrew, 'Eretz Israel') and to the grounds for reconstituting their National Home in that country (that is, in 'Eretz Israel') . . ."

In 1919, we also gained recognition of this right from the spokesman of the Arab People. The agreement of 3 January 1919, signed by Emir Feisal and Chaim Weizman, states:

"Mindful of the racial kinship and ancient bonds existing between the Arabs and the Jewish People, and realizing that the surest means of working out the consummation of their national aspirations is through the closest possible collaboration in the development of the Arab State and of Palestine . . ."

Afterwards, follow all the articles on cooperation between the Arab State and Eretz Israel. That is our right; its fulfillment-- the truth.

25   What happened to us when our homeland was taken from us?   I accompanied you this morning, Mr. President, to Vad Vashem. With your own eyes you saw what the fate of our People was when this Homeland was taken from it.   It is an incredible story.   We both agreed, Mr. President, that whoever has not himself seen what is found in Vad Vashem cannot understand what befell this People when it was homeless, robbed of its own Homeland.   And we both read a document, dated 30 January 1939, in which the word "vernichtung" appears--"if war breaks out the Jewish race in Europe will be annihilated."   Then, too, we were told to pay no heed to such words.   The whole world heard.   No one came to our rescue not during the nine critical, fateful months following this announcement--the likes of which had never been heard since God created man and man created Satan--and not during those six years when millions of our people, among them a million and a half small Jewish children were slaughtered in every possible way.

26   No one came to our rescue, not from the East and not from the West.   And therefore we, this entire generation, the generation of Holocaust and Resurrection swore an oath of allegiance: never again shall we endanger our People; never again will our wives and our children--whom it is our duty to defend, if need be even at the cost of our own lives--be put in the devastating range of enemy fire.

27   And further: ever since then it has been, and will continue
to be, our duty, for generations to come, to remember that certain things said about our People are to be related to with all
seriousness.   We must not, Heaven forbid, for the future of our
People, accept any advice suggesting that we not take such words
seriously.

28   President Sadat knows, as he knew from us before he came to
Jerusalem, that our position concerning permanent borders between
us and our neighbors differs from his.   However, I call upon the
President of Egypt and upon all our neighbors: do not rule out
the negotiations on any subject matter.   I propose, in the name
of the overwhelming majority of this Parliament, that everything
will be negotiable.   Anybody who says that, in the relationship
between the Arab People--or the Arab Nations in the area--and the
State of Israel there are subjects that should be excluded from
negotiations, is assuming an awesome responsibility.   Everything
is negotiable.   No side shall say the contrary.   No side shall
present prior conditions.   We will conduct the negotiations with
respect.

29   If there are differences of opinion between us, that is not
exceptional.   Anyone who has studied the history of wars and the
annals of peace treaties knows that all negotiations for peace
treaties have begun with differences of opinion between the
parties concerned, and that, in the course of negotiations, they
have reached solutions which have made possible the signing of
agreements or peace treaties.   That is the path we propose to
follow.

30   We shall conduct the negotiations as equals.   There are no
vanquished and there are no victors.   All the Peoples of the
region are equal, and all will relate to each other with respect.
In this spirit of openness, of readiness of each to listen to the
other--to facts, reasons, explanations--with every resonable
attempt at mutual persuasion--let us conduct the negotiations as
I have asked and propose to open them, to conduct them, to continue them persistently until we succeed, in good time, in signing the peace treaty between us.

31   We are prepared, not only, to sit with representatives of
Egypt and with representatives of Jordan, Syria and Lebanon--if
it so desires--at a Peace Conference in Geneva.   We proposed that
the Geneva Conference be renewed on the basis of Resolutions 242
and 338 of the Security Council.   However, should problems arise
between us prior to the convening of the Geneva Conference, we
will clarify them today and tomorrow and, if the President of
Egypt will be interested in continuing to clarify them in Cairo--
all the better; if on neutral ground--no opposition.   Anywhere.
Let us clarify--even before the Geneva Conference convenes---the

problems that should be made clear before it meets, with open eyes and a readiness to listen to all suggestions.

32   Allow me to say a word about Jerusalem. Mr. President, today you prayed in a house of worship sacred to the Islamic faith, and from there you went to the Church of the Holy Sepulchre. You witnessed the fact, known to all who come from throughout the world, that, ever since this city was joined together, there is absolutely free access, without any interference or obstacles, for the members of all religions to their holy places. This positive phenomenon did not exist for 19 years. It has existed now for about 11 years, and we can assure the Moslem world and the Christian world--all the nations--that there will always be free access to the holy places of every faith. We shall defend this right of free access, for it is something in which we believe--in the equality for every man and every citizen, and in respect for every faith.

33   Mr. Speaker, this is a special day for our Parliament, and it will undoubtedly be remembered for many years in the annals of our Nation, in the history of the Egyptian People, and perhaps, also, in the history of nations.

34   And on this day, with your permission, worthy and learned Members of the Knesset, I wish to offer a prayer that the God of our common ancestors will grant us the requisite wisdom of heart in order to overcome the difficulties and obstacles, the calumnies and slanders. With the help of God, may we arrive at the longed-for day for which our people pray--the day of peace.

35   For indeed, as the Psalmist of Israel said, "Righteousness and peace have kissed," and, as the prophet Zechariah said, "Love truth and peace."

"Prime Minister Begin's Speech at the Signing of
the Peace Treaty With Egypt."[6]

1   Mr. President of the United States of America, Mr. President
of the Arab Republic of Egypt, Mr. Vice President, Mr. Speaker of
the House of Representatives, Mr. Speaker of the Knesset, Members
of the Cabinets of the United States, of Egypt, and Israel,
Members of the Congress and the Knesset, your Excellencies,
Chairman of the Board of Governors of the Jewish Agency, Chairman
of the Executive of the Zionist Organization, Mrs. Gruber, the
mother of the sons, distinguished guests, ladies and gentlemen:

/2   I have come from the Land of Israel, the Land of Zion and
Jerusalem, and here I am in humility and with pride, as a son of
the Jewish People, as one of the generation of the Holocaust and
Redemption. The ancient Jewish people gave the world a vision of
eternal peace, of universal disarmament, of abolishing the teach-
ing and the learning of war. Two prophets--Isaiah and Micah--
having foreseen the spiritual unity of man under God with these
words coming from Jerusalem, gave the nations of the world the
following visions, expressed in identical terms: "And they shall
beat their swords into plowshares, and their spears into pruning
hooks. Nations shall not lift up sword against nation; neither
shall they learn war anymore." Despite the tragedies and disap-
pointments of the past, we must never forsake that vision, that
human dream, that unshakeable faith.

3   Peace is the beauty of life. It is sunshine. It is the
smile of a child, the love of a mother, the joy of a father, the
togetherness of a family. It is the advancement of man, the
victory of a just cause, the triumph of truth. Peace is all of
these and more, and more. These are words I uttered in Oslo on
December the tenth, 1978, while receiving the second half of the
Nobel Peace Prize--the first half went, rightly so, to President
Sadat. And I took the liberty to repeat them here, in this
momentous historic occasion. It is a great day in the annals of
two ancient nations, Egypt and Israel, whose sons met in battle
five times in one generation, fighting and falling. Let us turn
our hearts to our heroes, and pay tribute to their eternal
memory. It is thanks to them, to our fallen heroes, that we
could have reached this day.

---

[6]Menachem Begin, "Prime Minister Begin's Speech at the Signing of the Peace Treaty With Egypt," 26 March 1979, State of
Israel Government Press Office. Begin's statement was printed
all in caps.

266

4   However, let us not forget that in ancient times, our two nations went also in alliance. Now we make peace: the cornerstone of cooperation and friendship.

5   It is a great day in your life, Mr. President of the United States, and you have worked so hard, so insistently, so consistently, to achieve this goal, and your labors and your devotion bore God-blessed fruit. Our friend, President Sadat, said that you are the unknown soldier of the peace-making effort. I agree--but, as usually, with an amendment. A soldier in the service of peace, you are. You are, Mr. President, horrible dictu, an intransigent fighter for peace. But, Jimmy Carter, the President of the United States, is not completely unknown. And so is his effort, which will be remembered and recorded by generations to come.

6   It is, of course, a great day in your life, Mr. President of the Arab Republic of Egypt. In the face of adversity and hostility, you have demonstrated the human value that can change history: civil courage. A great field commander once said civil courage is sometimes more difficult to show than military courage. You showed both, Mr. President. But now it is time for all of us to show civil courage, in order to proclaim to our peoples and to others: no more war, no more bloodshed, no more bereavement--peace unto you, Shalom, Salaam forever.

7   And it is, ladies and gentlemen, the third greatest day in my life. The first was May the fourteenth, 1948, when our flag was hoisted. Our independence in our ancestors' land was proclaimed after 1,878 years of dispersion, persecution, humiliation, and ultimately physical destruction. We fought for our liberation alone, and, with God's help, we won the day. That was spring. Such a spring we can never have again. The second day was when Jerusalem became one city, and our brave, perhaps most hardened soldiers--the parachutists--embraced with tears and kissed the ancient stones of the remnants of the wall destined to protect the chosen place of God's glory. Our hearts wept with them in remembrance: "Now we stand within your gates, O Jerusalem, that is built to be a city where people come together in unity."

8   This is the third day in my life. I have signed a treaty of peace with our great neighbor, with Egypt. The heart is full and overflowing. God gave me the strength to persevere, to survive the horrors of Nazism and of a Stalinite concentration camp--and some other dangers. To endure--not to waver in or flinch from my duty. To accept the abuse from foreigners and, what is more painful, from my own people and even from my close friends. This effort, too, bore some fruit.

267

9   Therefore, it is the proper place and the appropriate time
to bring back to memory the song ad prayer of thankgsiving I
learned as a child in the home of father and mother, that doesn't
exist anymore--because they were among the six million people,
men, women, and children, who sanctified the Lord's name with
their sacred blood, which reddened the rivers of Europe from the
Rhine to the Danube, from the Bug to the Volga, because--only
because--they were born Jews. And because they didn't have a
country of their own, and neither a valiant Jewish army to defend
them. And because nobody, nobody, came to their rescue, although
they cried out, "Save us!   Save us!", de profundis, from the
depths of the pit and agony.

10   That is the song of degrees, written two millenia and five
hundred years ago, when our forefathers returned from the first
exile to Jerusalem and Zion:

> ("When the Lord brought back those that returned
> to Zion, we were like unto them that dream. Then
> was our mouth filled with laughter, and our
> tongue with singing; then said they among the
> nations: 'The Lord hath done great things with
> these.' The Lord hath done great things with us;
> we are rejoiced. Turn our captivity, O Lord, as
> the streams in the dry land. They that sow in
> tears shall reap in joy. Thou he goeth on his
> way weeping, that beareth the measure of seed, he
> shall come home with joy, bearing his sheaves.")

11   I will not translate. Every man, whether Jew or Christian
or Moslem, can read it in his own language, in the book of the
books. It is just Psalm 126.

268

Begin's Statement Folllowing the Golan Annexation[7]

1   Three times during the past six months the US Government has 'punished' Israel.

2   On June 7 we destroyed the Iraqi nuclear reactor 'Osirk' near Baghdad. I don't want to mention to you today from whom we received the final information that this reactor was going to produce atomic bombs. We had no doubt about that: therefore our action was an act of salvation, an act of national self-defense in the most lofty sense of the concept. We saved the lives of hundreds of thousands of civilians, including tens of thousands of children.

3   Nonetheless, you announced that you were punishing us--and you left unfulfilled a signed and sealed contract that included specific dates for the supply of (war) planes.

4   Not long after, in a defensive act--after a slaughter was committed against our people leaving three dead (including an Auschwitz survivor) and 29 were injured--we bombed the PLO head-quarters in Beirut.

5   You have no moral right to preach to us about civilian casualties. We have read the history of World War Two and we know what happened to civilians when you took action against the enemy. We have also read the history of the Vietnam war and your phrase 'body count'. We always make efforts to avoid hitting civilian populations, but sometimes it is unavoidable--as was the case in our bombing of the PLO headquarters.

6   Nonetheless you punished us: you suspended delivery of F-15 planes.

7   A week ago, at the instance of the Government, the Knesset passed on all three readings by an overwhelming majority of two-thirds the 'Golan Heights Law.'

8   Now you are once again boasting that you are 'punishing' Israel.

9   What kind of expression is this--'punishing Israel'? Are we a vassal-state of yours? Are we a banana republic? Are we youths of fourteen who, if they don't behave properly, are slapped aross the fingers?

---

[7]Begin's statement is reprinted in "Israel Hits Back After U.S. Sanctions," _Jerusalem Post International Edition_, 20-26 December 1981, pp. 1-2.

10   Let me tell you who this government is composed of. It is
composed of people whose lives were spent in resistance, in
fighting and in suffering. You will not frighten us with 'punishments.' He who threatens us will find us deaf to his threats.
We are only prepared to listen to rational arguments.

11   You have no right to 'punish' Israel--and I protest at the
very use of this term.

12   You have announced that you are suspending consultation on
the implementation of the memorandum of understanding on strategic cooperation, and that your return to these consultations in
the future will depend on progress achieved in the autonomy talks
and on the situation in Lebanon.

13   You want to make Israel a hostage of the memorandum of
understanding.

14   I regard your announcement suspending the consultations on
the memorandum as the abrogation (by you) of the memorandum. No
'sword of Damocles' is going to hang over our head. So we duly
take note of the fact that you have abrogated the memorandum of
understanding.

15   The people of Israel has lived 3,700 years without a memorandum of understanding with America--and it will continue to
live without one for another 3,700 years. In our eyes it (i.e.,
the US suspension) is an abrogation of the memorandum.

16   We will not agree that you should demand of us to allow the
Arabs of East Jerusalem to take part in the autonomy elections--
and threaten us that if we don't consent you will suspend the
memorandum.

17   You have imposed upon us financial punishments--and have
(thereby) violated the word of the President. When Secretary
Haig was here he read from a written document the words of President Reagan that you would purchase 200 million dollars worth of
Israeli arms and other equipment.

18   This is therefore a violation of the President's word. Is
it customary? Is it proper?

19   You cancelled an additional 100 million dollars. What did
you want to do--to 'hit us in our pockets'?

20   In 1946 there lived in this house a British general by the
name of Barker. Today I live here. When we fought him you
called us 'terrorists'--and we carried on fighting. After we
attacked his headquarters in the requisitioned building of the

270

King David Hotel, Barker said: 'This race will only be influenced by being hit in the pocket'--and he ordered his soldiers to stop patronizing Jewish cafes.

21   To hit us in the pocket--this is the philosophy of Barker. Now I understand why the whole great effort in the Senate to obtain a majority for the arms deal with Saudi Arabia was accompanied by an ugly campaign of anti-Semitism.

22   First the slogan was sounded 'Begin or Reagan'--and that was nice because it meant that whoever opposes the deal is supporting a foreign prime minister and is not loyal to the President of the United States.   And thus Senators, like Jackson, Kennedy, Packwood, and of course Boschowitz are not loyal citizens.

23   Then the slogan was sounded.   'We should not let the Jews determine the foreign policy of the United States.' What was the meaning of this slogan?   The Greek minority in the U.S. determined the Senate decision to withhold weapons from Turkey after it invaded Cyprus.   No one will frighten the great and free Jewish community of the U.S., no one will succeed in cowing them with anti-Semitic propaganda. They will stand by our side. This is the land of their forefathers--and they have a right and a duty to support it.

24   Some say we must 'rescind' the law passed by the Knesset. 'To rescind' is a concept from the days of the Inquisition. Our forefathers went to the stake rather than 'rescind' their faith.

25   We do not need to go to the stake: we, thank God, have strength enough to defend our sovereignty and to defend our rights.

26   If it were up to me (alone) I would say we should not rescind the law.   But as far as I can judge there is in fact no one on earth who can persuade the Knesset to rescind the law which is passed by a two-thirds majority.

27   Mr. Weinberger--and later Mr. Haig--said that the law adversely effects U.N. Resolution 242.   Whoever says that has either not read the Resolution, or has forgotten it or has not understood it.

28   The essence of the Resolution is negotiation to determine agreed and recognized borders.   Syria has announced that it will not conduct negotiation with us, that it does not and will not recognize us--and thus removed from Resolution 242 its essence. How, therefore, could we adversely effect 242?

271

29   As regards the future, please be kind enough to inform the Secretary of State that the Golan Heights Law will remain valid. There is no force on earth that can bring about its rescission.

30   As for the contention that we surprised you, the truth is that we did not want to embarrass you. We knew your difficulties. It was indeed President Reagan who said that Mr. Begin was right--that had Israel told the US about the law (in advance) the US would have said no--and then go ahead and apply Israeli law to the Golan Heights.

31   As regards Lebanon, I have asked that the Secretary of State be informed that we will not initiate a war, but if we are attacked by the terrorists or the Syrians we will launch a counter-attack.

SELECTED BIBLIOGRAPHY

Primary Resources: Menachem Begin and the Irgun Zvai Leumi

Begin Menachem.   "Address by Prime Minister Menachem Begin at a
Special Festive Ceremony Held at Knesset Plaza, to Mark the
Premier's Return Home Following the Signing of the Peace
Treaty With Egypt." Jerusalem: Press Bulletin of Israel,
29 March 1979.

----------.   "Address by Prime Minister Menachem Begin at the
Knesset Session in Honour of President Francois Mitterand of
France." Jerusalem: Israel Ministry of Foreign Affairs, 4
March 1982.

----------.   "Address by Prime Minister Menachem Begin on the
Occasion of the Centenary Year of the Birth of Zeev Jabotin-
sky, at a Memorial Meeting on Mt. Herzl, Jerusalem, on 30
July 1981." Jerusalem: Press Bulletin of Israel, n.d.

----------.   "Address by Prime Minister Menachem Begin to the
Egyptian People, Jerusalem, November 11, 1977." New York:
Consulate of Israel, n.d.

----------.   "Address by Prime Minister Menachem Begin to the
Knesset in the Debate on the Suggested Sale of American Arms
to Jordan and the Resulting Knesset Resolution." Jerusalem:
Israel Ministry of Foreign Affairs, 15 February 1982.

----------.   "Address by Prime Minister of Israel, Mr. Menachem
Begin at the Opening of the Winter Session of the Knesset,
Monday, November 2, 1981." Jerusalem: Press Bulletin of
Israel, n.d.

----------.   "Advance or Be Pushed Into the Sea." The Answer, 6
August 1948, p. 5.

----------.   "Basic Policy Guidelines of the Government of Israel
as Presented to the Knesset (Israel's Parliament) on June
20, 1977." Washington: Embassy of Israel, n.d.

----------.   "Beigin [sic] in Stirring Address at Waldorf-Astoria
Dinner." The Answer, 10 December 1948, pp. 4-5.

----------. "Begin Replies: Don't Give Comfort to Our Enemies."
Jerusalem Post International Edition, 27 July-2 August 1980,
p. 11.

----------. "Begin Replies: Shocking Frivolity Has Guided You."
Jerusalem Post International Edition, 1-7 June 1980, p. 10.

----------. Dialogue Rabbi William Berkovitz and Prime Minister
Menachem Begin. New York: Institute of Adult Studies of
Congregation Bnai Jeshulan, 1977.

----------. "Excerpts From the Address by Prime Minister Menahem
Begin Before the Central Committee of the Herut Party, Tel
Aviv, January 8, 1978." New York: Consulate of Israel,
1978.

----------. "Excerpts From the Address of Prime Minister Menachem
Begin Upon Presenting His Government to the Knesset on 5
August 1981." Jerusalem: Press Bulletin of Israel, 1981.

----------. "Excerpts From Begin's News Conference at National
Press Club in Washington." New York Times, 24 March 1979,
p. A10.

----------. "Excerpts From Carter-Begin Remarks." New York
Times, 23 March 1978, p. 16.

----------. "Excerpts From an Interview with Prime Minister
Menachem Begin on Israel Television's 'Moked.'" Jerusalem:
Press Bulletin of Israel, 15 April 1981.

----------. "Excerpts From a News Conference Given by Prime
Minister Begin at Ben-Gurion Airport, Upon His Return from
Ismailiya, on 26 December 1977." Jerusalem: Israel Infor-
mation Centre, n.d.

----------. "Excerpts From the Statement in the Knesset by Prime
Minister Menahem Begin." New York: Consulate of Israel.
15 February 1978.

----------. "The First Prerequisite of Freedom Is Complete Victory." The Answer, 28 May 1948, pp. 4-5.

----------. "Foreign Policy Section of a Speech Made at the 13th
Convention of the Herut Movement, Jerusalem, 6 January
1977." In Who Is Menahem Begin. Beirut: Institute for
Palestine Studies, 1977, pp. 56-59.

----------. "The Freedom Movement Speak!" The Answer, 15 October 1948, p. 6.

----------. "Highlights of an Address by Prime Minister Menachem Begin to the Knesset." Jerusalem: Israel Information Centre, 23 January 1978.

----------. "I Bring the Message of Peace." Jerusalem: Israel Information Centre, 25 September 1978.

----------. "The Inheritance of Our Fathers." The Jewish Herald, 28 March 1972, pp. 12-13.

----------. "Interview With Israel's Prime Minister Menachem Begin." Macleans, 6 February 1978, pp. 4, 8, 10.

----------. "Interview with Prime Minister Menachem Begin, Recorded Aboard the Plane En Route Home from the Treaty-Signing Ceremony in Washington, and Broadcast over Israel Radio's Morning Newsreel Today." Jerusalem: Press Bulletin of Israel, 30 March 1979.

----------. Israel and the USA: Friendship-Alliance Strategic Cooperation. Washington: Embassy of Israel, n.d.

----------. "Israel Hits Back After U.S. Sanctions." Jerusalem Post International Edition, 20-26 December 1981, pp. 1-2.

----------. "Israel Was Right in Attempt to Capture Habash." The Jewish Herald, 4 September 1973, p. 4.

----------. " Israel Will Yet Be Wholly Free." The Jewish Herald, Rosh Hashanah, 1952, p. 1.

----------. "Israel's Borders with Her Neighbors." Israel Digest, 15 July 1977, p. 33.

----------. "Jerusalem Waits and Hopes." The Answer, 8 September 1948, p. 5.

----------. "Jewish-Arab Relations in Israel." The Jewish Herald, 28 October 1969, p. 7.

----------. "The Jewish News Salutes the People of Israel on the 30th Anniversary of Their Independence." The Detroit Jewish News, 12 May 1978, p. 31.

----------. "Major Points from Prime Minister Menahem Begin's Speech to the Knesset, December 28, 1977." New York: Consulate of Israel, n.d.

----------. "Menachem Begin: Prime Minister of Israel." Meet the Press, 82 (25 April 1982).

----------. "Menachem Beigin [sic] Talks to the City of Jerusalem." The Answer, 20 August 1948, pp. 7-8.

----------. "The New Miracle of Chanukah." The Answer, 17 December 1947, p. 7.

----------. "New Year's Greetings." The Answer, 15 October 1948, p. 6.

----------. On the Road to Peace. Jerusalem: The Israel Economist, n.d.

----------. "Our Fight for Freedom." In Who Is Menachem Begin. Beirut: Institute for Palestine Studies, 1977, pp. 22-31.

----------. "Prime Minister Begin's Speech at the Signing of the Peace Treaty with Egypt." Jerusalem: State of Israel Government Press Office Bulletin, 26 March 1979.

----------. "Prime Minister Menachem Begin on Israel Radio September 6, 1977." Washington: Embassy of Israel, 12 September 1977.

----------. "Prime Minister Menachem Begin's Address to the Knesset at the Opening of Its Summer Session." Jerusalem: Israel Ministry of Foreign Affairs, 3 May 1982.

----------. "Prime Minister Menahem Begin's Press Conference--July 20, 1977, Old Executive Office Building, Washington, D.C." Washington: Embassy of Israel, n.d.

----------. "Prime Minister Menachem Begin's Speech to the Knesset Presenting the New Government and the Outlines of Its Policy." Washington: Embassy of Israel, 21 June 1977.

----------. "Prime Minister's Reaction to U.S. Senate Vote." Jerusalem: Press Bulletin of Israel, 17 May 1978.

----------. "Real Security." Jerusalem: Israel Information Briefing, 1978.

----------. The Revolt. Trans. Samuel Katz. Ed. Ivan M. Greenberg. New York: Nash, 1972.

----------. The Revolt. Rev. ed. New York: Dell, 1977.

----------. "Speech Made at the 11th Convention of the Herut Movement (excerpt). Tel Aviv, 29 September 1974." In Who Is Menahem Begin. Beirut: Institute for Palestine Studies, 1977, pp. 32-46.

----------. "Speech Made at the 12th Convention of the Herut Movement (excerpts). Hebron, 12 January 1975." In Who Is Menahem Begin. Beirut: Institute for Palestine Studies, 1977, pp. 47-55.

----------. "Statement by Prime Minister Begin in the Knesset, 7/9/79, Following the Visit by the Leader of the P.L.O. to Austria." Washington: Embassy of Israel, July 10, 1979.

----------. "Statement Delivered in the Knesset by the Prime Minister, Mr. Menachem Begin." Jerusalem: Press Bulletin of Israel, 13 March 1978.

----------. "Statement in the Knesset by Prime Minister Menahem Begin in Reply to Six Urgent Motions for the Agenda Concerning the Invitation to President Anwar Sadat of Egypt to Visit Jerusalem--15 November 1977." New York: Consulate of Israel, n.d.

----------. "Statement in the Knesset, on Behalf of the Government, by Prime Minister Menachem Begin, on the Political Situation." New York: Consulate of Israel, 29 March 1978.

----------. "Text of Address by Mr. Menahem Begin, Prime Minister of Israel, at a Special Session of the Knesset (Israel's Parliament)." Jerusalem: Embassy of Israel, 20 November 1977.

----------. "Text of Begin's Letter to Reagan Dealing with Lebanon and the West Bank." New York Times, 6 September 1982, p. A24.

----------. "Thousands Hear Beigin [sic] Outline Policies of Tenuat Hacherut." The Answer, 5 November 1948, p. 7.

----------. "The Time Is Now!" Jewish World, January-February 1956, pp. 4-5.

----------. "Transcript of a Press Conference with Prime Minister Menachem Begin at the Annual Luncheon of the Foreign Press Association." Jerusalem: Press Bulletin of Israel, 24 February 1981.

----------. "The Truth about the Altalena." The Answer, 9 July 1948, pp. 6-7.

----------. White Nights: The Story of a Prisoner in Russia. Trans. Katie Kaplan. London: Futura, 1977.

----------. "Why the Irgun Fought the British." The London Times, 14 April 1971, p. 6.

----------. "Why We Must Stand Fast." The American Zionist, January 1971, pp. 9-14.

Gruner, Dov. "Statement of Dov Gruner to the Military Court." The Answer, 16 April 1948, p. 17.

Gurion, Itzhak. Triumph on the Gallows. New York: Futuro, 1950.

Irgun Zvai Leumi. "American Lessons for Ben-Gurion." The Answer, 6 June 1947, p. 6.

----------. "Announces Creation of Freedom Movement." The Answer, 18 June 1948, p. 6.

----------. "An Appeal to the Citizens of the Hebrew Homeland." The Answer, 9 April 1948, p. 6.

----------. "Attack Is Best Defense against Rioting Arabs." The Answer, 26 December 1947, p. 6.

----------. "Attention: The Sixth Division." The Answer, June 1946, p. 11.

----------. "Ben-Gurion Issues Blank Checks to UN." The Answer, 27 August 1948, p. 7.

----------. "Blessed Be the Unified Resistance." The Answer, June 1946, p. 16.

----------. "A Bloody Performance." The Answer, 23 January 1948, p. 6.

----------. "British Law Holds Hebrew Patriots." The Answer, 27 August 1948, p. 7.

----------. "The Case Against Haganah." The Answer, 4 July 1947, p. 7; 11 July 1947, p. 5; 18 July 1947, p. 5.

----------. "Commander Hands Banner of Irgun to Troops in Jerusalem Areas." The Answer, 27 August 1948, p. 7.

----------. "A Decision is Near." The Answer, 11 April 1947, p. 6.

----------. "'Definite Targets' and 'Spectacular Exploits.'" The Answer, 23 January 1948, p. 6.

----------. "Dov Gruner." The Answer, 21 February 1947, p. 6.

----------. "Efforts of Jewish Agency to Intimidate Fail, Haganah, Hashomer Hatzoir Members to Contribute." The Answer, 19 March 1948, p. 6.

----------. "Facts and Conclusions." The Answer, 13 December 1946, p. 5.

----------. Fighting Judea, April 1946, pp. 1-19.

----------. "The Flogging Incident." The Answer, 21 February 1947, p. 6.

----------. "Fratricidal War." The Answer, 21 March 1947, p. 6.

----------. "From Kishenev to Acre: On the Sixth Anniversary of the Death of David Raziel." The Answer, 30 May 1947, p. 6.

----------. "The Great Lesson of the Exodus." The Answer, 3 October 1947, p. 6.

----------. The Hebrew Struggle For National Liberation. Presented to the United Nations Special Committee on Palestine, 1947.

----------. "How the Irgun Took Dir-Yasin." The Answer, 30 April 1948, p. 6.

----------. "In Broadcast Irgun Declares 'Attack Is Best Defense.'" The Answer, 9 January 1948, p. 6.

----------. "In Iron Lies Our Salvation." The Answer, 16 January 1948, p. 6.

----------. "The Irgun Appeals Against Partition." The Answer, 27 June 1947, p. 6.

----------. "Irgun Appeals for Financial Support; Gets 'Not a Penny' from Gov't Treasury." The Answer, 18 June 1948, p. 1.

----------. "Irgun Charges British Plan War of Attrition." The Answer, 26 December 1947, p. 6.

----------. "Irgun Commander Demands Aid for Hebrew Defense in Palestine." The Answer, 16 January 1948, pp. 1, 2.

----------. "Irgun Exposes British Lie about Soviet Agents." The Answer, 9 January 1948, p. 6.

----------. "Irgun Exposes British Tricks and Offers a Plan of Action." The Answer, 31 October 1947, p. 6.

----------. "Irgun Offers Plan of Action." The Answer, 24 October 1947, p. 6.

----------. "The Irgun Poses Some Questions to the Sons of Cain, Who Call Themselves 'Trustees of the Yishuv.'" The Answer, 9 May 1947, p. 6.

----------. "Irgun Proclaims Iron Fund for Liberation." The Answer, 19 March 1948, p. 6.

----------. "The Irgun Replies to Mr. Ben-Gurion." The Answer, 6 June 1947, p. 6.

----------. "The Irgun Replies to the Trusteeship Proposal." The Answer, 9 April 1948, p. 6.

----------. "Irgun Sets Forth Plan of Action for Hebrew Liberation." The Answer, January 1946, pp. 14-15.

----------. "Irgun Warning on Civil War." The Answer, 14 November 1947, p. 6.

----------. "Irgun Warns against Bloody British Intrigues." The Answer, 9 January 1948, p. 6.

----------. "The Irgun Z'vai Leumi Explains Its Stand." The Answer, 18 October 1946, p. 8.

----------. "Irgun's 'Iron Fund' Appeal." The Answer, 19 March 1948, p. 6.

----------. "Israel Will Be Free." The Answer, 9 July 1948, p. 3.

----------. "Jerusalem." The Answer, 6 August 1948, p. 6.

----------. "The Legend of Dov Gruner." The Answer, 16 May 1947, p. 6.

----------. "Let the People Judge." The Answer, 11 April 1947, p. 6.

----------. "Let This Be a Warning." The Answer, 25 July 1947, p. 6.

----------. "Majority vs. Minority." The Answer, August 1946, pp. 14-15.

----------. Memorandum to the United Nations Special Committee on Palestine. Presented to the United Nations Special Committee on Palestine, 1947.

----------. "A Message From the Commander-in-Chief of the Irgun to the Diaspora." The Answer, September 1946, pp. 11-12.

----------. "The Night of Blood at Acre." The Answer, 16 May 1947, p. 6.

----------. "Notice!" The Answer, 7 March 1947, p. 6.

----------. "Only Offensive Operations Can Defend Our Homeland." The Answer, 16 January 1948, p. 6.

----------. "Order of the Day for Passover." The Answer, 14 May 1948, p. 6.

----------. "Partition Will Never Be Recognized Says Irgun." The Answer, 12 December 1947, p. 6.

----------. "A Piece of Disgraceful Hypocrisy." The Answer, 7 May 1948, p. 6.

----------. "Prisoners of War: Hebrew Soldiers Teach the World." The Answer, 14 May 1948, p. 6.

----------. "Proclamation." The Answer, August 1946, p. 18.

----------. "Proclamation of Irgun Zvai Leumi Dated End of November 1946, British Desire Hebrew Civil War: Nation Wants Fight for Freedom." The Answer, 6 December 1946, p. 3.

----------. "Proclamation to the Jewish People in Zion." In The First International Quiz on Jewish Underground Activities: Chapters in the History of Jewish Underground Activities. Jerusalem: National Labour Federation in Israel, n.d., pp. 64-68.

----------. "The Rioters Must Be Crushed." The Answer, 16 January 1948, p. 6.

----------. "The 'Rise' of Jerusalem's Military Governor." The Answer, 6 August 1948, p. 6.

----------. "The Story of Dov Gruner." The Answer, 7 March 1947, p. 6.

----------. "Struggle for Hebrew Freedom to Continue." The Answer, 12 December 1947, p. 6.

----------. "The Ten Martyrs Under Cursed Britain Compared to 10 Martyrs Under Rome." The Answer, 15 August 1947, p. 6.

----------. "Ten Points." The Answer, 8 October 1947, p. 6.

----------. "These Are the Facts." The Answer, 9 July 1948, p. 3.

----------. ". . . Till The Enemy Has Gone." The Answer, 15 November 1946, p. 6.

----------. "Time to Act." The Answer, 23 October 1947, p. 6.

----------. "To All Soldiers: A Passover Message From the Irgun." The Answer, 8 April 1947, p. 6.

----------. "To Arms: With Faith in the Justness of Our Cause the First Step." The Answer, June 1946, p. 16.

----------. "To the Nation and to the Youth." The Answer, 7 March 1947, p. 2.

----------. "To Our Arab Neighbors." The Answer, 12 September 1947, p. 6.

----------. "To Our 'Exodus' Brothers." The Answer, 12 September 1947, p. 6.

----------. "To the People." The Answer, 21 March 1947, p. 6.

----------. "To the People of the United States." The Answer, 25 July 1947, p. 6.

----------. "The Trap Concealed in the Armistice Proposal." The Answer, 16 April 1948, p. 16.

----------. "Underground Blasts Partition." The Answer, 11 October 1946, p. 5.

----------. "We Demand Prisoner of War Status!" The Answer, 21 February 1947, p. 6.

----------. "We Have Begun to Retaliate." The Answer, 14 November 1947, p. 6.

----------. "We Must Choose: Combat or Death." The Answer, June 1946, p. 10.

----------. "We Want No Foreign Troops on the Soil of Palestine." The Answer, 16 April 1948, p. 16.

----------. "What Can Unify the Hebrew Resistance Movement?" The Answer, July 1946, p. 13.

----------. "Wishful Thinking." The Answer, 16 May 1947, p. 6.

Katz, Doris. The Lady Was a Terrorist During Israel's War of Liberation. New York: Shiloni, 1953.

Katz, Samuel. Days of Fire. Garden City, New York: Doubleday, 1968.

Merridor, Ya'Acov. Long Is the Road to Freedom. Teljung, California: Baral, 1961.

Begin and the Irgun

Abramowitz, Isidore, et al. Letter. New York Times, 4 December 1948, p. 12.

Avrech, Myra. "The Captain of the 'Altalena' Tells His Story." Jewish World, September 1956, pp. 14-16.

Bauer, Yehuda. From Diplomacy to Resistance: A History of Jewish Palestine 1939-1945. Trans. Alton M. Winters. Philadelphia: Jewish Publication Society, 1970.

"Begin and Bible: Moses' Lessons Applied to 1980." New York Times, 5 October 1980, p. A22.

"Begin Charges Zionist Abandoned European Jews." Jerusalem Post, indistinct date apparently 13 November 1961, Inter-Documentation Company microfiche, n. pag.

"Begin, Mao in Arabic Found in Gaza Strip." Jerusalem Post, 8 April 1969, Inter-Documentation Company microfiche, n.d.

"Begin, Menachem." Choice, June 1978, p. 603.

"Begin Presents Flag to I.Z.L." Jerusalem Post, 5 August 1948, Inter-Documentation Company Microfiche, n. pag.

Bell, J. Bowyer. Terror Out of Zion: Irgun Zvai Leumi, Lehi, and the Palestine Underground, 1929-1949. New York: Avon Books, 1977.

Benaron, S. "Passionate Account of I.Z.L.'s Exploits." Jerusalem Post, 22 April 1965, Inter-Documentation Company microfiche, n. pag.

Benvenisti, J. L. "Britain and Palestine." Commonweal, 14 February 1947, pp. 439-441.

Bercovici, Konrad, et al. Letter. New York Times, 15 December 1943, p. 32.

Bethell, Nicholas. The Palestine Triangle: The Struggle for the Holy Land, 1935-48. New York: Putnam, 1979.

Blitzer, Wolf. "Responsibility in the Middle East." New York Times Book Review, 29 January 1978, pp. 9, 29.

Bodner, Allen Joy. "Begin, Historian Said to Be Certain Third Parties Cannot Assure Life of Jewish Nation." The Jewish Week-Examiner, 21 May 1978, p. 25.

Borisov, J. Palestine Underground: The Story of the Jewish Resistance. Philadelphia: Judea, 1947.

Breindel, Eric. "The Many Wars of Menachem Begin." Rolling Stone, 3 November 1977, pp. 86-91.

Brewer, Sam Pope. "Irgun Bombs Kill 15 Arabs; 3 of 5 Attackers Are Slain." New York Times, 8 January 1948, p. 1.

Brilliant, Morris. "No Holds Barred." New Republic, 23 December 1946, pp. 855-856.

Bruzonsky, Mark. "The Mentor Who Shaped Begin's Thinking: Jabotinsky." Washington Post, 16 November 1980, Section L, p. 2.

Clarke, Thurston. By Blood and Fire: The Attack on the King David Hotel. New York: Putnam, 1981.

Cohen, Dov. The Conquest of Acre Fortress. Tel-Aviv: Hadar, 1977.

Cohen, Geula. Women of Violence. Trans. Hillel Halkin. New York: Holt, Rinehart and Winston, 1966.

Cohen, Moshe. "I.Z.L. Awards Captivity Medal." Jerusalem Post, 11 February 1964, Inter-Documentation Company microfiche, n. pag.

Crossman, R.H.S.   "War Criminals."   New Statesman, 13 October 1951, p. 411.

Currivan, Gene.   "Irgun Ship Afire in Tel Aviv; Battle With Israeli Army."   New York Times, 23 June 1948, pp. 1, 24.

----------.   "Israel Arrests 70 in Irgun Round-Up; 2 Ministers Resign."   New York Times, 24 June 1948, pp. 1, 14.

de Reyneir, Jacques.   "Deir Yasin."   In Who Is Menahem Begin. Beirut: Institute for Palestine Studies, 1977, pp. 16-20.

Dolav, Aharon.   "White Nights and Tempestuous Days in the Life of Menachem Begin."   Jerusalem: Embassy of Israel reprint of article in Ma'ariv, 10 June 1977.

"Ends and Means."   Times Literary Supplement, 5 October 1951, p. 623.

Farrell, William.   "A Day in the Life of Menahem Begin Reflects Fierce Loyalties of an Israeli Founder."   New York Times, 14 June 1977, p. 3.

----------.   "The New Face of Israel: Hawk on a Mission of Peace."   New York Times Magazine, 17 July 1977, pp. 11-52.

Gervasi, Frank.   The Life and Times of Menahem Begin: Rebel to Statesman.   New York: Putnam, 1979.

Gordon, Nahum L.   "Since the Exile, He's First Leader to Talk Judaism to the World."   Jewish Weekly American, 18 September 1977, p. 3.

Greenfield, Irving, and Richard Greenfield.   The Life Story of Menachem Begin.   New York: Manor Books, Inc., 1977.

Grandos, Jorge Garcia.   The Birth of Israel: The Drama as I Saw It.   New York: Knopf, 1948.

Gross, David C.   "Israeli Premier: Menachem Begin Seen as Tough Minded Blend of Soldier-Prophet."   Jewish Week-American Examiner, 24 September 1981, p. 31.

Haber, Eitan.   Menahem Begin: The Legend and the Man.   Trans. Louis Williams.   New York: Delacorte Press, 1978.

Halpern, Ben.   The Jewish Military Organization in Palestine. New York: Labor Zionist Organization, 1947.

Hirschler, Gertrude, and Lester Eckman. Menahem Begin: From Freedom Fighter to Statesman. New York: Shengold, 1979.

Hogdin, Edward. "Palestine Sensibility and Sense." The Spectator, 5 October 1951, pp. 448-449.

Hurwitz, Harry. Menachem Begin. Johannesburg, South Africa: The Jewish Herald Ltd., 1977.

Ignatius, David, et al. "Begin on Begin: Soon I'll Retire and Write My Book." Wall Street Journal, 9 July 1982, pp. 1, 9.

"Irgun Honours Dead." Jerusalem Post, 28 May 1962, Inter-Documentation Company microfiche, n. pag.

"The Irgun Revolt." Commonweal, 30 November 1951, pp. 196-197.

"Irgun Vows War if Arabs Attack." New York Times, 5 November 1947, p. 18.

Isaac, Erich, and Raël Jean Isaac. "The Impact of Jabotinsky on Likud's Policies." Middle East Review, 10, no. 1 (1977), pp. 31-48.

Jabotinsky, Vladimir. Prelude to Deliah. New York: Bernard Ackerman, 1945.

"Jabotinsky Memorial." Jerusalem Post, 26 July 1968, Inter-Documentation Company microfiche, n. pag.

Kirchwan F. "Battle of Palestine." Nation, 3 August 1946, pp. 117-120.

Kirk, George. "The Revolt." International Affairs, 28 (1952), pp. 516-517.

Koëstler, Arthur. Promise and Fulfillment: Palestine 1917-1949. New York: Macmillan, 1949.

----------. Thieves in the Night: Chronicle of an Experiment. London: Hutchinson, 1946.

Linowitz, Sol. "The Begin I Know." Newsweek, 14 September 1981, p. 42.

Malgo, Wim. Begin with Sadat. Hamilton, Ohio: The Midnight Call, Inc., 1978.

Meltzer, Julian Louis. "Political Terrorist Groups Keep Palestine in Turmoil." New York Times, 28 July 1946, p. 4E.

"Menachem." Jewish Herald, 12 May 1970, p. 10.

Merhav, Meir. "The Constancy of Menahem Begin." Jerusalem Post International Edition, 23 August 1977, pp. 7, 14.

----------. "Menahem Begin's Counter-Zionism." New Outlook, 22, no. 7 (October 1979), pp. 11-14.

"Monument to Men Executed by Turks and Britains." Jerusalem Post, 25 April 1968, Inter-Documentation Company microfiche, n. pag.

Morgan, Edward P. "Terror in Tel-Aviv." Colliers, 24 May 1947, pp. 23, 103-105.

"Palestine Raids Statements." New York Times, 30 June 1946, p. 18.

Paulding, C. G. "The Terrorists." Commonweal, 2 May 1947, pp. 53-54.

Rabinovich, Abraham. "Memorial to IZL Dead in Attack on New Gate." Jerusalem Post, Inter-Documentation Company microfiche, n. pag.

Safire, William. "The Authentic." New York Times, 4 August 1977, p. A19.

Safran, Nadav. "Makers and Witnesses of History." New York Times Book Review, 7 May 1978, pp. 9, 40-42.

Schechtman, Joseph B. Fighter and Prophet: The Vladimir Jabotinsky Story the Last Years. New York: Thomas Yoseloff, 1961.

Scherr, Julian M. "Begin, Menachem. The Revolt: Story of the Irgun." Library Journal, 15 October 1951, p. 1704.

Schmidt, Dana Adams. "200 Arabs Killed, Stronghold Taken." New York Times, 10 April 1948, p. 6.

Segal, Mark. "Herut 'Anniversary of the Revolt' Rally in Tel Aviv." Jerusalem Post, 9 April 1958, Inter-Documentation Company microfiche, n. pag.

----------. "Herut Brings Down the Roof." Jerusalem Post, 8 July 1966, Inter-Documentation Company microfiche, n. pag.

Sims, John F. Interview with J. Bowyer Bell. South African Jewish Times, 1 June 1977, p. 1.

St. John, Robert. <u>Shalom Means Peace</u>. Garden City, New York: Doubleday, 1950.

Stone, I. F. <u>Underground to Palestine and Reflections Thirty Years Later</u>. 1946; rpt. New York: Pantheon, 1978.

Sulzberger, C. L. "Irgun Still Seeks All Palestine." <u>New York Times</u>, 30 July 1948, p. 9.

Sykes, Christopher. <u>Crossroads to Israel</u>. Bloomington: Indiana University Press, 1965.

Teller, J. L. "Guerillas in the New Israel. <u>New Republic</u>, 3 January 1949, pp. 19-21.

----------. "The Revolt: Story of the Irgun." <u>The Middle East Journal</u>, 6 (1952), pp. 360-361.

----------. "The Tools of Jewish Resistance." <u>Commonweal</u>, 2 August 1946, pp. 375-378.

"10th Anniversary of Altalena Incident." <u>Jerusalem Post</u>, 8 June 1958, Inter-Documentation Company microfiche, n. pag.

"Text of the British Memorandum for Palestine Solution." <u>New York Times</u>, 11 February 1947, p. 12.

Weaver, Suzanne. "A Chat with Begin: Optimistic, Tough, a Sense of History." <u>Wall Street Journal</u>, 22 September 1978, p. 20.

Webster, Richard A. "Israel's Political Parties: the Zionist Heritage." <u>Middle East Review</u>, 11, no. 3 (Winter 1978-1979), pp. 5-10.

Wolf, Leonard. <u>The Passion of Israel: Interviews Taken and Edited in Collaboration with Deborah Wolf</u>. Boston: Little Brown, 1970.

Zionism, the Holocaust, Judaism and Israel

Ajami, Fouad. "The Oasis Goes Dry." <u>New York Times</u>, 21 June 1982, p. A19.

American Friends Service Committee. <u>A Compassionate Peace: A Future for the Middle East</u>. New York: Hill and Wang, 1982.

Anderson, Jack. "Secret Profile Provides a Closer View of Begin." <u>Lawrence Daily Journal World</u>, 26 May 1982, p. 4.

Arendt, Hannah. Eichman in Jerusalem: A Report on the Banality of Evil. New York: The Viking Press, 1964.

----------. The Jew as Pariah: Jewish Identity and Politics in the Modern Age. Ed. Ron H. Feldman. New York: Grove Press, 1978.

"Autonomy: What Israel Has in Mind." Jerusalem Post International Edition, 20-26 January 1980, p. 7.

Avineri, Shlomo. "History versus Security." Jerusalem Post International Edition, 1-7 June 1980, p. 13.

----------. The Making of Modern Zionism: The Intellectual Origins of the Jewish State. New York: Basic Books, Inc., 1981.

Avnery, Uri. Israel Without Zionists: A Plea for Peace in the Middle East. New York: Macmillan, 1968.

Avishai, Bernard. "Begin vs. Begin." New York Review of Books, 31 March 1979, pp. 35-41.

----------. "The Road to Disaster." The New York Review of Books, 10 June 1982, pp. 20-25.

Avruch, Kevin A. "Gush Enunim: Politics, Religion, and Ideology in Israel." Middle East Review, 11, no. 2 (1978-1979), pp. 26-31.

Bamberger, Bernard J. The Story of Judaism. New York: Schocken Books, 1970.

Barach, Nathan A. The Jewish Way of Life. Middle Village, New York: Jonathan David, 1975.

Bauer, Yehuda. The Holocaust in Historical Perspective. Seattle: University of Washington Press, 1978.

----------. The Jewish Emergence from Powerlessness. Toronto: University of Toronto Press, 1979.

----------. "Jewish Masochism." Jerusalem Post International Edition, 15-21 June 1980, p. 13.

"Begin at the End?" New Republic, 7 April 1982, pp. 7-9.

"Begin Is Criticized in Israel's Press." New York Times, 22 December 1981, p. A12.

"Begin's Tactics under Fire." Time, 6 March 1982, pp. 34-35.

Bell, Josef. "Words Not Enough." Jerusalem Post International Edition, 14-20 January 1979, p. 11.

Ben-Gurion, David. Rebirth and Destiny of Israel. Trans. Mordekhai Nurrock. New York: Philosophical Library, 1954.

Ben-Sasson, H. H., ed. A History of the Jewish People. Cambridge, Massachusetts: Harvard University Press, 1976.

Berenbaum, Michael. The Vision of the Void: Theological Reflections on the Works of Elie Wiesel. Middletown, Connecticut: Wesleyan University Press, 1979.

Berkovits, Eliezer. Faith after the Holocaust. New York: KTAV Publishing House, 1973.

Bettelheim, Bruno. The Informed Heart: Autonomy in a Mass Age. New York: Avon Books, 1971.

"B-G: Dayan to Stop Speeches." Jerusalem Post, 8 July 1966, Inter-Documentation Company microfiche, n. pag.

Brecher, John. "Arafat: Nowhere to Hide." Newsweek, 5 July 1982, p. 40.

Brecher, John, et al. "Beirut: A City in Agony." Newsweek, 16 August 1982, pp. 10-15.

----------. "A Roadblock to Peace?" Newsweek, 14 September 1981, pp. 36-41.

Brenner, Robert. The Faith and Doubt of Holocaust Survivors. New York: Collier Macmillan Publishers, 1980.

Breslauer, S. Daniel. The Ecumenical Perspective and the Modernization of Jewish Religion. Missoula: Scholars Press, 1978.

Bright, John. A History of Israel. London: S.C.M. Press, 1959.

Buber, Martin. Hasidism and Modern Man. Trans. Maurice Friedman. New York: Horizon Press, 1958.

----------. Israel and the World: Essays in a Time of Crisis. New York: Schocken Books, 1948.

----------. On Judaism. Ed. Nahum Glatzer. New York: Schocken Books, 1977.

290

Butler, David. "How Carter Did It." Newsweek, 26 March 1979, pp. 32-34.

Cargas, Harry James. In Conversation with Elie Wiesel. New York: Paulist Press, 1970.

Cargas, Harry James, ed. Responses to Elie Wiesel. New York: Persea Books, 1978.

Caroll, Raymond, et al. "Why Begin Is Tough." Newsweek, 30 January 1978, p. 42.

Claiborne, William. "Begin Refuses to Compromise Principles." Washington Post, 25 March 1979, pp. A1, A18.

----------. "Begin Rules Out Deal on Missiles, Assails Schmidt." Washington Post, 7 May 1981, pp. A1, A27.

"Clearing the Way for Peace." Time, 9 October 1978, pp. 50-51.

Cohen, Richard. "Holocaust Is Trivialized for Political Purposes." Washington Post, 29 June 1980, p. B1.

Collins, Larry, and Dominique Lapierre. The Fifth Horseman. New York: Avon, 1980.

----------. O Jerusalem. New York: Simon and Schuster, 1972.

Davis, Uri, Andrew Mack, and Nira Yuval Davis. Israel and the Palestinians. London: Ithaca Press, 1975.

Dawidowicz, Lucy S. The War Against the Jews. New York: Bantam Books, 1976.

Dayan, Moshe. Breakthrough: A Personal Account of the Egypt-Israel Peace Negotiations. New York: Knopf, 1981.

Deming, Angus, and Milan J. Kubic. "Getting Tough with the US." Newsweek, 4 January 1982, pp. 20-21.

----------. "A Jewish West Bank?" Newsweek, 30 November 1981, pp. 57-58.

Derogy, Jacques, and Hesi Carmel. The Untold History of Israel. New York: Grove, 1978.

Des Pres, Terrence. The Survivor: An Anatomy of Life in the Death Camp. Oxford: Oxford University Press, 1976.

Dimont, Max. The Indestructible Jews. New York: The New American Library, 1973.

Dinur, Ben Zion. Israel and the Diaspora. Philadelphia: Jewish Publication Society, 1969.

Dobsson, Christopher. Black September: Its Short Violent History. New York: Macmillan, 1974.

Eban, Abba. "Camp David—The Unfinished Business." Foreign Affairs, 157 (Winter 1978-1979), pp. 343-354.

----------. "UN's Rhetorical Pogrom." Jerusalem Post International Edition, 3-9 August 1980, p. 11.

Elazar, Daniel J. "Zionism and the Future of Israel." Middle East Review, 11, no. 3 (1979), pp. 19-24.

Elon, Amos. Flight into Egypt. New York: Pinnacle Books, 1981.

Elpeleg, Zvi. "PLO Calls the Tune." Jerusalem Post International Edition, 23-29 November 1980, p. 11.

Estes, Ted L. Elie Wiesel. New York: Frederich Ungar, 1980.

Evron, Boas. "The Demise of Zionism?" New Outlook, 23, no. 8 (1980), pp. 30-31.

Fackenheim, Emil L. God's Presence in History: Jewish Affirmations and Philosophical Reflections. New York: Harper & Row, 1970.

----------. The Jewish Return into History: Reflections in the Age of Auschwitz and a New Jerusalem. New York: Schocken Books, 1978.

"Fatah Again Affirms 'Liberation by Force.'" Jerusalem Post International Edition, 8-14 June 1980, p. 10.

Fighters for the Freedom of Israel. "Fighters for the Freedom of Israel (Stern Group): A Statement of Policy." The Answer, June 1946, pp. 14-15.

"Framework for Just, Comprehensive, Durable Settlement." Washington Post, 19 September 1981, p. A16.

Frank David O. "In Celebration of Peace: A Rhetorical Analysis of the Three Speeches Delivered at the Middle East Ceremony of Peace 26 March 1974." Paper presented at the Speech Communication Association Convention in Anaheim, California: 13 November 1981.

----------. "'Shalom Achshav'--Rituals of the Israeli Peace Movement." Communication Monographs, 48 (1981), pp. 165-182.

Friedlander, Albert H., ed. Out of the Whirlwind: A Reader of Holocaust Literature. New York: Schocken Books, 1976.

Gilbert, Martin. Exile and Return: The Struggle for a Jewish Homeland. Philadelphia: Lippincott, 1978.

Gilion, Philip. "The Feud in Labour." Jerusalem Post International Edition, 23-29 November 1980, p. 11.

Gittelsohn, Roland B. The Modern Meaning of Judaism. Cleveland: Collins S. Cleveland, 1978.

Glatstein, Jacob, et al. Anthology of Holocaust Literature. New York: Atheneum, 1977.

Goldman, Peter, et al. "A Glimpse of Peace." Newsweek, 26 March 1979, pp. 28-31.

Goldston, Robert. Next Year in Jerusalem. New York: Fawcett Crest, 1978.

Gonen, Jay Y. A Psycho-History of Zionism. New York: New American Library, 1975.

Gwertzman, Bernard. "Peace Treaty Signed by Egypt and Israel." New York Times, 27 March 1979, p. A10.

Haber, Eitan, Zeev Schiff, and Ehud Yaari. The Year of the Dove. New York: Bantam Books, 1979.

Haganah. "Haganah." The Answer, June 1946, pp. 12-13.

Halabi, Rapik. The West Bank Story. Trans. Ina Friedman. New York: Harcourt Brace Jovanovich, 1981.

Halpern, Ben. The Idea of a Jewish State. Cambridge, Massachusetts: Harvard University Press, 1961.

Harkabi, Y. The Palestinian Covenant and Its Meaning. Totowa, New Jersey: Valentine Mitchell, 1979.

Herberg, Will. _Judaism and Modern Man_. New York: Antheneum, 1980.

Hertzberg, Arthur. "Begin and the Jews." _New York Review of Books_, 18 February 1982, pp. 11-12.

----------. _Judaism_. New York: George Braziller, Inc., 1961.

----------. _The Zionist Idea: A Historical Analysis and Reader_. New York: Atheneum, 1959.

Herzberg, Arthur. "It Is Not Because of the Masada Zealots that the People of Israel Lives." _New Outlook_, 22, no. 2 (1979), pp. 45-46.

Hilberg, Raul. _The Destruction of the European Jews_. New York: Harper and Row, Publishers, 1961.

Hirst, David. _The Gun and the Olive Branch: The Roots of Violence in the Middle East_. New York: Harcourt Brace Jovanovich, 1977.

Hoffman, Stanley. "Israeli Self-Defense? No Self Deceit." _New York Times_, 16 June 1982, p. A31.

Hurewitz, J. C. _The Struggle for Palestine_. New York: Schocken, 1976.

Hurwitz, Roger, and Gordon Fellman. "U.S. Jews and Lebanon." _New York Times_, 26 June 1982, p. 25.

Hussain, Haten, ed. _Toward Peace in Palestine_. Washington: Arab Information Centre, 1975.

Isaac, Raël Jean. _Israel Divided: Ideological Politics in the Jewish State_. Baltimore: Johns Hopkins University Press, 1976.

----------. _Party and Politics in Israel: Three Visions of a Jewish State_. New York: Longman, 1981.

Israel Information Centre. _The Egypt-Israel Peace Treaty: Speeches and Interviews_. Jerusalem: Israel Information Centre, March 1979.

"Israeli Defense Minister Relaxes Tough Policies on West Bank, Gaza." _Washington Post_, 13 August 1981, p. A22.

"The Israeli Mess." _Washington Post_, 19 May 1977, p. A16.

Johnston, Leonard. _A History of Israel_. New York: Sheed and Ward, 1964.

Jureidini, Paul, and R. D. McLaurin. _Beyond Camp David: Emerging Alignments and Leaders in the Middle East_. Syracuse, New York: Syracuse University Press, 1981.

Kahn, Moshe. "Thoughts on the Holocaust." _Jerusalem Post International Edition_, 5 October 1978, p. 21.

Katz, Shmuel. "The Arab 'Peace Trap.'" _Jerusalem Post International Edition_, 3-9 August 1980, p. 11.

----------. _Battle Ground: Fact and Fantasy in Palestine_. New York: Bantam Books, 1973.

----------. _The Hollow Peace_. Jerusalem: Dvir and the Jerusalem Post, 1981.

----------. "Illusion of Security." _Jerusalem Post International Edition_, 11-17 March 1980, p. 11.

----------. "An Irresponsible Act." _Jerusalem Post International Edition_, 26 September 1978, p. 15.

----------. "Words versus Deeds." _Jerusalem Post International Edition_, 2-8 March 1980, p. 13.

Katzenstein, Constance A. "Israel--The Jewish Response to Feelings of Helplessness." _New Outlook_, 23, no. 1 (1980), pp. 31-34.

Kaufman, William E. _Contemporary Jewish Philosophies_. New York: Reconstructionist Press, 1976.

Keller, Werner. _Diaspora: The Post-Biblical History of the Jews_. Trans. Richard and Clara Winston. New York: Harcourt, Brace, and World, 1966.

Kempe, Frederick. "House Divided: Israel's War Costs Include an Increase in Internal Discord." _Wall Street Journal_, 12 July 1982, p. 11.

Kurzman, Dan. _Genesis 1948: The First Arab-Israeli War_. New York: World, 1970.

Langer, Lawrence L. _The Holocaust and the Literary Imagination_. New Haven: Yale University Press, 1975.

Laqueur, Walter. A History of Zionism. New York: Schocken
   Books, 1972.

Latour, Arnny. The Resurrection of Israel. Trans. Margaret S.
   Summers. Cleveland: World, 1968.

Learsi, Rufus. Israel: A History of the Jewish People. Westport, Connecticut: Greenwood, 1949.

Lewis, Anthony. "Combing the Wreckage." New York Times, 10 June
   1982, p. A31.

----------. "Might Makes Wrong." New York Times, 24 June 1982,
   p. A23.

----------. "The Price of Mr. Begin." New York Times, 2 July
   1981, p. A19.

----------. "Why the Palestinians Feel Left Out." Kansas City
   Times, 2 October 1979, p. 12A.

Lewis, Arnold. "The Peace Ritual and Israeli Images of Social
   Order." Journal of Conflict Resolution, 23 (1979), pp. 685-
   703.

Lindsay, John. "A Lively Discussion." Newsweek, 5 July 1982,
   p. 38.

Linowitz, Sol. "You Have to Level With Begin." Time, 28 June
   1982, p. 18.

Lippman, Thomas W. "Egypt Greets Peace Treaty with Mix of Joy,
   Indifference." Washington Post, 27 March 1979, p. A12.

Litvinoff, Barnett. Road to Jerusalem: Zionism's Imprint on
   History. London: Weidenfeil and Nicolst, 1965.

McGarry, Michael B. Christology After Auchwitz. New York:
   Paulist Press, 1977.

Meltzer, Milton. Never to Forget: The Jews of the Holocaust.
   New York: Dell Publishing Company, 1976.

Menuhin, Moshe. The Decadence of Judaism in Our Time. Beirut:
   Institute for Palestine Studies, 1969.

Milson, Menahem. "The PLO's Real Aims." Jerusalem Post International Edition, 7-13 December 1980, p. 11.

Mohs, Mayo. "Troubled Land of Zion." Time, 18 May 1981, pp. 32-43.

Montgomery, Paul. "Begin Tells Leading U.S. Jews of Invasion's Goals." New York Times, 18 June 1982, p. A6.

Morse, Arthur D. While Six Million Died: A Chronicle of American Apathy. New York: Random House, 1968.

Mroz, John Edwin. Beyond Security: Private Perceptions among Arabs and Israelis. New York: Pergamon, 1980.

Near East Reports. Myths and Facts 1978: A Concise Record of the Arab-Israeli Conflict. Washington: Near East Research, 1978.

Pawolczynska, Anna. Values and Violence in Auschwitz. Trans. Catherine S. Leach. Los Angeles: University of California Press, 1979.

Peled, Matityahu. "Autonomy as a Gambit." New Outlook, 22, no. 1 (1979), pp. 11-15.

Peretz, Martin. "Lebanon Eyewitnesses." New Republic, 2 August 1982, pp. 15-23.

Perlmutter, Amos. "Begin's Rhetoric and Sharon's Tactics." Foreign Affairs, 61 (1982), pp. 67-83.

Plotkin, Frederick S. Judaism and Tragic Theology. New York: Schocken Books, 1973.

"Retiring Envoy Doubts Peace under Begin." Lawrence Daily Journal World, 1 September 1981, p. 2.

Rosenfeld, Alvin H., and Irving Greenberg, eds. Confronting the Holocaust: The Impact of Elie Wiesel. Bloomington: Indiana University Press, 1978.

Roth, Ari, et al. "Treaty Ends 30-Year State of War." Jerusalem Post International Edition, 25-31 March 1979, pp. 1-2.

Roth, John K. A Consuming Fire. Atlanta: John Knox Press, 1979.

Rozenweig, Efraim M. We Jews: Invitation to Dialogue. New York: Hawthorne, 1977.

Rubenstein, Richard L. After Auschwitz: Radical Theology and Contemporary Judaism. Indianapolis: Bobbs-Merrill Company, 1976.

----------. The Cunning of History: The Holocaust and the American Future. New York: Harper and Row, 1975.

----------. "God as Cosmic Sadist: In Reply to Emil Fackenheim." Christian Century, 29 July 1970, pp. 921-923.

Sachar, Howard M. A History of Israel: From the Rise of Zionism to Our Time. New York: Knopf, 1979.

Sadat, Muhammad Anwar Al. "Text of Address by Mr. Muhammad Anwar Al-Sadat, President of the Egyptian Arab Republic, at a Special Session of the Knesset (Israel's Parliament) Jerusalem, 20 November 1977." Jerusalem: Israel Information Centre, 1977.

Safire, William. "The Jewish DeGaulle." New York Times, 30 August 1981, p. E17.

----------. "PLO Won't Be Talked Out of Propaganda Haven." Kansas City Times, 6 August 1982, p. A11.

Said, Edward W. "Begin's Zionism Grinds On." New York Times, 11 June 1982, p. A31.

----------. The Question of Palestine. New York: Vintage Books, 1980.

Scholem, Gershom G. Major Trends in Jewish Mysticism. New York: Schocken, 1941.

----------. The Messianic Idea in Judaism: And Other Essays on Jewish Spirituality. New York: Schocken, 1971.

Schwarz-Bart, Andre. The Last of the Just. Trans. Stephen Becker. New York: Bantam Books, 1978.

Segre, Dan V. A Crisis of Identity: Israel and Zionism. Oxford: Oxford University Press, 1980.

----------. "The Symbolic Sources of Begin's Power." Washington Post, 28 August 1977, p. B5.

Selzer, Michael, ed. Zionism Reconsidered. New York: Macmillan, 1970.

Shipler, David. "Begin Defends Raid, Pledges to Thwart a New 'Holocaust.'" New York Times, 10 June 1981, pp. A1, A12.

----------. "Begin Tells Cabinet to Ignore Reported U.S. Threat." New York Times, 17 June 1982, p. A22.

----------. "A Crisis of Conscience over Lebanon." New York Times, 18 June 1982, p. A6.

----------. "West Bank Is Israel's, Begin Asserts." New York Times, 4 May 1982, p. A3.

Sidey, Hugh. "In Celebration of Peace." Time, 9 April 1979, pp. 30-35.

Silver, Abba Hillel. Where Judaism Differed. New York: Macmillan, 1972.

Sommer, Theo. "'Will We Ever Be Forgiven?'" Newsweek, 18 May 1981, p. 63.

"Sounding Off with a Vengeance." Time, 18 May 1981, p. 37.

Steinberg, Milton. Basic Judaism. New York: Harcourt Brace Jovanovich, 1975.

Stone, I. F. "The Other Zionism." Harpers, September 1978, pp. 65-73.

Syrkin, Marie. "How Begin Threatens Israel." New Republic, 16 September 1981, pp. 23-27.

----------. "The Revisonist in Power." New Republic, 22 April 1978, pp. 20-23.

"Tale of One Death Camp." Palestine Post, 18 February 1944, p. 1.

"Tanks Close In: Vow Made to Step Up Pressure on PLO." Kansas City Times, 5 August 1982, p. A8.

"Text of Prime Minister Menachem Begin's Autonomy Plan for Judea, Samaria and the Gaza District as Presented in the Knesset, December 28, 1977." Washington: Embassy of Israel, n.d.

"Texts of Treaty, Accompanying Documents." Washington Post, 27 March 1979, p. A14.

Trepp, Leo. The Complete Book of Jewish Observance. New York: Schocken, 1976.

Turki, Fawaz. "To Be a Palestinian." In Israel and the Palestinians. Ed. Uri Davis, et al. London: Ithaca Press, 1975, pp. 188-195.

Ullman, Richard H. "The U.S. Should Press Israel to Pursue Peace." New York Times, 14 July 1981, p. A25.

Viorst, Milton. "It Isn't the Israel It Used to Be." Washington Post, 1 August 1982, p. B1.

Vital, David. The Origins of Zionism. Oxford: Oxford University Press, 1975.

Walsh, Edward, and Jim Hoagland. "30 Years of Strife Officially Ended." Washington Post, 27 March 1979, pp. A1, A13.

Weaver, Suzanne. "Somber Gladness Pervades Carter's Party for Peace." Wall Street Journal, 30 March 1979, p. 14.

Weitz, Yehiam. "The Holocaust Analogy." New Outlook, 20, no. 7 (1977), pp. 45-46.

Weizman, Ezer. The Battle for Peace. New York: Bantam Books, 1981.

"West Bankers Told: Bark but Do Not Bite." The Middle East, no. 49 (1978), p. 20.

Wiesel, Elie. The Accident. Trans. Anne Borchardt. New York: Avon Books, 1961.

----------. A Begger in Jerusalem. New York: Pocket Books, 1970.

----------. Dawn. Trans. Frances Frenaye. New York: Avon Books, 1960.

----------. The Gates of the Forest. Trans. Frances Frenaye. New York: Avon Books, 1966.

----------. A Jew Today. Trans. Marion Wiesel. New York: Random House, 1978.

----------. Legends of Our Time. New York: Avon Books, 1968.

----------. Night. Trans. Stella Rodway. New York: Avon Books, 1958.

----------. The Oath. New York: Avon Books, 1973.

----------. One Generation After. New York: Pocket Books, 1978.

----------. Souls on Fire. Trans. Marion Wiesel. New York: Random House, 1973.

----------. Zalmen or the Madness of God. Trans. Nathan Edelman. New York: Pocket Books, 1974.

Yehoshua, A. B. Between Right and Right: Israel: Problem or Solution? Garden City, New York: Doubleday, 1981.

Yodfat, Aryeh Y., and Yuval Arnon-Ohanna. PLO Strategy and Politics. New York: St. Martin's Press, 1981.

Zion, Sidney, and Uri Dan. "Untold Story of the Mideast Talks." New York Times Magazine, 21 January 1979, pp. 20-22, 46-53; 28 January 1979, p. 32-38, 42-43.

Myth and Rhetorical Criticism

Aiken, Henry D. The Age of Ideology. Boston: Houghton Mifflin, 1957.

Altizer, J. J. Oriental Mysticism and Biblical Eschatology. Philadelphia: Westminster Press, 1966.

Barrett, William. Time of Need: Forms of Imagination in the Twentieth Century. New York: Harper and Row, 1972.

Bass, Jeff D., and Richard Cherwitz. "Imperial Mission and Manifest Destiny: A Case Study of Political Myth in Rhetorical Discourse." Southern Speech Communication Journal, 43 (1978), pp. 213-232.

Bennett, Lance W. "Myth, Ritual, and Political Control." Journal of Communications, 30, no. 4 (1980), pp. 166-179.

Black, Edwin. "A Note on Theory and Practice in Rhetorical Criticism." Western Journal of Speech Communication, 44 (1980), pp. 331-336.

----------. Rhetorical Criticism: A Study in Method. New York: Macmillan, 1965.

Braden, Waldo W. "Myth in a Rhetorical Context." Southern Speech Communication Journal, 40 (1975), pp. 113-126.

Bultmann, Rudof, and Karl Jaspers. Myth and Christianity: An Inquiry into the Possibility of Religion without Myth. Trans. Norbert Guberman. New York: Noonday, 1958.

Burke, Kenneth. "Ideology and Myth." Accent, 7 (1947), pp. 195-205.

----------. Language as Symbolic Action: Essays on Life Literature and Method. Los Angeles: University of California Press, 1966.

----------. "Myth, Poetry and Philosophy." Journal of American Folk Lore, 73, no. 240 (1960), pp. 283-306.

----------. "The Rhetoric of Hitler's Battle." In his The Philosophy of Literary Form. 3rd ed. Berkeley: University of California Press, 1973.

Butcher, S. H. Aristotle's Theory of Poetry and Fine Art: With a Critical Text and Translation of the Poetics. 4th ed. New York: Dover, 1951.

Campbell, Joseph. Creative Mythology. Vol. 4 of The Masks of God. New York: Viking, 1968.

----------. The Flight of the Wild Gander: Explorations in the Mythological Dimension. South Bend, Indiana: Gateway Editions, 1969.

----------. The Hero With a Thousand Faces. Princeton: Princeton University Press, 1949.

----------. Joseph Campbell: Myths to Live By, Part 1. Narr. Bill Moyers. Prod. Randy Bean. "Bill Moyer's Journal." PBS, 17 April 1981.

----------. Joseph Campbell: Myths to Live By, Part 2. Narr. Bill Moyers. Prod. Randy Bean. "Bill Moyer's Journal." PBS, 24 April 1981.

----------, ed. Myths, Dreams and Religion. New York: E. P. Dutton, 1970.

----------. Myths to Live By. New York: Bantam, 1972.

----------. Occidental Mythology. Vol. 3 of The Masks of God. New York: Viking, 1962.

----------. Oriental Mythology. Vol. 2 of The Masks of God. New York: Viking, 1962.

----------. Primitive Mythology. Vol. 1 of The Masks of God.
New York: Viking, 1969.

Campbell, Karlyn Kohrs. "An Exercise in the Rhetoric of Mythical
America." In her Critiques of Contemporary Rhetoric. Belmont, California: Wadsworth, 1972, pp. 50-57.

----------. The Rhetorical Act. Belmont, California: Wadsworth,
1982.

Cassirer, Ernst. An Essay on Man: An Introduction to a Philosophy of Human Culture. New Haven: Yale University Press,
1944.

----------. Language. Vol. 1 of The Philosophy of Symbolic
Forms. New Haven: Yale University Press, 1955.

----------. Language and Myth. Trans. Susanne K. Langer. New
York: Dover Press, 1946.

----------. The Myth of the State. New Haven: Yale University
Press, 1946.

----------. Mythical Thoughts. Vol. 2 of The Philosophy of
Symbolic Forms. New Haven: Yale University Press, 1955.

Caws, Peter. "Structuralism." Dictionary of the History of
Ideas. 1973 edition.

Childs, Brevard S. Myth and Reality in the Old Testament.
London: S. C. M. Press, 1960.

Cohen, Percy S. "Theories of Myth." Man, NS 3 (1969), pp. 337-
353.

Connolly, William E. Political Science and Ideology. New York:
Atherton Press, 1967.

Cook, Albert. Myth and Language. Bloomington: Indiana University Press, 1980.

Corbertt Patrick. Ideologies. New York: Harcourt, Brace and
World, 1965.

Cornwell, George W. "Analyst Mixes Christianity with Freudian
Techniques." Lawrence Daily Journal-World. 24 October
1981, p. 8.

Cuthbertson, Gilbert Morris. Political Myth and Epic. Lansing:
Michigan State University Press, 1975.

Davidson, William C. "Sam Houston and the Indians: A Rhetorical Study of the Man and the Myth." Diss. University of Kansas, 1971.

Decker, Philip. "The Use of Classic Myth in 20th Century English and American Drama." Diss. Northwestern University, 1966.

DeGeorge, Richard, and Fernande DeGeorge, eds. The Structural-ists:From Marx to Lévi-Strauss. Garden City, New York: Doubleday, 1972.

deSantillana, Giorgio, and Hertha von Dechend. Hamlet's Mill: An Essay on Myth and the Frame of Time. Boston: David R. Godine, 1977.

Dickinson, Donald. "Problems of Religion and Myth in Modern Drama: 1914-1950." Diss. Northwestern University, 1961.

Dorson, Richard. "Current Folklore Theories." Current Anthro-pology. 4 (1963), pp. 93-112.

Douglas, Wallace W. "The Meanings of 'Myth' in Modern Criti-cism." Modern Philology, 50 (1953), pp. 232-241.

Drake, Carlos. "Jung and His Critics." Journal of American Folklore, 8, no. 313 (1967), pp. 321-333.

Dundes, Alan. "From Etic to Emic Units in the Structural Study of Folktales." Journal of American Folklore, 75 (1967), pp. 45-105.

Durcher, H. M. The Political Uses of Ideology. London: London School of Economics and Political Science, 1974.

Eliade, Mircea. Myth and Reality. Trans. Willard R. Trask. New York: Harper and Row, 1963.

----------. "Myth in the Nineteenth and Twentieth Centuries," Dictionary of the History of Ideas. 1973 edition.

----------. The Myth of the Eternal Return or Cosmos and History. Trans. Willard R. Trask. Princeton: Princeton University Press, 1954.

----------. Myths, Dreams and Mysteries: The Encounter Between Contemporary Faiths and Archaic Realities. Trans. Philip Mairet. New York: Harper and Row, 1960.

----------. Patterns in Comparative Religion. Trans. Rosemary Sheed. New York: Meridian Books, 1958.

----------. *The Quest: History and Meaning in Religion*. Chicago: University of Chicago Press, 1969.

----------. *The Sacred and the Profane: The Nature of Religion*. Trans. Willard R. Trask. New York: Harcourt Brace Jovanovich, 1959.

----------. *The Secular Scripture: A Study of the Structure of Romance*. Cambridge, Massachusetts: Harvard University Press, 1976.

Feder, Lillian. *Ancient Myth in Modern Poetry*. Princeton: Princeton University Press, 1971.

Feuer, Lewis S. *Ideology and the Ideologist*. Oxford: Basil Blackwell, 1975.

Fisher, Walter R. "Reaffirmation and Subversion of the American Dream." *Quarterly Journal of Speech*, 59 (1973), pp. 160-167.

Fontenrose, Joseph. *The Ritual Theory of Myth*. Berkeley: University of California Press, 1966.

Frazier, James George. *The Golden Bough: A Study in Magic and Religion*. New York: Macmillan, 1950.

Fromm, Erich. *The Forgotten Language*. New York: Grove Press, n.d.

Frye, Northrop. *Anatomy of Criticism: Four Essays*. Princeton: Princeton University Press, 1957.

----------. *The Critical Path: An Essay on the Social Context of Literary Criticism*. Bloomington: Indiana University Press, 1971.

----------. "Literature and Myth." In *Relations of Literary Study*. Ed. James B. Thorpe. New York: Modern Language Association, 1967.

----------. "Varieties of Literary Utopias." *Daedalus*, 94 (1965), pp. 323-347.

Gardner, Howard. *The Quest for Mind: Piaget, Lévi-Strauss and the Structuralist Movement*. 2nd ed. Chicago: University of Chicago Press, 1981.

Gaster, Theodore H. *Myth, Legend and Custom in the Old Testament*. New York: Harper and Row, 1969.

Graves, Robert. The White Goddess: A Historical Grammar of
    Poetic Myth. New York: Farrar, Straus and Giroux, 1948.

Halle, Louis J. The Ideological Imagination. Chicago: Quad-
    rangle Books, 1972.

----------. "Marx's Religious Drama." Encounter, 25, no. 4
    (1965), pp. 29-37.

Halpern, Ben. "The Dynamic Elements of Culture." Ethics, 65
    (1955), pp. 235-249.

----------. "Myth and 'Ideology' in Modern Usage." History and
    Theory, 1 (1961), pp. 129-149.

Hatfield, Henry. "The Myth of Nazism." In Myth and Mythmaking.
    Ed. Henry A. Murray. Boston: Beacon, 1968, pp. 199-219.

Heisey, D. Ray. "The Rhetoric of the Arab-Israeli Conflict."
    Quarterly Journal of Speech, 56 (1970), pp. 12-21.

Herd, E. W. "Myth Criticism: Limitations and Possibilities."
    Mosaic, 2, no. 3 (1969), pp. 69-77.

Herskovitts, Frances, and Melville J. Herskovitts. Dahomean Nar-
    rative: A Cross Cultural Analysis. Evanston, Illinois:
    Northwestern University Press, 1958.

Hoban James Leon. "Rhetorical Rituals of Rebirth." Quarterly
    Journal of Speech, 66 (1980), pp. 275-88.

----------. "The Structure of Myth in Rhetorical Criticism."
    Diss. University of Illinois at Urbana-Champaign, 1971.

Hooke, S. H., ed. Myth and Ritual. London: Oxford University
    Press, 1933.

----------. Myth, Ritual, and Kingship in the Ancient Near East
    and in Israel. Oxford: Oxford at the Clarendon Press,
    1958.

Itzkoff, Seymour W. Ernst Cassirer: Philosopher of Culture.
    Boston: Twayne Publishers, 1977.

James, E. O. "The Nature and Function of Myth." Folklore, 68
    (1957), pp. 474-482.

Janeway, Elizabeth. Man's World, Woman's Place: A Study in
    Social Mythology. New York: Morrow, 1971.

Jung, C. G., and C. Kerenyi. Essays on a Science of Mythology: The Myth of the Divine Child and the Mysteries of Eleusis. Trans. R. F. C. Hull. Princeton: Princeton University Press, 1963.

Jung, Carl G., et al., eds. Man and His Symbols. New York: Dell, 1964.

Kaplan, Abraham, and Harold D. Lasswell. Power and Society: A Framework for Political Inquiry. New Haven: Yale University Press, 1950.

Kelsey, Morton T. Myth, History and Faith. New York: Paulist Press, 1974.

Kirk, G. S. Myth: Its Meaning and Functions in Ancient and Other Cultures. London: Cambridge University Press, 1970.

----------. The Nature of Greek Myths. New York: Penguin Books, 1974.

Kluckhohn, Claude. "Myths and Rituals: A General Theory." Harvard Theological Review, 35 (1942), pp. 45-79.

----------. "Recurrent Themes in Myth and Mythmaking," in Myths and Mythmaking. Ed. Henry A. Murray. Boston: Beacon, 1968, pp. 46-60.

Knox, John. Myth and Truth: An Essay on the Language of Faith. Charlottesville: University Press of Virginia, 1964.

Koch, Klaus. The Growth of the Biblical Tradition: The Form Critical Method. Trans. S. M. Culpitt. New York: Scribners, 1969.

Kurzweil, Edith. The Age of Structuralism: Lévi-Strauss to Foucault. New York: Columbia University Press, 1980.

Langer, Susanne K. Philosophy in a New Key: A Study in the Symbolism of Reason, Rite, and Art. New York: The New American Library, 1951.

Larson, Stephen. Shaman's Doorway: Opening the Mythic Imagination to Contemporary Consciousness. New York: Harper, 1976.

Larue, Gerald A. Ancient Myth and Modern Man. Englewood Cliffs, New Jersey: Prentice Hall, 1975.

Leach, Edmund. Culture and Communication. Cambridge, England: Cambridge University Press, 1976.

----------. Genesis as Myth and Other Essays. London: Jonathan Cape, 1969.

----------. "Lévi-Strauss in the Garden of Eden: An Examination of Some Recent Developments in The Analysis of Myth." In Claude Lévi-Strauss: The Anthropologist as Hero. Ed. E. Nelson Haye and Tanya Haye. Cambridge, Massachusetts: MIT Press, 1970, pp. 47-60.

Lévi-Strauss, Claude. Myth and Meaning. New York: Schocken Books, 1978.

----------. The Origin of Table Manners. Vol. 3 of Introduction to a Science of Mythology. Trans. John Weightman and Doreen Weightman. New York: Harper and Row, 1969.

----------. The Raw and the Cooked. Vol. 1 of Introduction to a Science of Mythology. Trans. John Weightman and Doreen Weightman. New York: Harper and Row, 1978.

----------. The Savage Mind. Chicago: The University of Chicago Press, 1966.

----------. "The Structural Study of Myth," in The Structuralists From Marx to Lévi-Strauss. Ed. Richard De George and Fernande De George. Garden City, New York: Doubleday, 1972, pp. 169-194.

Lowry, Shirley Park. Familiar Mysteries: The Truth in Myth. New York: Oxford University Press, 1982.

McDonald, Lee C. "Myth, Politics and Political Science." Western Political Quarterly, 22 (1969), pp. 141-150.

McGee, Michael. "In Search of 'The People': A Rhetorical Alternative." Quarterly Journal of Speech, 61 (1975), pp. 235-249.

McGuire, Michael Dennis. "Mythic Rhetoric: A Case Study of Adolf Hitler's Mein Kampf." Diss. University of Iowa, 1975.

----------. "Mythic Rhetoric in Mein Kampf: A Structuralist Critique." Quarterly Journal of Speech, 63 (1977), pp. 1-13.

MacIntyre, Alasdair. "Myth." The Encyclopedia of Philosophy. 1967 edition.

MacIver, R. M. The Web of Government. New York: MacMillan, 1965.

McKenzie, J. L. "Myth and the Old Testament." Catholic Biblical Quarterly, 21 (1959), pp. 269-282.

MacKenzie, R. A. F. Faith and History in the Old Testament. Minneapolis: University of Minnesota Press, 1963.

Malinowski, Bronislaw. Magic, Science and Religion and Other Essays. Garden City, New York: Doubleday, 1948.

Mannheim, Karl. Ideology and Utopia: An Introduction to the Sociology of Knowledge. Trans. Louis Wirth and Edward Shils. New York: Harcourt, Brace and World, 1936.

Maranda, Pierre, ed. Mythology: Selected Readings. New York: Penguin Books, 1972.

Mechling, Elizabeth Walker. "Patricia Hearst: MYTH AMERICA 1974, 1975, 1976." Western Journal of Speech Communication, 43 (1979), pp. 168-179.

Mullin, Donald C. "Myth, Religion, and Meaning in Greek Tragedy." Quarterly Journal of Speech, 56 (1970), pp. 54-60.

Mullins, Willard A. "On the Concept of Ideology in Political Science." American Political Science Quarterly, 66 (1972), pp. 498-510.

Murray, Henry A., ed. Myth and Mythmaking. Boston: Beacon Press, 1960.

Newman, Robert P. "Lethal Rhetoric: The Selling of the China Myths." Quarterly Journal of Speech, 61 (1975), pp. 113-128.

Niebuhr, Reinhold. "The Truth in Myths." In Faith and Politics. Ed. Ronald H. Stone. New York: George Braziller, 1968.

Nietzsche, Fredrich. The Birth of Tragedy and the Genealogy of Morals. Trans. Francis Goltting. Garden City, New York: Doubleday, 1956.

Nimmo, Dan, and James E. Combs. Subliminal Politics: Myths and Mythmakers in America. Englewood Cliffs, New Jersey: Prentice-Hall, 1980.

Olson, Alan M., ed. Myth, Symbol and Reality. Notre Dame: University of Notre Dame Press, 1980.

Panikkar, R. Myth, Faith and Hermeunetics: Cross-Cultural Studies. New York: Paulist Press, 1979.

Pelto, Pertti, J. The Nature of Anthropology. Columbus, Ohio: Charles E. Merrill, 1966.

----------. The Structure of Inquiry. New York: Harper and Row, 1970.

Pike, Kenneth L. "The Etic and Emic Standpoints for the Description of Behavior." In Communication and Culture: Readings in the Codes of Human Interaction. Ed. Alfred G. Smith. New York: Holt, Rinehart, and Winston, 1966, pp. 152-163.

Prescott, Frederick Clark. Poetry and Myth. New York: Macmillan, 1927.

Propp, V. Morphology of the Folktale. Trans. Laurence Scott. Austin: University of Texas Press, 1968.

Raglan, Lord. The Hero: A Study in Tradition, Myth, and Drama. New York: New American Library, 1979.

Rahr, Philip. The Myth and the Powerhouse. New York: Farrar, Straus, and Giroux, 1965.

Rank, Otto. The Myth of the Birth of the Hero. Ed. Philip Freund. New York: Vintage Books, 1959.

Ritter, Kurt W. "The Myth-Making Functions of the Rhetoric of the American Revolution: Frances Hopkinson as a Case Study." Today's Speech, 23 (1975), pp. 25-31.

Robertson, James Oliver. American Myth, American Reality. New York: Hill and Wang, 1980.

Roelofs, H. Mark. Ideology and Myth in American Politics: A Critique of a National Political Mind. Boston: Little, Brown and Company, 1976.

Rogerson, J. W. Myth in the Old Testament. Berlin: Gruyter, 1974.

Rosenfield, Lawrence W. "The Anatomy of Critical Discourse." Speech Monographs, 25 (1968), pp. 50-69.

Runciman, W. G. "What is Structuralism?" British Journal of Sociology, 20 (1969), pp. 253-265.

Ruthven, K. K. Myth. London: Methuen and Company, 1976.

Scholes, Robert. Structuralism in Literature. New Haven: Yale University Press, 1974.

Seibold, David. "Jewish Defense League: The Rhetoric of Resistance." Today's Speech, 21 (1973), pp. 39-48.

Simons, Herbert W. "Requirements, Problems, and Strategies: A Theory of Persuasion for Social Movements." Quarterly Journal of Speech, 56 (1970), pp. 1-11.

Solomon, Martha. "The 'Positive Woman's' Journey: A Mythic Analysis of the Rhetoric of STOP ERA." Quarterly Journal of Speech, 65 (1979), pp. 262-274.

Sorel, Georges. Reflections on Violence. Trans. T. E. Hulme and J. Roth. Glencoe, Illinois: Free Press, 1950.

Stevens, Anthony. Archetypes: A Natural History of the Self. New York: William Morrow and Company, 1982.

Strelka, Joseph, ed. Literary Criticism and Myth. University Park: Penn. State University Press, 1980.

Swanson, David L., and Jesse G. Delia. The Nature of Human Communication. Chicago: S.R.A., 1976.

Sykes, A. J. M. "Myth in Communication." The Journal of Communication, 20 (1970), pp. 17-31.

Tucker, Gene M. Form Criticism of the Old Testament. Philadelphia: Fortress Press, 1971.

Watts, Alan W. Myth and Ritual in Christianity. Boston: Beacon Press, 1968.

Waxman, Chaim I., ed. The End of Ideology Debate. New York: Funk and Wagnalls, 1968.

Weins, Jill. "The Family of Women: A Mythological Analysis of Contemporary Feminist Songs." Diss. State University of New York at Buffalo, 1969.

Weisinger, Herbert. The Agony and the Triumph: Papers on the Use and Abuse of Myth. Lansing: Michigan State University Press, 1964.

Wheelwright, Philip. Metaphor and Reality. Bloomington: Indiana University Press, 1962.

Williams, Thomas Rhys. Field Methods in the Study of Culture. New York: Holt, Rinehart, and Winston, 1967.

INDEX

--A
Abraham, 34, 167, 169
Abraham, covenant of, 31
Acre fortress, 98, 125, 127
Akiba, Rabbi, 33
Allies, 61-2, 76, 104, 214
Altalena, 56, 58, 97, 108, 112, 114, 138, 159-60
Altizer, J. J., 10
Ammar ibn-Yasi, 192
anagogic phase, 14-5, 236-7
Anders, General, 51-2, 94
Anenauer, 59
Antiochus IV, 32
anti-Semitism, 6, 20, 31, 38-9, 41, 47, 62, 65, 72, 76-7, 182-3,
    201, 231, 233
Arab attacks, 142
Arab invasion, 133
Arab-Jerusalem, 172
Arab movement, 204
Arab peoples, 172, 176
Arab world, 5-6, 159, 172-4, 178, 180, 194, 202, 216
Arab youth, 193
Arabs, 50, 53, 56-7, 59, 61-2, 96, 98, 112, 129, 131, 141, 143,
    175, 191-2, 194, 203-7, 216-8
Arabs under Israeli rule, 129, 177, 200, 203, 205, 207, 214
Arafat, Yasser, 162, 192, 209
Archer-Cust, Colonel, 99
Argentina, 138
Aristotle, 9
Army of Israel--see Israeli army
Arnon-Ohanna, Yuval, 192
Aryans, 220
Ashbel, 98
assimilation, 20, 38-9, 41, 76, 138, 231, 233
Assyrians, 32
Auschwitz, 62-3, 65-6, 70-1, 75, 77, 105, 184, 212
AWACS planes, 183

--B
BBC, 61
Babylon, 32, 34, 76
Balfour Declaration, 5
Bar Kochba, Simon, 15, 33, 49, 133, 165, 197
Barker, General, 182, 184
Bauer, Yehuda, 61-2, 64
Beirut, 206, 208-9
Bell, J. Bowyer, 17-8, 20, 89

313

Benaron, S., 19-20
Ben-Gurion, David, 1, 40-1, 55-6, 58, 77, 96-7, 120, 132, 138,
    141, 143, 160, 196
Bennet, W. Lance, 8
Berenbaum, Michael, 75-6
Berkovits, Eliezer, 47, 62, 64, 66, 72-5, 78, 201, 222
Betar, 1, 3, 47, 49, 51, 58, 159, 166
Bethar, 33, 141, 214
Bethlehem, 168, 170-1
Bevin (British Foreign Minister), 112-3
Bialik, 124
Black, Edwin, 235-6
Blitzer, Wolf, 16, 20, 89
blood imagery/symbolism, 111-2, 114, 122, 163, 232
Brandt, Willy, 60
Brecher, John, 198
Brenner, Reeve Robert, 195, 213
Brest-Litovsk, Poland, 47
British, 1-2, 6, 16, 18, 20, 47, 50-8, 95, 97-100, 103, 105, 108,
    110, 113-4, 120-3, 125, 127-31, 133, 136, 141-3, 159-61,
    174, 183, 205, 214
British empire, 3, 143
British court, 139
British government, 3, 104, 121
British High Commissioner, 99
British Foreign Office, 105
Burke, Kenneth, 219-21
Buchenwald, 65

--C
Cairo, 172, 201
Camp David, xi, 177, 207
Campbell, Joseph, 21, 89-91, 219, 221, 232-4
Canaan, 32, 134
Carter, Jimmy, xi, 18, 177
Chancellor, John, 208
Childs, Brevard S., 12
Christian church, 204
Christianity, 11, 13, 38
Commanding Voice of Auschwitz, 70-1, 215, 222
Conference of Presidents of Major Jewish Organizations, 210
Collins, Larry, 216
Communists, 13, 58
Cyrus, 32

--D
David, 32
Dawidowicz, Lucy S., 64
Dayan, Moshe, 197
Diaspora, 34, 36-7, 48, 120-1, 123, 164, 169, 214-5, 231

Dir Yassin, 56-7, 96, 114, 174
Dolav, Aharon, 199
Dreyfuss affair, 39

--E
East Jerusalem, 1
Eastern Europe, 48-9
Eckman, Lester, 4
Eden, 232
Egypt, 6, 32, 34, 38, 63, 76, 111, 113, 132, 163-4, 167, 171-2,
    176-7, 179
Egyptian-Israeli Peace Treaty, 1, 164, 171, 176-7, negotiations,
    17, signing ceremony, 5, 18, 177-8
Egyptians, 178
Eliade, Mircea, 10, 231-4
Elijah, 75
Emergency Defense Regulations, 207
emic, 235-6
Ephrath, 168
etic, 235-6
Europe, 10-11, 31, 41, 131, 200
Exodus, 142

--F
Fackenheim, Emil, 47, 62, 66, 69-76, 78, 201, 214-5, 222
fascism, 13-4
Fatah, El, 192
Feinstein, Meir, 106, 139
First Zionist Congress, 36
Founding Conference of the New Zionist Organization, 48
France, 129, 201
Frank, David A., 18
French Revolution, 11
Freud, Sigmund, 14
Friedlander, Albert H., 75
Frye, Northrup, 8, 12, 14, 219, 221

--G
Gahal, 50, 195
Galad, 132
Ganzweick, Isaac, 139
Gardner, Howard, 8
Garibaldi, 50, 199-200
Garin, 94, 109
Gaster, Theodore, 7-8
Gaza, 197
Gentiles, 92
German church, 67
German war reparations, 50, 58-9, 77, 161
Germans, 62, 65, 67, 72, 102-4, 136, 204, 214

Germany, 48, 59, 63, 161, 214
Gervasi, Frank, 4
Gideon, 110
Gilion, Phillip, 15, 165
God of Progress, 69-70
Golan Heights, 1, 6, 171, 181-2, 201, 217
Gordon, David, 40
Government of National Unity, 2, 18, 58, 159, 195
Greeks, 7, 32
Greenberg, Irving, 64
Greenberg, Martin, 19
Gruner, Dov, 98, 109, 135, 159-60, 197, 213
Gulag, 1
Gypsies, 63

--H
Haber, Eitan, 3, 50, 58, 159
Habib, Philip, 208-9
Hadar, 49
Hadrian, 33
Haganah, 1, 49, 53, 55, 95-7, 100, 142
Haifa, 192, 205
Hannukah, 33
Hasmonean dynasty, 33
Hatikvah, 94, 109
Hebron, 168, 170-1, 202
Hefker, 125-6
Heisey, D. Ray, 18
Hertzberg, Arthur, 35, 39-40
Herut, 1, 15, 50, 58, 139, 160-1, 176, 195, 197, 200, 203, 213
Herut National Conventions, 15, 161-2
Herz, Theodore, 134
Herzl, 39
Hilberg, Raul, 64
Himmler, Heinrich, 61
Hirschler, Gertrude, 4
Hirst, David, 192, 194
Histadrut, 40, 232
Hitler, Adolf, 58-9, 63-4, 70-1, 104, 133, 209, 211-2, 214
Holy Writ, 36
Hurwitz, Harry, 4, 15, 162, 165-6

--I
Id el Adha, 172
inductive functionalist criticisms, 233-6
Iraqi nuclear reactor, 1, 59, 182, 184, 201-2, 216
Irgun media, 119, 127-9
Isaac, 167, 169, 172
Isaac, Erich, 48
Isaac, Raël Jean, 19, 40, 48, 232

Isaiah, 179
Islamic, 172, 192
Ismailiha, Egypt, 177, 207
Israel Defense Force, 57, 97, 170, 198, 202, 209
Israeli
    Air Force, 201, ambassadors, 7, 208, army, 167-8, 197, government, 22, 129, 169, 171, 183-4, intelligence, 172, peace movement, 18, U.S. relations, 17
Israelites, 32, 111
Italy, 199-200

--J
Jabotinsky, Vladimir Zeev, 1, 42, 47-50, 59, 135, 159, 163-4, 166
Jacob, 31, 167, 169
Jaffa, 100, 103, 106, 111, 114, 192, 205, 212
Jehoiakim, 32
Jerusalem, 12, 32-3, 56, 167-72, 176, 178, 180-1, 204-5, 214
Jerusalem death cell, 126-7
Jewish Agency, 1, 53, 95-7, 100, 106, 142-3
Jewish Defense League, 18
Jewish history, 31-4, 131
Jewish secularists, 70-1
Jews
    European, xi, 38-9, 48-50, 107, 201, Palestinian, 64, 107, traditional, 31, 36, 77, 137-9, 169-70, U.S., 119-20, 123
Job, 8
Jonas, Hans, 75
Jordan, 133, 165
Jordan River, 95, 122, 132, 141
Joseph, 31
Judaism, traditional, 20, 36, 41, 43, 76, 136, 138, 169-71, 196, 231
Judah, 5, 32, 174
Judea, 3, 134, 170, 191, 202, 207, 216
Judges, the, 32
Jung, C. G., 12, 233-4

--K
Kahn, Moshe, 64
Katyusha, 210
Katz, Samuel, 19-20
Kfar, Maccabia Hotel, 161
Kibbutz, 40, 232
King David Hotel, 97, 160, 182
Kishenev, Russia, 124-5
Knesset, 1, 5, 58, 139, 171-2, 176,
Koëstler, Arthur, 99, 216
Kohn, Han, 214
Kook, Rabbi Abraham Isaac, 35
Kripitchnkoff, David, 140

317

318

--T
Tabernacles, 37
Talmud, 35
Tel Aviv, 100
Teller, Judd L., 19
Terzi, 193, 195
Tireh, 205
Tomb of Rachel, 168, 170
Torah, 35
Tower of David, 132
Trans-Jordan, 133, 141
Treblinka, 106, 132-3, 139-41
Trepp, Leo, 38
Trumpeldor, Joseph, 134
Tsongas, Paul, 6-7
Turki, Fawaz, 193
Turks, 7

--U
Uganda, 39, 138
United Nations, 57, 112, 193, 202
UN peace-keeping forces, 209
UN Special Committee on Palestine, 99
United States, 6, 20, 62, 112, 129, 131, 171, 181-5, 197, 200-2,
     209-10, ambassador, 183, intelligence, 182, Senate, 183,
     Senate Foreign Relations Committee, 6-7, 209

--V
Vad Vashem, 172
Vietnam war, 182-3
Vilna, Poland, 51
Vital, David, 37
Voice of Fighting Zion, 127

--W
Wailing Wall--see "Western Wall"
Warsaw ghetto, 60, 143
Weaver, Suzanne, 5
Weissmandel, M.D., 62
Weitz, Yehiam, 218
Weizman, Ezer, 40, 141, 172, 197
West Bank, 3, 4, 169-72, 185, 195, 197-8, 202, 207, 216-8
West Bank Palestinians, 177, 199
West Germany, 4, 201
Western Europe, 38, 202
Western Wall, 54, 95, 167-71
White Russians, 94
Wiesel, Elie, 21, 65-6, 71, 75-6, 215
William, Thomas Rhys, 234-5
Wolf, Leonard, 192